CREATIVE TEACHING IN CHRISTIAN EDUCATION

CREATIVE TEACHING IN
CHRISTIAN EDUCATION

Rev. Alfred A. McBride, O.Praem.
Director, National Forum of Religious Educators
National Catholic Educational Association

Allyn and Bacon, Inc. — Boston, London, Sydney

Nihil Obstat: Rev. John R. Mulvehill, S. T. D.
DIOCESAN CENSOR DEPUTATUS

Imprimatur: †Humberto Cardinal Medeiros
ARCHBISHOP OF BOSTON

July 8, 1976

Library of Congress Cataloging in Publication Data

McBride, Alfred.
    Creative teaching in Christian education.

    Bibliography: p.
    Includes index.
    1. Christian education.   2. Catholic Church—
Education.   I. Title.
BX926.M25   268'.8'2   77–22144
    ISBN 0-205-05842-6

CONTENTS

CHAPTER 5 – LITURGY   113

CHAPTER 6 – ADULT EDUCATION   133

CHAPTER 7 – DELPHI TECHNIQUE AND FUTURES PLANNING 163

CHAPTER 8 – TEACHER TALK   175

CHAPTER 9 – PARENTS ARE "THE PEOPLE" TOO   199

CHAPTER 10 – THE TOOLS OF THE TRADE: WHICH TOOLS?
HOW MUCH TRADE?   227

PREFACE

Catechetical training is meant to make men's faith become living, conscious and active through the light of instruction.

Decree on the Bishops' Pastoral
Office in the Church, n.14

It is essential that the students acquire an understanding of and lively feeling for values. They must acquire a vivid sense of the beautiful and morally good. Otherwise, with their specialized knowledge, they resemble well trained dogs more than harmoniously developed persons.

Albert Einstein

Christian education, be it in a school or a center, possesses a mission to minister to the growth of a living faith in Christ and to help people see the link between faith and moral behavior. The purpose of this book is to offer some insights on how to do this. The audience I envision is Christian educators and administrators in Catholic schools and Religious Education Centers. I see the book as both a self-help for this audience as well as a teaching manual to be used in college and university departments of education as well as by diocesan and parish programs for teacher training.

Since the Church is the basic context for Christian education, the opening chapter dwells on the absolute necessity for a community of faith for the effectiveness of such education. The second chapter, on Basic Teachings, attempts to liberate them from a narrow intellectualist, "propositional faith" view and place them against the broader horizon of religious experience, Church history, the dynamic of inner believing and outer expression, and the variety of languages that this outer expression may take.

The third chapter, on Moral Education, takes into account the current developments in valuing processes and the stages of moral thinking as well as the specifically religious horizon that makes any Christian moral and value training a possible, pertinent project. In the fourth chapter, on Spiritual Education, I draw attention to the elements of growth of faith and the role of prayer.

Chapter 5 shows how Christian education is related to liturgy. I present guidelines for worship that Christian educators should keep in mind as they prepare people to celebrate the Church's supreme moments of contact with the Christ of Easter, especially at Eucharist. With our promised seventy-five–year life span, we all have an actuarial possibility of spending fifty-five years as adults. Chapter 6 looks at the stages of adult growth and outlines twenty ideas for helping adults to keep growing as maturing Christians.

Alvin Toffler's *Future Shock* and Herman Kahn's *Year 2000 Scenarios* have correctly set the style of *future think* for our planning and programming. Chapter 7 delineates two ways of adapting this for Christian education. The Delphi technique and Futures Planning provide a fresh look for planning processes.

Chapter 8, on Teacher Talk, seeks to relate ideas about education, content, and methods to Christian education. Secular educational theory can be put at the service of our religious endeavors. Chapter 9 looks to the role of media in Christian education. Mrs. Janet Bennett, author of this and the following chapter on the family, is one of America's most knowledgeable students of the media and a sharp critic thereof. Her essay on the role of the family, Chapter 10, should do much to show how Christian adults can sort out their hopes in these changing times, so that they can, despite the doomsayers, present to the young an adulthood worth looking forward to.

I have ranged over a wide number of areas in this book. The very breadth of the subject matter will necessarily preclude all the deep soundings that would be possible. I have taken a forthright generalist approach with the conviction that seeing the Big Picture is every bit as important as analyzing the individual parts. I have done this with the encouragement of a saying from one of the world's great specialists, Albert Einstein, who once wrote: "Education should always have as its aim that the young person leave it as a harmonious personality, not as a specialist ... The development of general ability for independent thinking and judgment should always be placed foremost, not the acquisition of special knowledge."

I trust that I have written the book in the spirit of faith in Jesus who lives and speaks to the Church and the world today. I share the spirit of St. Paul, who wrote, "Yet preaching the gospel is not the subject of a boast. I am under compulsion and have no choice. I am ruined if I do not preach it!" (1 Cor.9:16) I hope — and may it not be a vain expectation — that this book will cheer and encourage all those engaged in Christian education today.

Acknowledgments

I am enormously grateful to Mrs. Janet Bennett for her writing the final two chapters of this book, namely, the ones on family and media. She is a woman of extraordinary sensibility and wit and she brings to her topics a transcendental humaneness, a rare sense of poise and deeply felt compassion. She knows how to be "far from the madding crowd" while speaking to them with an inviting sanity.

I am also deeply appreciative for the assistance given me during the writing by Sr. Kathleen Marie Shields, C.S.J. There is probably no woman in America more experienced in the field of teacher training for Christian education. Time and again she gave me the right turn to take, the apt insight, and the unfailing encouragement to complete the work.

I owe a special debt to Father Leo Farley, both for an enduring friendship as well as for the continual light he sheds on the area of Christian ethics. Throughout this book you will find the themes of Christ's living vulnerability and his abiding redemptive forgiveness. I owe the formulation of this salvation language to Father Farley, and I thank him for it.

It has been my special good luck these past years to be associated with the staff of the National Catholic Educational Association and especially with its president, Father John Meyers. He has been a quiet shaker and mover for the field of Christian education. Together with NCEA's National Conference of Directors of Religious Education, he has been instrumental in producing for the field a heady set of clearly useful documents such as Focus on American Catechetics and Giving Form to the Vision. I value both his friendship and the direction I have been able to take due to his work.

I cannot speak enough praise for my secretary, Mrs. Isabella Casey, whose perfectionist approach to the typescript has both called lapses to my attention and eased some of the tedium that such final preparation requires.

Thank you all!

Rev. Alfred McBride, O.Praem.
NCEA

CREATIVE TEACHING IN
CHRISTIAN EDUCATION

COMMUNITY OF BELIEVERS

They devoted themselves to the apostles' instruction and the communal life, to the breaking of bread and the prayers.

Acts 2:42

Community is at the heart of Christian education not simply as a concept to be taught but as a reality to be lived.

TJD 23

It is clear that for Pope John the human race is not a cold abstraction, but a single precious family, whose life, interests, responsibilities and well being are a constant and loving preoccupation.

Adlai Stevenson

Pentecost started it all. The religious experience of the Spirit, sent by Jesus, transformed a frightened and fragmented group of people into a community of believers. The initial fervor yielded a consummate vision of community—selfless sharing, joyous proclamation, and simple worship. The "brief and shining hour" fixed a memory of ideal community so that the personal effort to achieve and sustain it would not imagine it was chasing a fitful mirage.

The word *community* presents a problem. People tend to speak of it in production terms. Find the right recipe and it will inevitably appear. Not so. Like office morale and school spirit and military *esprit de corps*, community escapes any effort to program it. Cruise directors of the spirit debase the ideal of community with their smugness and smiles and organized joy. Incurable optimists are no help either. Better that *they* be cured.

Pentecost clearly shows that community is a gift, a miracle, and a grace. The people in the Upper Room prayed for it because they instinctively knew that is how it ultimately comes. Cheerleading may help. Positive assertions doubtless buck up hopes. But in the last analysis it is a radical, prayerful yearning that best opens people to the possibility of the gift of community.

One must distinguish community from organization. A hungering faith summons community. Intelligent reasoning creates organization.

Community is a gift. Organization is a product. The experience of community is like ecstasy, an untrammeled joy wherein everyone senses effortless friendship and unity.

What is the purpose of organization? First, to give external and enduring shape to the vision experienced in community. Second, to provide the believers with a structure for living out the consequences of community. Thirdly, to keep alive the possibility of community.

The Acts of the Apostles tell the story of a community of believers struggling to organize themselves. They establish a Church order of deacons and presbyters. They institutionalize the method of missionary endeavor. They develop norms and rules for gentile converts and for Christian living in a pagan society.

They live quite well with the tension between community and organization, knowing that each needs the other. A community without organization results in chaos. The good wine is spilled. An organization without the possibility of community becomes a depressing, self-serving bureaucracy. The good wine sours.

Why all this talk about community and organization in a book about how to teach religion? There are several reasons. Unless the administration and faculty of a school or parish center are striving to become a community of believers, there will be little point in their trying to teach religion to the young. A lived faith automatically implies a common religious philosophy and a unified approach to facing life's dilemmas and challenges.

The failure of a faculty and administration to hammer out common religious goals and to make some decent effort to live by them assures the demise of any attempts to teach religion. What student is going to believe in a group of adults who do not agree on a common religious philosophy? Why follow the confused?

How many youth can be expected to feel the joy of Christ in their hearts when they see a faculty and administration that show no real sense of compassion and fraternity for each other? Religion invariably comes round to speaking about love, justice, peace, and friendship. Your students hear your impassioned pleas for a better world. Their eyes scan your nonverbal sermons. If the body talk of the adult teaching and administering group does not match the God talk, then the students' receptivity to the gospel will obviously be diminished.

A word about the perfectionist trap. These observations about the need to have a community of believers assumes that we are still on this side of paradise. The Bible says we are a pilgrim people, meaning that we are still in transit—we have not yet arrived. Aquinas was fond of the expression *Homo Viator* (the traveling person). Vatican II documents dwelt on the image of the Exodus, a people in progress, as describing the general condition of Christians.

The Declaration of Independence says that one of our basic rights is the pursuit of happiness. The critical word is *pursuit,* the right to search out the myriad ways to win the coveted mantle of happiness. Similarly, it is the pursuit of the ideal of being a community of believers that is at issue here. Never perfectly achieved on earth, this ideal demands the tedious daily effort to work and yearn and pray for it. Erich Fromm, in *The Art of Loving,* says that it is one thing to fall in love, but it is another matter to stand in love. God has graced us with the gift of community. We have fallen into it. Now we must stand in it.

Students frankly do not expect choirs of angels to be running Catholic schools and parish centers. But they do look for people who uphold a community ideal and clearly attempt to make it work. Their native, youthful love of the ideal sends up a silent shout to every group mouthing the gospel to them, "Tell us if you must, but above all, show us. We know you are not perfect. But we love to see you try."

The community of believers is the Church. If so, the believers should possess some understanding of the meaning of the Church. Vatican II's constitution on the Church, "The Light of Nations," outlines the central points of this self-understanding. Commentaries and theological explanations of all kinds have followed in abundance. The upshot of the discussions is that appreciation of the meaning of the Church ought not to be restrictive. Its spiritual reality requires a variety of models for adequate expression.

Why use the word *model?* Because a spiritual mystery of uncommon depth will not be amply expressed in any one set of words or ideas. Shakespeare once asked his girl friend, "Shall I compare thee to a summer's day?" Beautiful as a warm sunlit day amid the scent of roses on the English downs might be, is it enough to encompass the meaning of his beloved? His answer was, "No, thou art more lovely and more temperate." Comparisons must be used, otherwise we would be speechless.

Shakespeare's girl was incomparable. Still he went on to use many models and images to speak of her. The gathering of images reflected the wonder of her mystery. Romeo told Juliet, "You do hang upon the cheek of night like a jewel on an Ethiop's ear." Nice as that was, he didn't stop there. Juliet was more than an earring even though the image did express some of her beauty and mystery.

It is the same in speaking of the mystery of the Church. Models, images, and metaphors rejoice in the beauty of their limitations. They uncannily catch a glimpse of the glory and graciously yield to yet further ways of proclaiming the beauty. Avery Dulles outlines five such models in his book *Models of the Church.* Here is a summary of those models:

1. The Church as Institution

I have already alluded to the need for an organizational side to the Church. It should be self-evident that a Church would require responsible officers and approved procedures for a stable, lasting, and effective mission to the world. This institutional aspect of the Church possesses the advantage of linking the present with the origins of Christianity and helping the membership to develop a sense of religious identity. In this age of future shock with its witness to the collapse of so many traditions, this contribution of the institutional model is very appealing.

Still, the institutional model that dominated Catholic consciousness for so long is not the whole story. The other models bring dimensions missing here and provide a richer view of the spiritual mystery of the Church.

2. The Church as Mystical Communion

The institutional Church is an international society of people with a formal organization, officers, and structures. The second image of the Church as Mystical Communion moves away from the governmental aspect to one of community. I view the Church in terms of its local groupings where there is face-to-face association, relative permanence, a comparatively small number of people, and a relative intimacy among them.

Before Vatican II the move to this view was caught by the popularity of the image of the Mystical Body of Christ. Since Vatican II the metaphor of People of God has gained a widespread support. This populist insight offsets the tendency of the official institution to depersonalize the meaning of the gospel. It is within this model that community of believers finds its rationale.

3. The Church as Sacrament

Sacrament is a word that has acquired layers of meanings throughout Church history. It can mean religious mystery. It can also signify visible events, rituals, and institutions that point to religious mystery, as well as being sacred processes that put us in contact with the life of Christ. For a long time the term *sacrament* denoted mainly the seven major rituals that occasion our contact with the grace of Jesus (baptism, confirmation, marriage, and the rest).

Today the term is also applied to the meaning of the Church. It combines very well the models of institution and mystical communion. It curbs tendencies of the institution to be self-serving and instead puts it at the service of Jesus reaching out to save people. It limits the tendencies of the community of believers to lapse into a mere cozy fraternity by reminding them of their responsibilities to bear the love of Jesus to their fellow human beings.

The Church as Sacrament, therefore, is visible witness of the grace of Christ in the world. Since Christ has entered into a covenant with the world, the Church as Sacrament is a living reminder of what that can and should be like. It goes without saying that this witness runs hot and cold—and even tepid—depending upon the spiritual quality of the membership in any given age.

4. The Church as Herald

Jesus commissioned the apostles to preach the gospel to all nations. The Church, built upon the foundation of the apostles, fulfills this mission by proclaiming God's word to the world. Certainly the Church cannot help it if the Word is not accepted, but it fails in its vocation should it cease to preach that Word with persistence, conviction, and boldness.

It is a living Word that is preached. The power of the Holy Spirit is present in that Word. The Church must remain faithful to the meaning and spirit of the Word and pray that its announcement will be an occasion of grace and conversion for the listeners. Hence the Church is always a missionary group, announcing the joyful fulfillment possible in Christ and trusting the Spirit's power to touch the human heart.

5. The Church as Servant

Make justice your aim. Redress the wronged. Hear the orphan's plea, defend the widow.

Isa. 1:16

The first four models are specifically "Churchy." Religious structures, mystical communicants, visible signs of grace, and evangelical proclamation all point to the beyond and its divine coming into our midst. At the same time the arts and sciences of an emancipated secular culture have developed outside the world of the Church. For a long time a hostility existed between the Church and secular culture. Now, however, a dialogue between the two groups is beginning.

The humanitarian goals of the arts and sciences deserve the respect and support of the Church. When the Church participates in such humanitarian endeavor it should do so with a selfless interest for the universal good.

In identifying with genuine humanitarian goals the Church acts as a servant to the human community. In this servant role it reflects the Old Testament prophetic call to bring justice and peace to the earth and the New Testament mandate to act with love and compassion toward all individuals. The model of the Servant Church puts into concrete form the divine response to the deepest hopes and aspirations of the human community.

A community of believers will pursue the ideals implicit in these five models. It will engage in the tedious tasks of organizing, hammering out common goals, and identifying roles and relationships of the people involved. It will acknowledge the mysterious nature of community and beg for its grace to appear. It will hope that the Spirit will endow it with the ability to be a sign of Christ's grace to those within the group.

It will not be hesitant in making known the Word of God clearly and joyously. It will honor and celebrate the achievements of the arts and sciences and will join with all people of good will in the effort to make this weary world a planet of hope and human fulfillment.

The models themselves are nonverbal teaching devices. The processes of organizing (writing philosophies, arguing roles, developing guidelines, providing evaluation procedures) teach a great deal to those who are involved. That is why the maximum number of people should participate. In a certain sense the process is almost more important than the product, though obviously the product is central as well.

In particular, such organizing processes provide two important elements for community, namely, listening and an appreciation of continuity. These processes require extensive discussions, which will falter if the participants are unwilling to listen. In themselves these discussions are training grounds for listening and the acquisition of flexible thinking. The Church as Herald calls the world to "hear" the Word of the Lord. But if the preachers have never learned to listen to each other, it is not likely they will have the simple ability to hear the Lord speaking to them. Then they should not be surprised to find an unresponsive world. Physician, cure thyself.

Continuity is another value absorbed from the collegial processes. Since Vatican II we have begun to possess an embarrassment of riches. 1962 to 1970 was like one vast religious experience. Almost universally the members of the Church, despite disappointments and excesses, have viewed the events as the authentic work of the Holy Spirit. It was a charismatic time—not charismatic in the sense of Pentecostal Catholicism, but in the broader sense of a magnificent grace that provided the Church universal with a divine impetus to enter into a new and loving communion with the citizens of spaceship earth.

But this new wine of the Spirit requires new wineskins, new structures to keep it from being lost. We don't want the whole experience to stop in 1980, 1990, or 2000. No need to freeze-frame that religious experience and sentimentalize it nostalgically. The human way to continue a divine experience is to institutionalize it so that it can have historical continuity and be reexperienced by future generations.

Undramatic as organizing processes may seem, they do provide people with the sense of how to make possible the continuity of profound insights. Many would want to dismiss this duty and return to a paternalistic, simplistic view. They cite the quarrelsome polarizing and undignified bumbling of parish councils, boards of educations, liturgical committees, and music experts as the unhappy products of such efforts.

But this is a shallow and unfair evaluation. It is shallow because it lacks any sense of what foresight and planning in a complex society involves. It does not possess the forgiving and patient perception of how long it takes for a group of people wrestling with new ideas to reduce them to manageable proportions. It is unfair since it runs scared while the others stay and fight. It is sidelining and armchairing at its worst. If the founding fathers of the American republic had been as put off by such quarrels and failures at first sight, they would have gone back to mere grumbling and left us with a colonial status at best or settled for disruptive revolving-door governments.

Allied to the processes of organizing that teach so well are the efforts at spiritual consciousness raising that stretch out for that nimble will-o'-the-wisp community. In the 1960s people were fond of using the term "happening" for spontaneous and surprising events. Let it be admitted that some of the "happenings" were carefully programmed. Yet the insight, though occasionally degraded, was quite valid. Happening was the secular word for the religious counterpart known as grace.

The community of believers, when they exist, are a grace-happening. Organization creates the possibility; grace occasions the reality. The kinesthetic teaching of an existing community of believers is a teaching motivator of a high order. Spiritual processes of prayer and religious yearning must always be in motion to plead for this most precious of gifts. Have confidence. It will come when least expected. And it will never seem as though produced by self-conscious human effort. Grace never is.

The community of believers will be heralds of the Word. The Bible, with its meaning and message, will be clearly and boldly proclaimed. At the same time the words *proclamation* and *boldness* need the tempering that would save the heralds from smugness and any hint of self-righteousness. Aggressive preaching is done for the sake of being noticed. It can make the herald seem like a huckster.

A modesty of endeavor will be acquired when the herald realizes that it is the Spirit that converts the hearts of the listeners, not the preacher. A reverence for the freedom of the listeners and the complexity of their motivations and receptivity, as well as a respect for their goodness and uniqueness, will do much to make such proclaiming a temperate and humble object. It is a truism to say that the strongest are the gentlest and the mightiest are the most humble. Let this attitude prevail in proclaiming the Word.

The community of believers do not need the knowing looks of the saved. They will be far better off with the awesome wonder that such a gift could come to them at all. Hence the heralds will not fume with the zeal of a crusader so much as with the quiet confidence and relaxed conviction that the Lord will reach out through them with tender compassion, if they will but have the decency to let Him do it His way. This is a supreme teaching value that will shine through to listeners, be they students within the fold or others whom we wish to share in the life of the Church.

The teaching possibility of the Church as Sacrament is closely related to the communication power of symbols and ritual behavior. Consult the chapter on liturgy for the expansion of this concept.

The instructive potential of the Church as Servant is particularly compelling in a time when so many social problems, both local and international, cry out for intelligent and long-range solutions. The local community of believers should evidence, through practice, an awareness of the kinds of service that would be possible to anyone in need both nearby and on the world scene.

Several cautions must be borne in mind, however. Whatever service is undertaken ought to be something that can truly be accomplished. Beware of the fashionable causes and parlor liberalism, the so-called "radical chic." Take up a cause because your perceive it as worthy, not just because it is *news*worthy. Tackle something you can handle, otherwise you will be reduced to family room "hot talk" and not much accomplishment.

The second caution is: don't heat up the young people too soon. By *young* we mean especially anybody under fourteen years of age. Certainly there ought to be a gradual sensitizing of these young people to social issues, but their ability to cope with cosmic problems should be related to their mental and emotional readiness. Religion types can be great guilt producers. In the past guilt was heaped on the young in the area of personal moral matters. Today the tendency is to shame them on social moral issues. The old Romans remind us, *ne quid nimis* (never too much too soon). Surely all young people need to learn some measure of moral and civic responsibility—but let it be according to their age, stature, and receptivity.

Thirdly, consider the uniqueness of the call to social concern. Each person will respond according to talents, inner psychology, and the particular lead offered by the Holy Spirit. The move to social action is a complex affair involving the varieties of human readiness and the mystery of divine influence. Mandates, motivational appeals, and friendly nudgings all help to bring to the surface the possibilities of humanitarian service. A combination of prayerful reflection and reasonable review is also needed to fulfill the role of a Servant Church.

Now, with all this discussion about a community of believers, let us speak a word for the loner. Most people are gregarious and social. There is little need to fear that the bulk of humankind will crave isolation from their fellow human beings. Without question, however, some people are more private than others. This is not the same as bashfulness or a neurotic fear of meeting people. The ego strength of the private person apparently does not require too many support strokes, and in fact flourishes well in relative isolation. Some professions, such as writing and certain kinds of research, literally demand withdrawal.

It is not a question of absolute isolation, but rather a preference for private, individualistic endeavor and a positive dislike of all the goings and comings of communal behavior. The community of believers should favor and support individualists and should not attempt some modern form of imposed uniformity under the slogan "To be is to be communal." The loner can often be one of the community's most productive and helpful persons, a sort of thinker in residence.

The activities discussed in this chapter are directly aimed at the adult community of believers. Indirectly this would affect the teaching-learning processes for the youth. The assumption is that if the faculty and administration and the full parish executive group is not a community, then religious education of the young will falter accordingly. In a sense this is a chapter on how to teach the meaning of the Church by becoming a local evocation of the reality of the Church.

I speak of the parish executive group since the community of believers involves more than administrators and teachers in the school or parish center. Clearly, the pastor, the associate clergy, the school principal, the parish religious education coordinator, the members of the parish council, board of education, liturgical and music committees, parish ministers, adult education people, and all who are teaching (whether professional or volunteer) are involved in decisions that either promote or retard the reality of a community of believers. In one way or another this group influences the goals of religious education and lives out in some form the models of institution, commu-

Processes toward developing a community of believers

Chart Models

Types	Meaning	Teaching Applicability
Institution	Organizing necessity	Values of listening, continuity
Community	Mysterious gift	Value of spiritual yearning
Sacrament	Sign of Grace	Power of ritual behavior
Herald	Mission stature	Bold yet reserved
Servant	Social conscience	Moral responsibilities

nity, sacrament, herald, and servant. This is scarcely a plea for the Garden of Eden. It is simply an acknowledgment that a new wineskin needs to be sewn to sustain the fresh wine of the Spirit. The prophet Amos once wrote, "The juice of grapes shall drip down the mountains, and all the hills shall run with it. Plant vineyards and drink the wine." (9:13–14) The juice of the grapes has come. We still have to plant the new vineyards.

Men trust their eyes rather than their ears. The effect of precepts is, therefore, slow and tedious, while that of examples is summary and effectual.

Seneca

Models are for the eyes more than the ears. When they are lively they persuade. Following are some checklists on each of the five models suggested, as pieces of the puzzle known as community of believers. Ideally, the whole parish is the community of believers. But the leadership should show the way. In a best-of-all-world's scenario the full executive group of a parish would enter into processes to establish the possibility of community.

Who is this parish leadership group?

· Pastor
· Associate clergy
· School principal
· Coordinator of religious education
· Youth minister
· Chairpersons of board of education, liturgical and music committees, social concern and budget committees, home school associations, and any other committees developed by the parish.
· Presiding officers of spiritual development groups such as charismatic renewal, cursillo, Legion of Mary, sodality, Holy Name, ushers, choirs, Knights of Columbus, Catholic Daughters, etc.
· Adult education personnel

Going through the checklists and writing goals should begin with this group. In the second phase the principal, coordinator, chairpersons, and presiding officers should take their faculties, student representatives, and membership through the processes. The third phase calls for involving as many interested parishioners as possible. Phases one and two are the most necessary since they compel the leadership to make conscious, intelligent, and faith-motivated decisions about purpose and direction in religious education.

These processes assume that the leadership acts as an adult group, hence is respectful of each other's talents and possible contributions. The image is therefore not that of a lectern and desks, but of a round table.

The communication will thus be lateral and not vertical.

The checklists are not complete coverage of every element. They are starter lists to enable you to begin thinking about your strengths and shortcomings as a community of believers.

Each statement is preceded with two blanks: "Is So" and "Ought to Be So." The former tells the fact of the matter. The latter is a value judgment as to whether the item in question should be present in your group.

Complete the checklist for one model and use it as a basis for discussion. This is not a test to be scored, but a consciousness raiser to prompt the imagination and thinking of the participants.

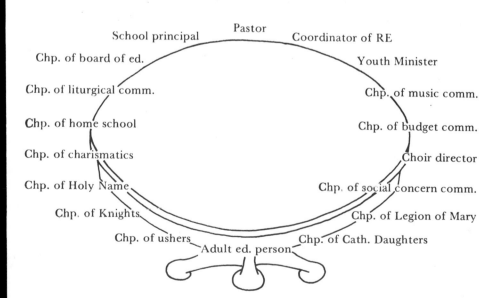

At the completion of the discussion of each list, write out your understanding of the model as it relates to your situation. List areas that need improvement and suggest how to bring them about (goals and programs).

Take plenty of time with these discussions. Avoid the temptation to arrive at quick solutions. Allow the processes to work their magic on the participants.

After you have finished the five models, begin working on a synthesis of the materials and compose a provisional philosophy of religious education, goals, and programs for your parish. We advise the composition of a provisional document at first so as to allow time later on for reconsideration and new or revised input.

You must decide what kind of a schedule to follow. We offer you one here simply as a guide. We recommend that each meeting be no less than two hours. We believe that the process should begin in September, since that is usually the beginning of the formal educational year.

September: *Institution*
October: Review previous meeting and revise written statement.
November: *Community*
December: Review and revise as before. Note tensions and conflicts between institution and community. Seek resolutions.
January: *Sacrament.* Face up to the need for coordination of catechetical efforts and liturgical celebrations.
February: Review. Revise. Compare. Cope with tensions that come to light.
March: *Herald.* Call for a smooth relationship in biblical proclamation in the pulpit and the study of the Bible in religious education.
April: Review. Revise. Compare. Resolve tensions.
May: *Servant.* Remember that justice, like charity, begins at home. A parish community that practices intramural justice has a better chance of credible social concern when exercised toward others.
June: Long session. Review. Revise. Compare. Reduce tensions. Write first draft of philosophy of Religious Education.
Take a summer rest.
September: Review the previous year's work. Rewrite the philosophy, goals, and programs in light of second thoughts.

Begin new cycle with *Institution*.
Where should you go from here?
I suggest your taking a second year to go through the same processes

with your faculties, student groups, the members of your board, home-school association committees, and spiritual development groups. You might also at this time want to invite as many other parish members who are interested to join in. Taking another whole year might seem much too drawn out. Interest will have peaked and perhaps died out. That will have to be a prudential judgment on your part. I urge the two-year plan because I believe the results will be richer and more lasting. Initial enthusiasms may wane, but to borrow from the language of joggers, I believe there is plenty of "second wind" out there. Most gold lies deep in the ground. The first digging usually yields little.

I don't promise miracles with this approach. I concede that the results can be occasionally awkward, as illustrated by the definition of the camel as a horse put together by a committee. Nothing is perfect in this life. Yet, if even a shred of community is to exist, people must work together. I am offering a systematic way of bringing that about.

Who should initiate these processes? The pastor, the school principal, the religious education coordinator, and the chairperson of the board of education—these four people have the initial leadership responsibility, so it is their duty to draw up the agenda and decide on the distribution of responsibilities.

With all these items in mind, here are the checklists and meeting outlines.

Institution

Is So	Ought to Be So	
——	——	1. Major decisions about religious education in our parish involve widespread participation of the concerned groups.
——	——	2. Consultation is a normal procedure for our decision making.
——	——	3. Hiring procedures (interviews, contracts, benefits) for school principal, coordinator of religious education, and faculty are clearly spelled out and developed.
——	——	4. We have a budgeting and planning committee that is both knowledgeable and competent.
——	——	5. Our budget allows a fair allocation of funds for the religious education of all the young people in the parish.
——	——	6. The identity, roles, and relationships of the various members of the parish leadership group are delineated and evidently thought through.

____   ____   7. Our planning procedures for the parish look ahead on a five-year projection.

____   ____   8. The participants in our meetings are, by and large, good listeners.

____   ____   9. We appreciate the value of continuity in Church life.

____   ____   10. We retain a sensitivity to the needs of the diocesan and universal Church in our deliberations.

____   ____   11. We know the difference between authority and authoritarianism.

____   ____   12. We try to remain open to new ideas.

____   ____   13. Communications between the various institutions of the parish (viz., school, rectory, convent, religious education center, board, committees, societies, etc.) are fluid and effective.

____   ____   14. Sideward, rather than downward, communication is the norm.

____   ____   15. Inevitable tensions are seen as opportunities for growth rather than occasions of divisive polarization.

____   ____   16. Representation on committees is satisfactory (i.e., proportionate and reflecting maximum interests).

____   ____   17. Generally the majority of officers of the various committees and societies are elected.

____   ____   18. We perceive our efforts at organization as a service to the religious life of the people.

____   ____   19. We affirm that our organizing is not an end in itself.

____   ____   20. Systematic organizing has vastly improved our religious education program.

A. Each member should go through the checklist privately.
B. Follow this with a discussion of the replies.
C. Make a list of your organizational strengths that become evident as a result of the discussion.
D. Itemize areas that need improvement.
E. Call for organizational details not mentioned in the checklist.
F. Ask for ideas that could go into a statement by your parish concerning the community of believers as an institution.
G. Write out a provisional statement of your perception of institution. (As you can see, this could well take much more time than the model schedule calls for. Don't try to finish this task in one meeting, if that be the case. Be sure to plan a social period to go with the evening.)

Follow-up Session

A. Review the discussion about institution and the provisional statement.

B. Revise your statement where needed. Ask if there are still more ideas that should be included.

C. Begin a list of goals and programs to implement institution.

Community

Is So	Ought to Be So	
——	——	1. We realize that a community of believers is a gift of God.
——	——	2. We regularly pray the Holy Spirit will abide with us and help us to become community.
——	——	3. We understand that the work of institutionalizing helps create favorable conditions for community.
——	——	4. If asked, most of the members of our parish would agree that we already have some sense of Christian community.
——	——	5. The experience of faith community in our parish makes the work of religious education much easier.
——	——	6. Our Eucharistic celebrations are regular high points of faith community for us.
——	——	7. Our people are aware that their baptismal commitment involves a dedication to seeking community.
——	——	8. Confirmation events in our parish clearly help us to deepen our sense of community.
——	——	9. Weddings do much to intensify the sense of community among us.
——	——	10. Wakes and funerals raise community consciousness among our people.
——	——	11. Fund raising has helped unite our people through common effort.
——	——	12. Consistent and generous response to social crises in our midst has created a parishwide sense of fellowship.
——	——	13. Tensions in our parish have resulted in creative solutions rather than polarization.
——	——	14. We have been successful in minimizing the problems of cliques and factions.
——	——	15. Most of our parishioners see the connection between growth in grace and the spiritual life with an integrated personal and social life.

____	____	16. All of our adults feel some sense of responsibility for the religious education of all our children.
____	____	17. Our penance celebrations have done much to reconcile people to each other where needed.
____	____	18. We realize the value of neighborhood ties, ethnic identification, and family loyalty. But ultimately we affirm that it is the Spirit that brings us together as one people.
____	____	19. We have succeeded in making community more than a concept to be taught. It is a reality to be lived.
____	____	20. Our parish senses a bond of community with the universal Church.

A. Begin with a personal view of the checklist.
B. Discuss the results.
C. List your community strengths.
D. List your community weaknesses.
E. Indicate aspects of community not covered by the checklist.
F. What tensions are now apparent between the institutional and community models?
G. What productive solutions do you offer to resolve these tensions?
H. Compose a provisional statement of your vision of the meaning of Christian community.
  · Avoid rushing the discussion.
  · Take time to think the items through.
  · Allow the values of process and interaction to work their own magic.

Follow-up Session

A. Review the discussion of community.
B. Revise your written statement where needed.
C. Keep probing for more ideas.
D. Itemize goals and programs to implement the move to community.

Sacrament

Is So   Ought to Be So

____	____	1. Our parishioners understand the broader use of the word *sacrament* as applied to the Church as a sign of grace.
____	____	2. This grace appears in the evident sense of interior unity in our parish expressed through mutual love and friendship.

—— ——   3. There is a clear desire for personal holiness and integrity in our people.

—— ——   4. We rejoice in our Catholic identity and act it out with a catholicity of concern for all our fellow human beings.

—— ——   5. We reflect the apostolic spirit of the early Church with a joyful forward looking effort to communicate the Good News of Christ to all.

—— ——   6. While knowing that Christ continually abides with the Church, we discern the constant need of the membership to improve their personal spiritual lives. (The holiness of Christ must find a counterpart in the members.)

—— ——   7. Our liturgical celebrations genuinely help our people improve their personal and spiritual lives.

—— ——   8. Without question, our people are a prayerful community.

—— ——   9. We have many active prayer groups in our parish.

—— ——   10. Unembarrassed religious belief is a special mark of our congregation.

—— ——   11. The element of mystery in religion is widely appreciated by our people.

—— ——   12. While our people do not speak about it very often, they would, if asked, affirm their religious experience of Christ's presence.

—— ——   13. Our parish is so much a grace to the local scene that outsiders have remarked about it.

—— ——   14. The majority of our people regularly attend Saturday evening/Sunday mass.

—— ——   15. The number of new converts to our faith is impressive and consistent.

—— ——   16. A significant number of our people meditate daily.

—— ——   17. Idealism, flowing from a religious motivation, is a pervasive characteristic in our parish.

—— ——   18. Our parishioners see the connection between religious education and spiritual growth.

—— ——   19. Our parish life is a symbol of the union of people with the Lord.

—— ——   20. We always understand our role as a sign of grace to be a gift of God.

A. Start with an individual review of the checklist.

B. Discuss the results in your group.

C. Number the ways you see yourselves as Sacrament, a community of believers that is a sign of grace.

D. Where do you need improvement in this regard?

E. Is your liturgical life consistent with your overall responsibility to be a sign of grace?

F. Are there tensions between institution, community, and sacrament? How will you resolve them?

G. Again write out a provisional statement about your view of how you fulfill the Sacrament model.
   · Slowly does it.
   · Keep open to more ideas.
   · Reflect on how the process itself is helping you.

Follow-up Session

A. Review the discussion on Sacrament.
B. Revise your statement on this subject.
C. Write out goals and programs in reference to Church as Sacrament.
D. Evaluate your progress to this point.

Is So	Ought to Be So	
____	____	1. Continuous Bible study is popular in our parish.
____	____	2. This Bible study makes use of up-to-date commentaries.
____	____	3. All Bible study groups combine prayer with the study.
____	____	4. Our people realize the spiritual power of the Word of God.
____	____	5. The mass homilies shed continuous and meaningful light on the texts of scripture.
____	____	6. The approach to the interpretation of the Bible is consistent between the study groups, the religious education programs, and the mass homilies.
____	____	7. It is understood that the Church has the responsibility to preach the Word of God to all nations.
____	____	8. It is equally appreciated that conversion resulting from this preaching occurs in an atmosphere of freedom. The listeners cannot be forced to accept.
____	____	9. It is further grasped that conversion is always an event of grace—i.e., God's free gift to a freely accepting person.
____	____	10. It is clear that prayerful study of the Bible is deepening the faith life of our people.
____	____	11. All our families own Bibles, but over half never read them.
____	____	12. Hearing and interpreting the Word of God helps our progress toward a sense of community.
____	____	13. The interpretation of scripture is always within the Catholic context.

____	____	14. The central saving message of Calvary and Easter dominates all considerations of the Word of God.
____	____	15. The Spirit of the Word of God has given our people a renewed enthusiasm for missionary endeavor.
____	____	16. This missionary consciousness begins at home and then extends worldwide.
____	____	17. Our religious education program contains a well planned and developed curriculum for teaching the Bible.
____	____	18. Biblical awareness noticeably affects the devotional life of our people.
____	____	19. All Bible study attempts to relate the Word of God to daily life.

A. Allow time for each member of your group to do the checklist alone.
B. Follow this with group discussion of the results.
C. Your community of believers is to be a herald of the Word of God. In how many ways is your community doing this?
D. List the forces that restrain you from this goal.
E. Compose a provisional statement that describes your role as herald.
F. What tensions do you find between herald and the other models of institution, community, and sacrament? Are there tensions in interpretation? Is there consistency between pulpit, home study, and religious education programs?
  · Make haste slowly.
  · Never stop reaching for more ideas.
  · Stop to evaluate all you have done to this point.

Follow-up Session

A. Review your previous discussion.
B. Revise your herald document.
C. Work on goals and programs to follow up on your herald role.
D. Call for yet more ideas.

Servant

Is So   Ought to Be So

____	____	1. Social concern is a continuous preoccupation of our parish.
____	____	2. We seek justice not only for Catholics but for all people who need fair and equitable treatment.

____   ____   3. We are sensitive to multicultural expressions and try to eliminate any prejudicial behavior in this regard.

____   ____   4. Through study groups, homilies, and other forms of adult education we have brought our people to appreciate the problems created by unjust social structures.

____   ____   5. We cooperate regularly with local community efforts to help people in need.

____   ____   6. As far as we can see, the value system of our people is consistent with the Church's social teachings.

____   ____   7. Our people take a lively and active interest in solving the moral dilemmas that affect the life of the parish.

____   ____   8. We know that both personal moral integrity and social moral awareness are necessary.

____   ____   9. We see that the pursuit of justice is intrinsic to our religious commitment.

____   ____   10. There is a clear relationship between our worship and prayer lives and the search for justice.

____   ____   11. The training in value and moral education in our religious education program for the young is consistent with the homilies and the various adult education programs.

____   ____   12. Salary scales and benefits for persons hired by the parish are enlightened and just.

Below is a list of moral and social issues. Note the ones you are facing.

a. ____ Preservation of privacy   j. ____ Neighborliness
b. ____ Poverty   k. ____ Pornography
c. ____ Racial discrimination   l. ____ Family unity
d. ____ Population control   m. ____ Divorce
e. ____ Women's rights   n. ____ Abortion
f. ____ Minority concerns   o. ____ Drugs
g. ____ Senior citizens   p. ____ Alcoholism
h. ____ Crime   q. ____ Honesty
i. ____ Prisons   r. ____ Other?

A. Do a personal review of the checklist.
B. Discuss the results.
C. You may find the discussion of your community of believers as "servant" seeking justice for all to be more lively and extensive than previous interactions. The issues are more concrete and closer to home. They are also more complex and less easy to

solve. Take plenty of time to talk out the implications of how your parish can be an effective witness to social concern.

D. List your strengths.

E. List your shortcomings.

F. Write a provisional social concern statement. Include the dimensions of individual moral values.
- Don't hurry this process.
- Probe for more ideas.
- Surface the tensions and face them.

When you have finished your coverage of Model 5, recess the meetings for several months. Time is needed for distance and perspective. When you resume the gatherings, allow for a warm-up period by a patient review of the previous work. Prepare a goals and program statement on social concern. Conclude that session by a rewriting of your statement on social concern. After this, appoint two people to take your five statements and write up an overall philosophy of your community of believers and a synthesis of the goals and programs suggested. Let this be a working document for your next session, where you try to hammer out just such a philosophy for yourselves.

Still, this is not the end of the project. Another year should be taken in which those of you who participated in this process will now involve selected groups from your membership, namely, faculty, board and council people, parish societies, student groups, and people in the parish who want to participate. Only after all this should you be ready to make your "final" statement and begin the work of implementing what you have decided to do. Review this philosophy each year. Amend it wherever needed. After five or ten years a thorough review should take place.

You may as well face the possibility that the meetings will not always be peaceful gatherings. Conflicts and tensions are inevitable. Combat and catharsis often mark productive meetings. Don't be put off by this factor. We all know that each person is different. At the round table there will be a wide range of personal psychologies and competencies. Ideally, the project should benefit from this diversity. Both religious motivation and an abiding regard for the opinions of others ought to prevail. Prayer and the spirit of faith should provide the needed hope that you can transcend inevitable impasses and find a common mind and heart.

Your philosophy will be responding to the following questions:

1. What institutional values and structures will best serve the growth of faith in the lives of our people?

2. How do we keep in mind the gift quality of community and the radical spiritual yearning that keeps us open to it?
3. What does it mean for us to be a Sacrament to the world? How do we generally illustrate this?
4. Why must we have a dedication to the Word of God and how do we maintain a long-range missionary spirit?
5. What principles of social concern will animate our consciousness?
6. How do we integrate these five models? How do we handle the tensions they involve?

The philosophy should be mainly a statement of principles. Follow it up with a list of goals and programs.

Spiritual Renewal Weekend

Community is a gift. Organization is a product. The former flourishes in a mood of inner reaching and spiritual sensitivity. The latter results from clear and conscious efforts to assemble and interrelate. We have offered a lengthy process for organization. Here we present a model spiritual weekend whose purpose is to nourish the spiritual dimensions that should be underpinning all the comings and goings of the organizational processes.

Community came to the 120 in the Upper Room at Pentecost as they were absorbed in nine days of prayer. While none would presume to predict that the gift of community will automatically descend upon you who embark on a spiritual weekend, still such an experience is a necessary part of reaching out for that ideal. The following outline is simply meant to give you some ideas of how you could create your own spiritual renewal weekend.

One Mind, One Heart

Friday Evening

7:00 PM   *Arrival:* settling in.

7:30   *Introduction:* housekeeping details; process and goals for the weekend.

          Hymn: COME HOLY GHOST

          Reading: Pentecost story (Acts 2)

          Prayer: Come to us, Spirit of the Lord. Grant us the gift of community. Open our minds to see the grounds of unity in the midst of diverse points of view. Enlarge the capacity of our hearts to love with simplicity and loyalty. Draw us together in the common bond of grace. This we ask through Jesus our Lord, Amen.

Film: (filmstrip, slide, movie) Something on community or Holy Spirit, or commentary on Acts of Apostles.

Talk: "Community is a Gift." Stress the mysterious way that community appears; never forced; seems always to arrive as a miracle and a grace. (15 minutes)

Sharing session: Call upon all participants to offer their thoughts about the community of believers.

Hymn: AMAZING GRACE

Social hour

Saturday

9:00 AM   *Breakfast*

10:00   *Meditation*

11:00   *Group session*

Hymn: ALL THE EARTH SING PRAISE TO GOD

Prayer

Talk: "What is a Believer?" How believing is part of all life, whether arts, sciences, religion, sports, or personal relations. How believing is behind all thinking and is in fact the deeper side of thought. Relation of believing to God and religious truths and daily living. (30 minutes)

Film, etc., if available.

Sharing session: Invite everyone personally to speak up. Don't pressure people to talk, they may either have nothing to say, or simply don't feel like it at the moment. Keep a relaxed atmosphere.

1:00 PM   *Lunch*

2:00   *Quiet time*

4:00   *Hymn:* HOW GREAT THOU ART

Reading: "They devoted themselves to the communal life, to the breaking of bread and prayers. Those who believed shared all things in common. They would sell their property and goods, dividing everything on the basis of each one's need. They went to the temple area every day, while in their homes they broke bread. With exultant and sincere hearts they took their meals in common, praising God and winning the approval of all the people. Day by day the Lord added to their number those who were being saved."

                                                                                      (Acts 2:42–47)

Personal response of each participant:

1. This scene from the early church

    a. ____ depressed me   b. ____ puzzled me   c. ____ struck me as unreal

    d. ____ inspired me   e. ____ appears too ideal   f. ____ encouraged me to trust that our group can become a community of believers.

2. I am impressed by (rank order)
   ___ their common ownership of goods.
   ___ the way they centered their lives on prayer and Eucharist.
   ___ their linking of prayer at the Temple and Eucharist at home.
   ___ the closeness of their relationships.
   ___ the daily increase of their numbers.
   ___ their evident personal joy.
3. The difference between their community and ours is (check three)
   ___ We don't have common ownership of goods.
   ___ Nor do we want that kind of common life.
   ___ We almost never pray together.
   ___ We approach Eucharist as a formality, not a sign of unity.
   ___ We feel no need for each other.
   ___ We're basically strangers.
   ___ We close our eyes to each other's opinions and needs.
4. My best memories of community were
   ___ Ski holiday.
   ___ Caribbean cruise.
   ___ High school retreat.
   ___ Thanksgiving with my family.
   ___ Graduation party.
   ___ Winning a sports championship.
   ___ Working together on a social action project.
   ___ Other.
5. What do I fear about becoming a member of community as described in Acts?
   ___ The expectations are too high.
   ___ I don't want any more close relationships.
   ___ I don't think I can believe as deeply as they can.
   ___ They seem to put more trust in prayer than I am willing to.
   ___ The incompatability factor in our group is too extensive.
   ___ I will not be ready or able to offer the emotional support that some people will demand of me.

Let each person ponder these items and then use them as a basis for discussion. Relax, however. Let people join in the discussion according to their inclination.
   ___ Prepare for mass.
   ___ Use the mass of the day. Select hymns and practice them.
   Write out prayers of petition.

7:00 PM   *Supper*

8:15   *Evening session*
Hymn: FAITH OF OUR FATHERS
Ask each member to volunteer an entertainment for the group. Time for hidden talents to emerge. Tell a story, funny or sad, mocking or serious. Sing a song. Dance a dance. Pose a riddle. Play a musical instrument. Recite a poem or something else that

has been memorized. Pantomime. Don't push anyone. Let involvement be comfortable and free.
Quiet time together. (15 minutes)

Sunday

9:00 AM   *Breakfast*

10:00   *Talk: "Jesus."* He was able to create a community out of twelve unlikely people. His risen presence abides to call unlikely people such as ourselves to the possibility of community.

        Film, etc.

        Reactions

        Mass time: Use mass of day. Select hymns. Practice them. Write out prayers of petitions. During the communion meditation period, invite participants to verbalize their thoughts and feelings about the weekend, if they so choose.

        Light Lunch

        Departure

Here are some comments about this model. 1) Normally your parish executive group will be small enough for group participation without splitting up. If you are in your second year with much larger numbers, use small groupings for the discussion times, but not for the entertainment evening. 2) Condense the affair to a one-day gathering or several evenings, or expand it to more days should you desire. 3) Avoid the temptation to intrude on people's feelings or privacy. 4) Hope for a happy time but beware of "organizing" the joy.

Honor Thy Friend and Neighbor

Remembrance events and recognition ceremonies do much to create the simple tug that draws people closer to each other. Your parish has many ways in which this can be done. Following is a list of suggestions along these lines.

1. Remember people's birthdays and anniversaries.
2. Praise individual achievements. (Some people have a hard time getting such words out of their mouths. Perhaps they think it is beneath them or that the achiever doesn't want, need, or deserve it. True, it's all water off a duck's back. But the duck likes it. So does almost everyone.)
3. *Recognition ceremonies*
   a. Aquinas medal for college graduates.
   b. Cardinal Newman award for those who have received their master's degree.

c. John XXIII medal for completion of doctorate. (When the parish takes time to recognize academic excellence and achievement, there will be a better relationship between the intellectual community and the parish at large.)

d. Golden rose for couples completing their fiftieth year of marriage.

e. Silver rose for silver wedding anniversaries. (Marriages today need all the support they can get. There is so much news about marriages breaking up. Let there also be some attention paid to marriages that have matured and survived contemporary pressures.)

f. *Families of the week.* Display pictures of parish families on bulletin board in church vestibule, with names and a story about them.

g. *Singles of the week.* Display pictures of single people in the parish and a story about their interests and achievements. (Young singles in particular often feel left out of parish life because of the heavy family orientation—with parents and children dominating the scene.)

h. Use the parish bulletin to describe the progress being made by groups engaged in the community of believers processes.

i. Implement (h) by encouraging words from the pulpit from time to time.

j. If economically reasonable, create a parish yearbook or album with pictures of all your parishioners and items of human interest.

4. Don't overlook the traditional socializing functions of picnics, pot luck suppers, dances, card parties, bazaars, bingo. Granted, these affairs may be simpler to run in rural settings than in urban or suburban situations, but variations can be devised.

5. Gratitude night for special donors in the parish (pews, windows, etc.).

6. Graduation mass for all the students.

7. *Variation for Lenten sermons:* Ask families to speak of family and religion in their experiences.

8. Corpus Christi ice cream party for all the year's first communicants.

9. Christmas and Valentine parties for the special education children of the parish.

10. Honor Roll of parents of priests and members of religious orders in the parish.

11. Appreciation dinner for CCD teachers and their spouses.

12. Appreciation dinner for Catholic school faculty, spouses, and personnel.

13. Four times a year, conduct welcome gatherings for newcomers in your parish.
14. Ecumenical night for local personnel of other religions.
15. Weekly coffee for the senior citizens.
... and many more.

Summary

We have tried to set out the theory behind a community of believers. We followed this with a description of a two-year process that should help formulate a philosophy, with goals and programs to implement the idea of such a community. This was followed by a description of a model spiritual renewal weekend, and lastly, by a listing of some simple human ways to encourage the appearance of a community spirit. We well know that nothing guarantees the appearance of community. We also know that people must work intelligently and prayerfully to make it possible.

BASIC TEACHINGS

How are men to call upon him in whom they have not believed? And how are they to believe in him of whom they have never heard? And how are they to hear without a preacher? Faith comes from what is heard, and what is heard comes by the preaching of Christ.

Rom. 10:14, 17

The Christian faith requires explanations.
GCD, 25

Every institution has a charter that articulates the fundamental principles and beliefs upon which it is based. America roots its expectations and identity in the Declaration of Independence and the Constitution—"We hold these truths to be self evident. . . ." So also the Church stands on an articulated charter by which she expresses her meaning. This charter is expressed in the Bible, the Creeds, the dogmas, and moral principles.

The literature of the charter is extensive. This is why educators (and others) try to express a statement of belief that is concise, yet complete and thorough at the same time. In the early period of the Church, the creation of the Creeds (Apostles, Nicene, Athanasian) realized this aim. In the post-Reformation Church, catechisms, with their question-and-answer format, spoke to this need.

Once again, in the wake of so much creative thinking spurred by Vatican II, the Church asks for an expression and a reaffirmation of its basic beliefs. The term Basic Teachings normally arises as the embodiment of this hope. In this chapter I intend to summarize the Basic Teachings. I will be guided by the three major bases—the Bible, Creed, and dogmas—in outlining them.

I wish to pose four questions before getting to this task. Where do Basic Teachings come from? What is the context for teaching these basics? What is the link between Basic Teachings and faith? What kind of talk is used for these teachings in a) the Bible, b) the Creeds, c) the catechism, and d) today's personalism? The purpose of these questions is to put Basic Teachings in some kind of perspective. Unless they are given some kind of setting such as suggested by these questions, they are liable to be misused and misunderstood.

First Question: Where Do Basic Teachings Come From?

The most obvious answer for most of us is—the Church. My question
is deeper. Where did the Church find the Basic Teachings? In the
Bible. All right, but how did they appear in the Bible? From the
prophets and apostles. Yes, but what moved the prophets and apostles
to utter these teachings?

I submit that religious experience is the basic event to keep in mind.
Religious experience means that the prophets and apostles met the
Lord. When asked why he said what he said, Isaiah replied: "I saw the
Lord ... One of the seraphim flew to me, and holding an ember,
touched my mouth with it." (Read about Isaiah's vision/religious ex-
perience in Chapter 6 of his book.)

The prophets clearly maintain that their teachings originated from
an experience of God. Jeremiah tells us the Lord came to him. That
is religious experience. Ezekiel sees a space spectacular by the river
Chebar. The Lord comes to him in that vision, offers him the scroll of
the Holy Word, and commands the prophet to eat the Word of sweetness. This is religious experience. An interior meeting with God precedes an exterior expression of the Lord's teaching.

The utterances of the prophets are first delivered in sermons—in
Holy Spoken Word. Lest those teachings be lost, the prophets' words
are then written down—Holy Written Word, Holy Writ, Scripture.

It is the same with the apostles. For three years they enjoy the
privilege of a religious experience of Jesus the Lord. Their relationship
with Jesus is not just at the external level of a fraternity but at the
more profound level of "heart to heart." True, they are exposed to the
external deeds and words of Jesus, but it is their inner union with him
that makes the experience of his personal teaching and works "religious" in the best sense of that term.

The summit of their experience of Jesus lies both in their pitiful and
dark reaction to his passion and death, and in their ecstatic meeting
with him as Easter Lord. Their experience of the events of redemption
unutterably heightened their association with Jesus during the years of
the Galilean and Judean ministry.

As the prophets moved from their experience of God to the public
utterance of His word, so also the apostles proceeded from their experience of Jesus to the public utterance of his word. The Old Testament
utterance is prophecy. The New Testament proclamation is gospel.

Religious experience is the name given to a meeting between God
and a human person. The prophets met God. The apostles met Jesus,
the Son of God. The name given to their spiritual response is faith.
God comes in love to the consciousness of the prophet. The prophet

opens his heart to God. This act of opening and adherence is faith. Abraham believed in God. Isaiah believed in God.

Jesus came in love to each apostle as he called him to discipleship. In trust and faith, each apostle responded. The Gospels describe the deepening of that belief, particularly as it grew to enduring firmness in the events of redemption.

Faith not only refers to personal adherence to and trust in God, but also to the public expression thereof. The words of prophecy and gospel are words of faith. In the religious experience, faith is the act of personal conviction that opens one up and lovingly welcomes the Lord. In prophecy and gospel, faith is the preached and written word that expresses the meaning of the experience of God. Hence the word *faith* operates at two levels, the interior (experience of God) and the exterior (public utterance).

When the Blessed Virgin was pregnant with Jesus, she rejoiced in the experience of her Lord. On the summit of Ain Karim she met her cousin Elizabeth, who solicited from her an unforgettable public expression of her interior union with God. Every cloister and monastery in the world echoes with her words each evening at Vespers:

My soul magnifies the Lord!

The Bible asserts that this religious experience may occur privately or in public. Jeremiah's basic experience seems to have occurred while he was in solitude. Gabriel's annunciation to Mary happens while she is alone.

On the other hand, the Israelites crossing the Red Sea, experience God in a tumultuous historical event. Isaiah meets the Lord at a public temple liturgy. The apostles experience Jesus in a variety of social and fraternal gatherings, both before and after the resurrection. The obvious conclusion, then, is: One may meet the Lord alone or with others.

The answer to my first question, then, is that religious experience is the primordial event from which comes, eventually, the public utterance—the Word of the Lord. The Basic Teachings, with which we will soon deal, are a summary of that Word of the Lord. The root of Basic Teachings is the result of the faith-filled human experience of God. Let me reflect again that I speak of faith in two senses: 1) personal adherence to God, 2) public expression in Holy Word. I must add that we also speak of faith in terms of moral behavior. If Basic Teachings are a Word expression of faith, loving and moral behavior is the Body Talk of faith. Hence I witness my faith both by preaching and by performing.

Second Question: What is the context for teaching the Basics?

Here, again, the answer is—the Church.

Several refinements are in order here. First, the Church is itself, like Basic Teachings, a result of the experience of God. That is why tradition speaks of the event of Pentecost as the birthday of the Church, the day the Church was born. Pentecost was a communal religious experience of the Spirit of God. However, the Church was already coming into existence prior to Pentecost.

Jesus labored to form the apostles into a community of believers. His words and deeds shaped them and his personal impact upon their lives gradually welded them into a spiritual community. His appointment of Peter as the rock upon which the Church would be built emphasizes his intention that they become a communal continuation of his life and teachings and Spirit.

Hence a series of religious events led to the creating of the Church. Just as God willed Israel to be a people and brought it about by graciously giving them an experience of Himself, His power, and His love, so also Christ willed, through the apostles, a new people, graciously giving them an unmatched experience of himself, his power, and his love.

The Church is a public community born from (and willed by) the experience of God's Son.

The Church is a community of believers.

The Church is also an institution, an organization.

Every community has its structural and institutional aspects. As a community, the Church is the living witness of Christ. As an institution, it embraces the organizational methods and tools to sustain its ideal of being the Body of Christ. The institutional side of the Church maintains the public memory of the events of salvation (the Bible), celebrates that memory in sacraments, implements it through moral guidance, strives to speak the basic message in "thoughts that burn and words that breathe."

The institutional Church canonizes and protects the Sacred Word, ritualizes the holiest moments of people in sacraments, theologizes that God may be touched by people from diverse cultures and ages. Since the chapter on Community of Faith touches this distinction at great depth, I will not linger on it here.

I simply want to set the background for saying that the Church is the context for Basic Teachings. If there were not a community and an institution standing for the Basic Teachings, no individual would ultimately succeed in proclaiming them. The Church stands as a support system for the individual's work in teaching Christ. A local parish — a mini-Church — is the local support system for teaching religion. This involves not only finanical support, but, more importantly, moral and spiritual support.

Where do Basic Teachings come from?

First, they come from religious experiences described in my first answer. Secondly, they come from the Church as context, namely, the memory carrier and sociological sustainer of the public utterances of the prophets and apostles (who proclaim the words and deeds of Jesus).

Third Question: What is the relationship between Basic Teachings and faith?

The Basic Teachings originated in a faith event. They grew out of a special relationship between God and people. The faith relationship begins as personal, spiritual, inward and moves to external utterance in Holy Word and Holy Deed. Since speaking and doing are confined to the moment of history when they occur, it is the institutionalized written expression that lives on.

To us, then, the Basic Teachings are written testimonies of faith that once were spoken in prophecy and gospel resulting from religious experience and lived out in Christian witness.

What is their value for us?

Their purpose is to introduce us to the Son of the living God. The Basic Teaching about redemption is not meant just to be a raw, cold statement, but an invitation to experience Jesus as savior and redeemer. Merely as a piece of grammar and sentence structure, a Basic Teaching is nothing more than a concept. Our belief is that it can point us to Jesus and invite us to spiritual union with our Easter Lord.

Hence the ultimate purpose of a Basic Teaching is spiritual and moral. It may indeed, and often does, possess a secondary purpose of giving us some words to use when we want to tell someone in concise conceptual form the substance of our belief. The mistake is made when we make this secondary usage the primary one. On the other hand, it is equally erroneous to so concentrate on its primary aim that we ignore its secondary practicality.

Education dwells so much on concept mastery — on memory and organization — that it could easily mix up the priorities inherent in Basic Teachings. I assert once more that the principal reason for Basic Teachings is spiritual enlightenment, union with Jesus as savior, and the moral consequences for personal witness flowing therefrom. Its secondary value, as an articulation tool and memory jogger, remains clear.

Fourth Question: What kind of talk is used for these Basic Teachings in a) the Bible, b) the Creeds, c) the catechism, and d) today's personalism?

Bible writers use the narrative art form to express Basic Teachings. They present a faith-informed history of Israel and Jesus.

The catechism writers employ an abstract art form and wed it to a teaching technique of question and answer.

The personalist writers employ the concrete language of relationship.

Each approach speaks for a cherished value. The Biblical Word, coming closest (as it does) to the actual events of salvation and enjoying the privilege of inspiration, offers us the most complete expression in terms of the original moment.

The Creedal word is crisp, hieratic, liturgical in tone. It declares the events of creation and salvation in the general sequence in which they are found in the Bible. It is a recital of the major acts of God that our faith both affirms and responds to. Invariably incorporated into the Sunday mass, the Creedal words partake of the continuing mystery of God's power made present and available to every age.

The catechism word possesses the advantage of condensing the full picture of salvation into a clearly ordered sequence. Its use of abstract vocabulary enables the user to acquire clear concepts in order to distinguish the explanation of the reality from confusing or misleading ones.

The personalist word captures the meaning of salvation in concrete relational terms. It also strives to relate God and people in the immediacy of the contemporary situation, not by using modern props but by communicating the sense of invitation to spiritual union implied by the teaching.

Each approach also has its limits.

The Bible presents the Basic Teachings in extensive, rich narrative. It tells the events at length. It does not offer us neat condensations. It requires the reader to excerpt and tape together the principal events of salvation. Unhappily, and in spite of all the excellent Bible aids and new translations available today, many people do not and cannot approach the Bible in any meaningful way.

Like the catechism word, the Creedal word condenses the Biblical announcement. Even more so than the catechetical word, it provides the quickest overview of the acts of God. On the other hand, the Creedal word has almost too much brevity. And it speaks not of sacraments nor of morality nor of spirituality — elements of belief that must be included in order to portray the whole picture.

The catechism condenses and sequences very well. However, its language may obscure what it intends to communicate. Being so abstract, it does not speak to the heart naturally. Sometimes its terms are heavily technological to the point where even continuous explanation still does not seem to help.

The personalist approach can suffer from vagueness. Even though relationship as a category would seemingly have universal appeal (and it does), it also participates in the ebb and flow of what every relationship does. If the catechism in its abstractness may appear to be too far from life, the personalist approach in its concreteness can be so close up to life that meaning can become muddled.

So now you know my four questions and responses. Basic Teachings grew out of the religious events described in the Bible. They are sustained within the context of the Church as a living and structured Body of Christ. Their major purpose is to awaken the life of faith and lead to spiritual enlightenment and union with Christ. They are articulated in the Bible, the Creeds, the catechism, and in today's personalist categories, each of which expressions has advantages and disadvantages for catechesis.

Now a new question: What are the Basic Teachings? I will venture to list them. My language will waver between biblical and personalist, but the brevity will cause a certain leaning toward the abstract. In my suggestions about teaching, following this section, I hope to help you ascertain the primary and secondary goals for referring to Basic Teachings as a catechetical guideline.

Please keep in mind that the following list is that and nothing more. I have added some thoughts to go with each teaching. They are clearly an insufficient comment on the full extent of the teaching. I have not tried to touch all bases in speaking of each truth claim. I am hoping that at every moment you keep in mind the aspect of faith as spiritual union with Christ and a moral posture toward life in both its personal and social aspects.

I have chosen to present the sequence from a transcendental point of view. First, let us consider God's actions through the events of creation and redemption. Then, let us look at our faith response in Church, Sacrament, Morality, and Spirituality. I use an "I believe" format to emphasize the personalist dimension.

A List of Basic Teachings—With Some Comment

1. I believe in God, the Father Almighty, the creator of heaven and earth.

    a. I believe in God.

    We begin immediately with a testimony of faith. This is an announcement of one's personal experience of the Lord. It affirms to the world that we do not know ultimate loneliness, for we perceive God's pervasive presence in the universe and in our own lives. We appreciate the psalmist's observation that the earth is full of the glory of God.

b. I believe God is my Father.

This means that my experience of God is one of origin. I assert that God made me to know, love, and serve him here and to enjoy his presence hereafter. I find in God's fathering me a purpose for my existence in the world. I also note that he never ceases to communicate life to me. God is my enduring shepherd. He is my origin and destiny.

c. I believe that God is the creator of the universe.

King David wrote that the heavens declare the glory of God and the firmament speaks to all of us about its being his handiwork. I believe this and know that all that is speaks of that which is beyond. The world is a sounding board of the divine presence,

Creation is not to be presented as a truth by itself, but ordered toward the salvation wrought in Jesus Christ. The creation of visible and invisible things, of the world and of angels, is the beginning of the mystery of salvation. The creation of man is to be regarded as the first gift and first call that leads to glorification in Christ. (GCD 51)

telling us of the God who created it. God speaks to us through the wonders of nature. I see that God has not only created the cosmos, he sustains it and presides over its development.

Teaching Guideline   Note that this rich affirmation of one's faith in God is a fundamental declaration of our spiritual experience of his transcendent presence. Critics have said we may sometimes teach about a God who is "out there." That may be. This statement of belief speaks of a God who is "right here," the Father and creator who dwells in the midst of life.

Believe and praise, before you prove.

In your teaching, show that a faith in God precedes rational proofs of his existence. This is like falling in love. This mysterious and happy event happens first. Then the lovers work to prove that their love is real.

2. I believe in Jesus Christ, Son of God, Savior and Lord.

a. I believe Jesus is the Word made flesh.

From the outset I testify that Jesus is the Son of God made man, conceived by the Holy Spirit and born of the Virgin Mary. I find that my experience of the Christmas mystery is expressed by and associated with the matchless words used by Matthew and Luke in their infancy narratives. With shepherds and kings I stand in awe before this mystery of Incarnation. I see in this unity of God and man the basis of being open to the marvels of divine indwelling.

b. I believe Jesus is my savior.

Clearly Christ's life, with its teachings, parables, and miracles, his death, and resurrection constitute the substance of his saving work. Through his saving work I know I can be and have been forgiven my sins. By overcoming evil* Jesus both gives me the possibility of liberation from evil as well as the positive side of growth to the highest form of self-fulfillment in union with him. I know that nothing is more central to me than to identify with and be gratefully open to Jesus as my savior.

c. I believe Jesus is my Lord.

He ascended into heaven where he sits at the right hand of the Father and will come to judge the living and the dead. My experience of Jesus as Lord draws forth from the sentiments of awe, reverence, and adoration. "When Christ shall come, mid shouts of jubilation, to take me home, what joy shall fill my heart! And I shall bow in humble adoration, and there declare, 'My God, How great thou art!'" I do not see adoration in any way a groveling or a dehumanizing act. Quite the opposite. I find that awe and reverence for the Lord fills me with immense self-respect and enables me to reverence all of life.

Teaching Guideline   Jesus is the center of all religion teaching. The fullest meaning of God, Church, Sacrament, and morality is rooted in him. He is the alpha and omega of all we are trying to do.

Center your catechesis in Christ.

Affirm him as God made man, Savior, and Lord.

---

* Dramatically illustrated during his life by overcoming the devil's temptations in the desert experience at the beginning of his ministry, by his many acts of exorcism of devils, and by the miracles that deposed the kingdom of evil. Note the Isaian prophecy, "How you are fallen from heaven, O Day Star (Lucifer), son of dawn." (14:12) See also the war between Michael the archangel and the dragon in Revelation: "Now a war arose in heaven, Michael and his angels fighting against the dragon . . . And that great dragon, who is called the devil and Satan, the deceiver of the whole world—he was thrown down to the earth and his angels were thrown down with him." (Rev. 12:7-10)

3. I believe in the Holy Spirit, Lord and Giver of Life, who proceeds from the Father and the Son. With the Father and the Son he is worshipped and glorified.

   a. I believe in the Spirit as Gift.

      I bless Christ our Lord who filled the apostles with wisdom by sending the Holy Spirit upon them. I bless Jesus for the personal gift of the Spirit. I understand this as grace, God's free graciousness in giving himself to us, being ever ready to communicate spiritual power that I may have a pure heart and the strength of Christian witness.

   b. I believe that Spirit is God's dynamic presence.

      The Holy Spirit awakens within me the sense of the divine presence, the Father Creator and Jesus as Savior and Lord. The wisdom the Spirit brings enables me to sense Christ present in others.

Teaching Guideline   The story of Pentecost begins the rich story of the work of the Spirit in the Church. Over and over, the apostles testify to the fire that comes from his inner presence that gives them unbelievable courage as they engage in the mission of the Church.

Link the Spirit with grace, religious experience, and courage.

O Comforter, equal in majesty and nature with the Father and the Son, glory unto you.

4. I believe in the Holy Trinity.

I experience God as my Father, origin, and destiny.

   I experience the Son of God as my savior and Lord.

   I experience the Spirit of God as Gift/Grace giver and encourager.

   Come all you nations of the world: Let us adore God in three holy Persons, Father, Son, and Holy Spirit—Three in One.

   I believe that from all eternity, the Father begets the Son, equal to him in majesty, equal also to the Holy Spirit, glorified with the Son in the Father—Three Persons, and yet a single power and essence and Godhead.

   In deep adoration, let us praise God.

   Holy is God, who made all things through the Son with the cooperation of the Holy Spirit.

   Holy is the Lord Jesus, through whom the Father was revealed to us and through whom the Holy Spirit came into this world.

   Holy is the Spirit, the Counselor who proceeds from the Father and reposes in the Son.

All Holy Trinity, glory to you!
(See the *Byzantine Daily Worship*, p. 892)

Teaching Guideline This is perhaps the most difficult teaching to put into words. I think it is a mystery perhaps too awesome for discourse. Still, I believe that the most light is shed by speaking of the Persons and their relation to us as Creator, Savior, Sanctifier.

Emphasize each Person's relation to us, while retaining a sense of the unity of Godhead.

5. I believe in the one, holy, catholic, and apostolic Church.

a. I believe in the one Church.

It is through the context of the Church that I regularly come to know Christ. It is in his Spirit that I can see how there can be Christian unity amid a diversity of nations, languages, cultures, and ministries. I know that this unity is something that must always be prayed and worked for. We respond to Christ's prayer that we all work to become one in him.

b. I believe in the holiness of the Church.

The Holy Spirit dwells in the Church ever ready to communicate holiness to the members. Clearly, the Church is like the gospel image of the wheat and the weeds. The saints, the holy ones, are the wheat. The sinners are the weeds. The Church has always been graced with living saints—her signs of holiness. But the Church also receives the saving forgiveness of Jesus and holds it out to all who are in need thereof.

c. I believe in the catholicity of the Church.

The universal Church is broad enough to include every nation, language, and culture. Her mission is to the ends of the earth, announcing Christ in a diversity of tongues and encouraging worship of him in a myriad of cultural expressions.

d. I believe the Church is apostolic.

This means the Church is always evangelical, ready to preach Christ, in season and out of season, prepared for a healing ministry and standing as a sign of hope to the poor and dispossessed and every human being hungering for God.

Teaching Guideline These notes on the four marks of the Church give a hint as to the many possibilities implicit in our faith and how we shall realize it.

Translate the four marks of the Church into action plans.

6. I believe in the Virgin Mary, Mother of God, image of the Church, and immaculately conceived.

a. I believe in the Virgin Mary, Mother of God.

The story of the Annunciation tells how the incarnation of Jesus occurs. God, who made the world without the aid of man or woman, now through his Spirit conceives his Son, Jesus, without the aid of a male spouse. Mary's Amen to God's intention illustrates both her remarkable openness to God's will, her perception to see it when it is spoken, and her practical readiness to act on it when it is clear.

b. I believe in Mary, the image of the Church.

Mary is a privileged model of how members of the Church should respond to Christ and bear his presence to the world. As an Ark of the Covenant she brought Christ to the world. The members of the Church bear the living Christ and have the responsibility to let his light shine to all nations.

c. I believe in Mary's immaculate conception.

Daughter of Joachim and Anne, Mary was created in grace, free from original sin. Pius IX declared this to be an official dogma of the Church in 1854.

Teaching Guideline   The two parts of the *Hail Mary* illustrate the basic approach to this teaching. Part one celebrates her mystery and meaning. Part two calls upon her intercessory power.
Take the Hail Mary *as the basis of your catechesis.*

7. I believe in the life of the world to come—and the judgment that awaits us.

a. I believe in immortality.

Death is not the end. It is the beginning of a new experience. A consciousness of death is a reminder of the short time allotted to us here to develop our personal potential and fully realize a growth in spiritual union with Christ. In his Cross and Resurrection, Jesus has broken the bonds of death and invited us to eternal life with him.

b. I believe in the judgment.

Beyond death we face the possibility of Heaven or hell. This is the judgment. It is not an arbitrary experience. As we live so shall we die. God's loving forgiveness awaits us to the very end—as in the case of the Good Thief. For those who have loved people and the Lord, there will be eternal life in Heaven. For those who have failed to love, who remain fixed in sin, there will be eternal death in hell.

Tradition distinguishes a particular and general judgment. Particular judgment occurs at the moment of individual death. The general judgment is to come at the end of time. It is primarily a celebration of the final glorification of Christ.

c. I believe in purgatory.

The Vatican Council speaks of purgatory in these words. Until Christ's arrival in majesty, "Some of his disciples are pilgrims on earth, some have finished this life and are being purified, and others are in glory." (Constitution on the Church #49) Funeral liturgies, prayers for the dead, and the Feast of All Souls speak to this mystery.

Teaching Guideline   In affirming immortality and the judgment we will not be able to describe life after death in anything but the most general terms. We can speak of Heaven and hell, but no concrete descriptions are available to us other than hell fire and divine glory. We do well to be modest and to refrain from using unwarranted realisms about the future life.

Better to concentrate on the relationship of death to life, which is the time of our personal spiritual growth, and remain comparatively reticent about life beyond the grave.

While affirming immortality, speak of death as the challenge to spiritual growth here on earth.

The following points refer to the Sacraments. A Sacrament is an event in which a person meets Christ and experiences his saving power. The ceremonial signs accompanying each Sacrament illustrate its meaning. Each Sacrament brings a spiritual depth to the person's human experience, whether it be birth, growth, fellowship, marriage, ministry, repentance, or sickness and death. Sacramental moments solemnize the major human experiences and unite them to the realm of the sacred. Religious educators should help people understand the fundamental meaning of Sacrament and explain the significance of the ceremonial signs accompanying each Sacrament, as well as awakening the faith of the person in the Jesus they are about to meet.

8. I believe in Baptism.

In the rite of Baptism I declare my faith and commitment to Jesus Christ, and my renunciation of the powers and forces of sin and evil.

Reborn again, in water and the Holy Spirit, I receive from Christ the grace of innocence and freedom from captivity of original sin and am made a member of the Church.

✦ **Teaching Guideline**   Since the majority of Baptisms are of infants, great care must be taken to instruct the adults involved about the meaning of Baptism and their religious responsibilities to the child.   If an adult is to be baptized, the new rite of Baptism for adults and the Lenten catechesis are in order.

In either case, prepare the adults.

9. I believe in Confirmation.

In the rite of Confirmation I reaffirm my Baptismal commitment and promise that I will remain faithful to Christ until my death.   I receive an inpouring of the Holy Spirit, his gift of wisdom, and particularly his gift of courage to live the Christian life with conviction and perseverance.   This Sacrament signals my entry into adult Christian life and my resolve to grow in faith in cooperation with the Spirit's guidance.

✦ **Teaching Guideline**   A living Christian must always be a developing person of faith.   Whether the Sacrament of Confirmation is celebrated for preadults or adults, religious educators should emphasize its relation to inner spiritual growth.

Treat Confirmation as Sacrament calling for lifelong spiritual growth.

10. I believe in the Eucharist.

Perhaps no Sacrament is more central to the spiritual life of the people than the Eucharist.   In the Eucharist I offer adoration, praise, gratitude, sentiments of repentance, and heartfelt petition to my Father through Jesus in the Spirit.   I enter into communion with Jesus, with both a consciousness of my individual need for him and my sharing with the Church in the table of the Lord.   Jesus binds me closer to himself by his offered love and deepens my sense of fellowship and partnership with all members of the Body of Christ.

I find that his abiding and real Eucharistic Presence, outside times of mass, invites me to meditation and continued spiritual enlightenment. I stand in faith-filled awe before the mystery of bread and wine being changed into Christ's Body and Blood and I look forward each time to being touched by the saving power of his Passion, Death, and Resurrection in this Most Holy Sacrament.

Teaching Guideline The Eucharist is the Sacrament most often contacted, because the mass is the daily and weekly worship service of the Church. Relate the Eucharist to the mysteries of Christ celebrated and made present, especially the events of redemption. Emphasize the possibilities of spiritual growth implicit in worship and communion. Relate worship to the moral witness and social consciousness of the people.

Link the Eucharist with worship, individual and communal growth, and moral consequences.

11. I believe in Confession of sins.

In the Sacrament of reconciliation I confess my sinfulness and receive divine forgiveness. Just as the Easter Christ conferred peace of heart and soul on his apostles in the Upper Room on Easter night, so here he waits to forgive, console, and lift from me the weight of guilt. After Baptism I felt like a new man. But I have sinned since then. But God is always in Christ reconciling us to himself. I am also thereby reconciled to the Church and am fully a member again of the believing and developing community.

Teaching Guideline The new rite of penance needs extensive explanation. It is important that Confession not be a mechanical moment, that the Lord's forgiveness be stressed, and that the communal dimension be included.

Proclaim an ever-forgiving Lord and reacceptance into community.

12. I believe in the Sacrament of Marriage.

Sacraments speak to the depth implicit in major moments in life. Few moments are more central than entry into marriage. The love of the partners reflects and will take strength from the love of Christ for the Church. Christ's commitment to the community of believers is absolute. His love is unfailing and it will be with us all of our days. The power of his kind of commitment is viable through this Sacrament and the renewal of its intention in the ensuing years.

Teaching Guideline The complexity of marriage in modern culture requires extensive preparation. No attempt will be made to outline it here. Since the currently greatest need appears to be the possibility of maximum fidelity in marriage, the link between that need and the grace of this Sacrament should be highlighed.

As Christ unfailingly loves the Church, so can the spouses share in that grace of enduring commitment.

13. I believe in the Sacrament of Holy Orders.

An ordained ministry is an intrinsic part of Church order. In the rite for the ordination of Bishops, Priests, and Deacons (both transitional and permanent) the candidates affirm their special calling to the ministry of Word, Sacrament, and Service and receive from Christ a share in his ministry and the power to celebrate Word and Sacrament in liturgy.

Teaching Guideline   The singularity of the priestly office should be distinguished from the general priesthood of all believers. The moral and spiritual responsibilities and duties of those who stand at the altar and engage in such proximity to the Sacred should be explained.
Explain the role of ordained ministers of Word, Sacrament, and Service.

14. I believe in the anointing of the sick.

In recent years the rite of anointing has been expanded from application only to dying persons to all who are in grave illness, with the idea that the Sacrament is one of spiritual and physical healing. While the latter may not occur, the former is always a possibility. The sick person reaches out to Christ for healing and hope, whether to simply get well – or if to die – to journey into his loving presence in the afterlife.

Teaching Guideline   Enlighten sick people and their families about the change in the usage of the Sacrament of anointing and encourage communal celebration wherever possible.
Highlight the consoling, healing, and communal aspects of anointing of the sick.

The next section is concerned with moral principles that relate to moral living. Moral principles stand between the religious experience of covenant and the human experience of dilemma situations.
Israel's covenant with God at Sinai led to the moral principles evidenced in the Ten Commandments and the principles enunciated in Deuteronomy, Leviticus, and the prophetic writings.
Christ's covenant with the Christian people occurs in his death and resurrection. The moral principles flowing from it appear in the Eight Beatitudes and the principles found primarily in the Sermon on the Mount, the Last Supper discourse, the teachings of Paul, and certain other New Testament writings.
The covenants of love give rise to the moral principles that express the meaning of covenant. The changing situations of life are where

those principles are to be applied. When applied correctly, the covenant of love is maintained and God's will is manifested.

15. I believe there are moral principles flowing from God's covenant with Israel and Christ's covenant with the world that are meant to guide us in solving moral dilemmas and living a Christian witness.

They are as follows:

a. "Therefore, you shall love the Lord your God with all your heart and with all your soul and with all your strength." (Deut. 6:5) and (Matt. 22:37)

b. "You shall love your neighbor as yourself." (Lev. 19:18) and (Matt. 22:39)

c. The Ten Commandments. I will not list them here, as they are well known. I do point out, however, that each commandment stands for a value:

   1. Value of acknowledging transcendence and radical dependence on God.
   2. Value of never reducing God to any set of words. He is greater than all we can say about Him. To reduce Him to one set of words is to take His name in vain.
   3. Value of worship, reverence, and awe.
   4. Value of family and mutual respect and cooperation among all the members.
   5. Value of the sacredness of life.
   6. Value of the dignity of the human person. Sexuality should not reduce a person to a thing.
   7. Value of ownership and respect for property.
   8. Value of candor, honesty, and trust.
   9. Value of freedom from obsession with sex.
   10. Value of freedom from avarice and greed.

d. The Eight Beatitudes. Again, they are well enough known not to need listing here. However, they too speak of values:

   1. Value of detachment from things.
   2. Value of bearing the purification of sorrow in redemptive silence.
   3. Value of repudiating authoritarian power to force the gospel on others.
   4. Value of making spiritual growth the highest priority.
   5. Value of inexhaustible compassion.
   6. Value of single-minded purpose.
   7. Value of an ideological and practical passion for peace and justice.

8. Value of the courage to suffer and die for what we believe and for those we love.

There are many other refinements of these moral principles to be found in other parts of the Bible, as indicated above.

❀ Teaching Guidelines

1. Always see these moral principles as growing out of and leading toward covenant fulfillment.
2. Examine seriously the full impact of the human situation to see how the principles can be applied, covenant be achieved, and God's will be disclosed.
3. Read the chapter on moral education in this book, concerning the psychological development of people and the relative maturity of their moral consciousness.

The final set of belief statements deals with spirituality. Even though this is a separate section, there is no question that spirituality is related to all that has gone before.

16. I believe in faith in Christ.

It is a little awkward to say it this way (I have faith in faith), but this is what is meant when people say we have the "gift of faith." The very ability to believe in anything that has been said above is itself a belief affirmation and a favor from the Lord. The capacity to believe in Christ comes from Christ. In the words of the old hymn, it is an "Amazing Grace." Such faith automatically includes *hope and love*, for a living faith will trust in Christ and love him.

Faith, hope, and love in Christ enables us to believe in, trust, and love people.

Faith also implies the belief in the kinds of statements that have been set out in this Basic Teaching list.

❀ Teaching Guidelines

1. Review the distinction between faith as conviction and a response in religious experience and faith as articulation and commitment to belief statements.
2. Never lose sight of one or the other: the faith that trusts, commits, loves, the faith that yields public utterance in belief statements.

17. I believe in prayer.

This means prayer in its wide variety, whether formal prayers such as the *Our Father*, the *Hail Mary*, and the *Rosary* (and other devotional forms) or spontaneous prayer, or the whole range of meditative, contemplative, and ascetical disciplines.

Teaching Guidelines

1. Read the chapter in this book on spiritual education, which offers a ladder of psychological consciousness in reference to believing and the capacity to be spiritual relative to our personal maturity.
2. Clarify the distinctive kinds of prayer, show the usefulness of each, and encourage spiritual living as a primary goal of life.

Here is the above belief list in a shorter form without comment:

1. God, our Father and Creator
2. Jesus Christ, Son of God, Incarnate Savior and Lord
3. Holy Spirit, Lord and Giver of Life
4. Holy Trinity
5. One, holy, catholic, and apostolic Church
6. Virgin Mary, Mother of God, Image of Church, Immaculately Conceived
7. Immortality: Judgment
8. Baptism
9. Confirmation
10. Eucharist
11. Reconciliation
12. Marriage
13. Orders
14. Anointing
15. Morality flowing from Covenant
    a. law of love
    b. moral principles (Ten Commandments, Eight Beatitudes, etc.)
16. Spirituality
    a. faith, hope, love
    b. prayer

How are Basic Teachings supposed to be taught?

I reply to this question at different levels.

The *how* should keep in mind the four preunderstandings of the origin, language, and purpose of Basic Teachings. They originate in religious experience of God in both personal and communal events.

The inner act of faith in those religious events is moved to external utterance by prophets, apostles, and evangelists, and takes shape within a community of believers that remains a context for their articulation, understanding, and maintenance throughout time. In a word, the People of God is the continual context for the Basic Teachings.

The term *faith* must always be understood in both its personal-

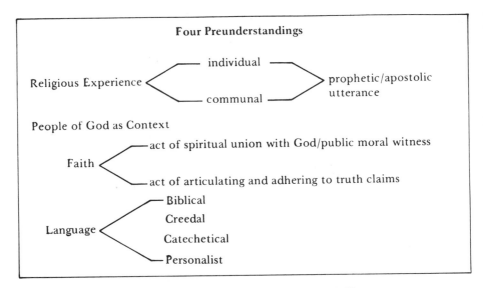

conviction/commitment-interpretation aspect as well as in its move to name the reality in religious truth claims and to adhere thereto.

The language of the Basic Teachings appears in Bible Talk, Creedal Affirmation, Catechism Expression, and today's Personalist Categories.*

Use these four preunderstandings as a mindset. Whatever pedagogy is chosen, it should be consistent with the preunderstandings.

· What kind of pedagogy is available?
· Lecturing
· Preaching
· Question and Answer *cum* rote memory
· Dialogue
· Inquiry-Discovery
· Valuing Processes
· Independent Study
· Individually Guided Instruction
· Team Teaching
· Grouping
· Others

If you examine the teacher's manuals of practically all textbooks today, you will find the emphasis is on student involvement in the teaching-learning situation.

McLuhan's famous adage "The process is the product" is echoed im-

---

* Some would call for an even further modern way, namely, political-liberation style language for the truth claims, reflecting the Latin American efforts in this regard.

plicitly and partially in most teaching methods today. Some have exaggerated the adage to claim that the process is everything and nothing else is needed. Such a naive view of process denies a fundamental human hunger for purpose, statement, and provisional articulation.

One of my preunderstandings, namely, religious experience as a basis for articulation, shows that the religious experience is a process. I have quite clearly emphasized its primacy. I have done the same with faith as spiritual union with Christ and public moral witness. That process is primary. But there are also products other than mysterious ecstatic unions and valid spiritual commitments. There is a clearly recognizable product called the People of God and truth claims uttered by them. There is also the product of observable body talk in realms of moral stance on issues of personal freedom and matters of public justice and peace. The placards and speeches at social concern demonstrations are plainly and simply product—apart from the process that brought them about.

The term *product* takes two forms: 1) the web of interrelationships, dialoguing, decision making, and maturing that goes on in process experiences; 2) the visible, though admittedly temporary (at least in some cases) slogans, statements, ideologies, philosophies, fraternities, clubs, alliances, graffiti, theologies, etc., that are the observable and identifiable public speech of the participants in the process.

Process pedagogy—be it inductive, dialogical, or experiential—dominates the talk about teaching today. I think of this as the enlightened and pleasing result of numerous breakthroughs in teaching method in this country. My own experience tells me that process style teaching is not as widely practiced as it is universally praised. It seems to suffer from the same problem as saints—everybody admires them, but imitating them is a different question.

I don't think anyone is arguing against process education today. If anything, people should argue more for it and help to see its implementation, especially in the field of teaching religion.

N.B. *Please do not confuse process pedagogy with process philosophy and theology. I am not speaking of process philosophy and theology here. Those two speculative disciplines are quite separate from the present discussion.*

I have one small fear. It is based upon parent dissatisfaction with the product of religion teaching. Parents are only looking at one half of one of my preunderstandings, namely, faith as articulator and adherent to truth claims. The parents say, "My child can't even speak a coherent sentence about certain forms of religious information, let alone spout a memorized one."

Frankly I don't blame the parents. If I were paying someone to teach my son how to repair a TV set and he emerged from the course knowing neither the vocabulary of the innards of the set, nor their relationships—let alone how to fix it—I might rightly complain. I expect that one of the goals of religion teaching is a decent ability to speak about religious information (truth claims, Bible ideas and stories, moral principles, etc.) in some knowledgeable and coherent way.

That isn't the only thing I want, though. I also hope the course has helped the student inch a bit toward spiritual and moral living and retain a hunger for worship. By emphasizing process as the *only* product many teachers have ignored articulation as another product. Hence there is an impasse between teachers and parents on my pre-understanding number (3):

Some teachers stress Faith as spiritual union, conviction, and
moral witness

Spurring the overreaction of

Some parents who stress Faith as articulated and adhering to
truth claims

The pity is that the naive teaching of *some* produces the naive reaction of *some.* And that upsets the purposes of all the rest.

I think the real problem is not that there is too much naive processing going on, but rather that process pedagogy (inductive learning, experience based approaches, dialogue, etc.) has not yet taken sufficient hold, whether naively or otherwise. I am not sure why, but I believe that deductive forms of education still dominate the educational scene.

Who is to blame?

Not the schools of education (including religious education). Examine their approaches and practicums, and you find that they lean heavily on the process.

Surely not the philosophy, goals, and objective statements submitted to accrediting agencies. Their literary form echoes process.

Nor is it the administrators who mouth the process gospel quite enthusiastically and clearly.

And few contemporary teachers would confess to outright deductivism. (However, some do. The success even today of the fantastic lecturer with the tightly disciplined class is a story still told. Some grouse about what success means here and complain (with some degree of legitimacy) that the students are left with no ability to think for themselves. My own observation of the star lecturer is that such a person possesses some inherent dramatic flair, with the captivating skills of an actor. I have found that the best of these types do in fact inspire their students to think and to self-realize. The worst ones do not, since they use their stage presence for some inner ego gratification and try to turn out rubber stamps.)

Where do I stand?

I put my chips with the varying forms of process teaching/learning. I think the star lecturer who does prompt inner self-realization in students is certainly welcome and effective. But this breed is rare and should not be considered normative.

I ask, however, that the process approach retain in its consciousness the four major preunderstandings I have consistently returned to here. Religious experience, the Church as context, the two kinds of faith, and the four major languages of catechesis should help process to avoid exaggerations and bring a rich and total format to catechesis.

How are the Basic Teachings to be taught?

The other chapters of this book provide one answer to this query. This chapter sets out certain guidelines. The other chapters provide Basic Teachings with the variety of contexts in which they can be taught.

The chapter on Community of Believers is built out of my second major preunderstanding, namely, the Church as context. The chapter on moral education assumes a process and developmental approach, while not ignoring articulated moral principles, the affirmation of spiritual covenant, or the need to become a responsible and accountable moral person, both to oneself and to society.

The chapter on spiritual education again takes up the developmental nature of people, the provisional stages and models that help one to gain some angle on the kinds of development that can occur, as well as the relationship to prayer, worship, and the styles of spiritual living that witness the gospel.

The chapter on family draws a distinction that is often forgotten by both home and school. Formal education (school/CCD) can do things that homes can't do. Homes can do things that formal education can't do. In our society, families transmit values in a way that cannot be communicated in any other manner. Formal education communicates values in a manner different from, but not opposed to, the family. Both entities must work together.

The chapter on moral education draws attention to the many ranges of consciousness involved when helping people to arrive at moral decisions. It speaks to the relationship between principle and situation, between covenant and personal maturity, between fundamental option and the suboptions, between sin and divine judgment.

The chapter on liturgy brings back into focus the events of revelation and their active presence in the mysteries of worship. The chapters on media, curriculum, and resources point to the embarrassment of riches we possess in teaching aids and some attempts at systematizing all of it.

Teaching Levels

It is also useful to think of at least six major levels of teaching:

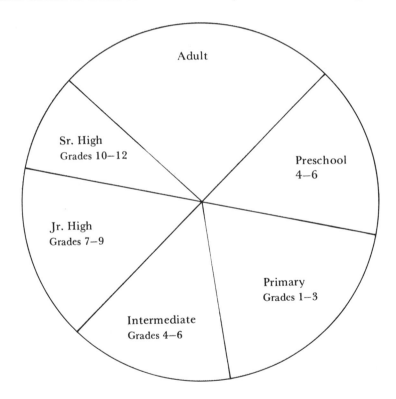

The above diagram lists the levels as:

- Preschool—Ages 4-6
- Primary—Grades 1-3
- Intermediate—Grades 4-6
- Junior High—Grades 7-9
- Senior High—Grades 10-12
- Adult

Most of the formalizing so far is between primary and senior high. There is a small growth at the preschool level, especially spurred by the Montessori movement. There is a larger growth and intense interest in adult education, with a specification for family education, which is searching for a way to continue what is called "traditioning"—how to communicate values as only families can do.

Catholic schools are showing a growing interest in preschool religion programs to go with a growth of "kindergartens" in many Catholic grade schools. The rapid rise of the single parent family has caused an expansion of day care centers under secular, religious, and independent auspices.

The primary level introduces the first expressly formalized approach to religion for the student. Needless to say, the communications of Basic Teachings at this level will be simple, nonthreatening, couched in terms that invite the student to be enchanted by the love of Jesus. The method will be strongly relational, rooted in the concrete.

At the intermediate level, religion as information moves to the center. Youngsters' minds are quick to retain data about the fresh world that opens before them. Nevertheless, relate the information to its spiritual purpose in worship, prayer, and moral living.

At the junior high level, when the students are a tense mix of logic and emotion, it is time to help them acquire their first systematic grasp of the data acquired at the intermediate stage, while at the same time helping them to stabilize their emotional life and to search for personal identity by encouraging them to a depth of spiritual living and a commitment to idealism.

At the senior high level, as the students move into a real sense of their future involvement in society, enable them to formulate their life goals and expectations in terms of their developing interior spiritual life and external moral behavior and the decision to be responsible and accountable adults.

The mystery of God is never exhausted. Neither is the mystery of the human person and the love of which people are capable. Adult religious education is a self-commitment to a lifelong deepening of the ultimate meaning of life.

"Too Much Too Soon"

It has often been said that we tend to give our students too much too soon. One unfortunate reaction to this concern is to give them too little too late. I agree that it is a mistake to try to bring the full impact of religion to a preschooler or a primary age child. For the very young, prayer, love, worship, encouragement to good behavior ("Play nice, don't fight"), and just the barest introduction to the big picture, mainly via storytelling, is a sufficient start.

For the intermediates, part of the game is really "information, please." Most youngsters of those ages are like psychic blotters in a wonderland of facts. What better time than this to unfold the religious information with some interpretation—while always encouraging their inner growth. Even here, not all the data is needed, but enough to stimulate them to continue on.

The junior high youngsters can begin their work of personal synthesis both of the data previously acquired and of the data related to their personal lives. Their minds are discovering the pleasure of arranging and sequencing. Let them do these tasks with the fund of data in their well furnished brains, as the result of their intermediate days. Their hearts are filled with passions and loves and ideals, obviously shaking them. Yet they have already over twelve years of prayer and worship and "good behaving" behind them. Help them to bring their mind systems and their heart systems together.

The high school age people, still fairly shaky but gaining minds of their own, needing to shape principles and goals for their lives and lisping ultimate questions (as they once did in their primary years), are discovering the joy of managing life through principles as well as the sorrow of bending principles and abandoning them at times. Here is where the personal spiritual and moral guidance of the teacher becomes central. They need the adult modeling of principled and spiritual people more so at this phase than at any other. (Obviously, every student always needs some of this modeling at any age.)

I see this approach as one way to avoid the "too much too soon" and the "too little too late." The primary age child is walked through religion as a time of wonder. The intermediates enjoy the movable feast of facts. The junior highs wrestle with the task of logic and arrangement along with fusing their hearts with their minds. The senior highs resolutely grapple with the efforts to become principled people. Hence there are four mirrors through which religion will be seen:

Wonder	Data	Logic	Principles
Spiritual, moral, and prayerful living			

The Charters for Religious Education

The complexity of religious education will never be lost sight of if teachers keep in mind the charters that the Church offers as guides. These are:

- *General Catechetical Directory*
- "Justice in the World"
- "To Teach As Jesus Did"
- *National Catechetical Directory*

The *General Catechetical Directory* offers guidelines for all religious education efforts around the world. It advises that each nation adapt its own culture to the principles outlined by the *GCD*. The American Bishops began this adaptation with a pastoral letter entitled "To Teach As Jesus Did." It sets forth the goals of religious education:

1. Proclaim the message of Jesus.
2. Create a community of faith.
3. Be witnesses of Christian service to all in need.

The document named five means to these three goals:

1. Adult Education
2. Young Adult and Campus Ministry
3. CCD (Continuing Christian Development)
4. Catholic Schools
5. Education and Liturgical Committees of Parish Councils and Parish/Diocesan Boards of Education

The document rested the three goals and five means on two themes:

1. *Total Education*
   The three goals of message, community, and service should be interrelated (i.e., not just messages with no service—or community with no message, etc.).
2. *Team Ministry*
   The five means (institutions) should work together to achieve the implementation of the three goals.

We also have the document on "Justice in the World," which expands on the service theme in *TJD*. Social concern and a passion for justice and peace must be an integral part of all catechetical effort.

The publication of the *National Catechetical Directory* draws together the many strands that must join in order that a complete religious education occur. Basic Teachings is part of that, but they function within:

1. An appreciation of our culture.
2. A sensitivity to religious experience and spiritual living implied by revelation and faith response.
3. An awareness of the Church as context.
4. The celebration of faith in Liturgy and Sacrament.
5. The quest for peace, justice, and personal moral integrity.

6. The proper training of catechists.
7. A proper application of the principles of behavioral science in education.
8. The creation of a pastoral organization that will be at the service of all these needs.

Summary

I have situated Basic Teachings in a context of four preunderstandings:

- Religious Experience
- Church as Context
- Faith: act of trust
             act of enunciating
- The Varying Languages

I have ventured a list of Basic Teachings with some comment.
I have suggested approaches to communicating the "teachings." This involved:

1. Remembering the preunderstandings.
2. Identifying six levels of learning: Preschool, Primary, Intermediate, Junior High, Senior High, Adult.
3. Operating within the major charters of catechesis provided by the Church.

That is prologue. The task is yet to be accomplished. I have tried to determinedly keep before you the complexity of the task. We all do our best. Ultimately, it is God who will touch the persons whom we are privileged to serve. I have tried to keep moving between the realms of faith and reason, between the kingdom of mysterious spirituality and the kingdom of clarity illustrated by lists and categories. This mood is articulated by Pascal:

> If we subject everything to reason, our religion will have nothing mysterious and supernatural.
> If we violate the principles of reason, our religion will be absurd and ridiculous.

3

MORAL EDUCATION

Let us with caution indulge the supposition that morality can be maintained without religion. Reason and experience forbid us to expect that national morality can prevail in exclusion of religious principle.

George Washington

The following is a paraphrase*:

Meno: Tell me, Socrates. Is virture acquired by teaching or by practice? If by neither, then how?

Socrates: If you know a virtue, you will practice it. By knowing I do not mean just an intellectual mastery. Knowing means being seized by the dream, by the vision for which the virtue stands. [Cf. Martin Luther King's "I have a dream!"]

Meno: Then I cannot teach virtue?

Socrates: You can if you are seized by the dream. You must become a philosopher king.† This means you must be a moral leader.

Meno: How then do my students learn virtue?

Socrates: They hunch its possibility. They are heuristic, that is, born expectations of virtue. In their hearts they are radically inclined to moral perfection.

Meno: How do I teach them?

Socrates: Don't devote all your energy to instruction. Summon them to the virtue that is already a nucleus in their hearts. Exhort them. Lead the way. Show them what moral leadership is like by your behavior. The moral leader is the best moral teacher.

Meno: Do I lecture?

Socrates: You can. But better to question them like a lawyer, drawing their inner truth out of them little by little. Then point them to the idcals.

Meno: Then, in a sense, I can teach virtue?

*Plato, *Meno*, trans. by Benjamin Jowett, intro. by Fulton Anderson (Indianapolis: The Bobbs-Merrill Co., 1949).
†Cf. Mary Renault's description of how Plato taught Dionysius to be a philosopher king in her novel *The Mask of Apollo* (New York: Bantam Books, Inc., 1974).

Socrates: Actually not. Ultimately, virtue is a gift of the gods. The best we can do is set the condition for its appearance and beg the gods for the gift.

Plato sets the right educational tone for moral and value education. In brief his teaching is: 1) Assume your students are born with an inner drive toward moral idealism. 2) Through dialogue, help your students become aware of their inner potential. 3) By means of personal moral leadership, model for them the realization of virtue.

There are two movements in education today that prove central to the topic at hand — valuing processes and teaching procedures based on a knowledge of how moral thinking develops. I will review these two movements and then locate them within a religious context.

Valuing Processes

Developed and popularized by Sidney Simon, the valuing processes enjoy the immense advantage of introducing a conversation about values without threatening any of the participants. Simon achieves this goal by a simple piece of advice: "Don't impose your values on the students. Don't depose their values. *Expose* their values." By avoiding implicit authoritarianism in imposition and deposition, the teacher is freeing the student to speak without fear about that which he prizes most in life.

Simon has developed an astonishing range of useful techniques to assist teachers and learners engaged in the valuing process. By calling them games, Simon clothes them with a playfulness that somewhat lightens the moral seriousness of such classes and enables the teacher to escape the didacticism and moralism that can sometimes distastefully characterize preoccupation with value and moral issues.

This approach to dealing with values bypasses both the grim moralizing just mentioned as well as the equally deplorable approach in education, which is to ignore values and morality altogether. This latter device is known as *value free learning.* Here the teacher commits himself to teaching only the facts with no reference to values hovering around the facts.

Strict objectivity is the order of the day. Like a scientist excising an amoeba for observation, all teachers are to preserve a conspiracy of silence about values and concern themselves with raw data. Of course this is an ideal never fully achieved. By deliberately ignoring values, some teachers have implicitly taught an amorality (and immorality) that is plaguing public life today.

Simon boldly thrust values right into the center of education in so disarming a manner that any teacher with both a conscience and a reserve of common sense could see the wisdom of his intervention. Simon's valuing processes have mercifully laid the myth of value neutral education to a well deserved rest.

As I mentioned earlier, Simon created a series of techniques to move teachers into the question of values. Here are some examples:

Forced Choice

a. **Seat Belt.** Who would you rather be? Drive-in Dan, who loves his seat belt so much that he even uses it at the drive-in movies? Or Scissors Stan, who so hates seat belts that he secretly cuts them out of other people's cars? On a rating scale of 1 to 10 ask your students to make a choice.

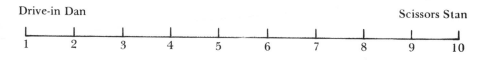

Drive-in Dan   Scissors Stan

1   2   3   4   5   6   7   8   9   10

Normally you would find in the ensuing discussion a series of anecdotes about car accidents in which seat belts figured in the life, death, or degree of injury to the occupants. But at a further level you would hear about the degree of freedom or law to which your students plan to commit themselves at this time. Their values are on the table.

b. **Control/Fate.** Ask your students which column better characterizes their approach to life — the external events of life, or inner mastery.

1. Getting along with people is a skill that must be practiced.

2. If you know how to deal with people, you can easily lead them.

3. I am the master of my fate.

1. It is almost impossible to figure out how to please some people.

2. I have little influence over the way others behave.

3. A great deal that happens to me is probably a matter of chance.

The discussion that flows from this will help you and your students to notice the degree of inner and outer directedness that holds the ascendancy in your personal lives at this time.

Literature is often a gold mine for value discussion. For example, Hamlet's soliloquy "To be, or not to be," is a splendid parable of the difficulty of decision making. Hamlet is faced with the temptation of suicide, "not to be . . . to die, to sleep, and by a sleep to say we end the thousand natural heartaches the soul is heir to." Like so many moderns, he is afflicted with a habit of indecision caused by too much thinking. "The native hue of resolution is sickly'd o'er with the pale cast of thought." Yet, not to decide is itself a decision.

Rank Order

One of Simon's more engaging games is the "Thanksgiving Ploy." On your chalkboard write:

- Pizza
- Twelve dollars
- Twelve minutes

Ask your students: Would you rather have pizza than turkey this Thanksgiving? Or would you prefer your dad gave you twelve dollars so you could go out and buy your own meal? Or would it be better to eat the meal, which took your mother a long time to prepare, in twelve minutes and then watch the football game on TV?

While none of these choices are especially admirable, all of them will evoke a fairly lively discussion about values. Pizza will raise the matter of world hunger. The twelve dollars will remind everyone of the need to express family solidarity from time to time. The twelve minutes will speak of the travesty of gratitude on a day supposedly devoted to giving thanks.

What is the origin of Simon's technique?

Basically, it is the application of Carl Rogers's nondirective, nonthreatening client-centered therapy to a group situation. Just as Rogers's empathetic listening helps a client to ventilate his fears and anxieties without experiencing further threat, so Simon's "games" facilitate the students' ability to verbalize their values in a nonjudgmental situation.

This valuing process is an excellent first step in restoring the dignity and prominence of moral discourse. The beauty of the system is that it provides a content for moral discussion and raises the questions about good and bad, right and wrong, true and false. The absence of threat creates a mood of confidence that moral issues can and should be dealt with as part of a student's educational and personal development.

Stages of Moral Thinking—Teaching Procedures

Simon establishes the possibility of clarifying values that can in turn become the substance of moral discourse. Lawrence Kohlberg charts the guidelines for discerning the ranges of consciousness that people bring to a discussion of morality. Simon works from a context of counseling psychology. Kohlberg operates from the perspective of experimental psychology—in particular, its developmental aspect.

Kohlberg is indebted to the pioneer work of Piaget and to the University of Chicago school of developmentalists, especially Havighurst. The center of concentration critical for our discussion is the development of human thinking. Hence emotional and behavioral development are not at issue here.

Regarding thinking, the developmentalists like to speak of stages. The theory is that human intelligence advances from childlike to mature perception in identifiable stages. Building on this assumption, Kohlberg contends that moral thinking (the capacity to think in moral patterns) pursues the same pattern of development as all human thinking.

If thinking in general moves from a vague, undifferentiated state to varying levels of analytic prowess, moral thinking treads pretty much the same path. By now, his ladder of moral thinking growth is quite well known. In the following illustration, I rephrase his stages in non-technical language: 1) Punishment; 2) Ego Building; 3) Good Boy/Girl; 4) Law and Order; 5) Why Law?; and 6) Conscience and Principle. (*See Kohlberg's Stages of Moral Thinking*, p. 62.)

According to the theory moral thinking begins at a very primitive level, namely, that of *punishment*. The person judges behavior to be bad simply because one is punished for it. ("Don't steal the candy because the police will get you.") Such a person is not thinking in terms of rules or concepts. He or she sees the strap, not the rule.

The *self-interest* stage allows for some initial ability to think abstractly and appreciate rules. The punishment motive is still strong. Ego building or self-interest is the criteria of good and bad. Things go badly when they fail to bolster self-growth.

This is not necessarily mean-minded selfishness or reproachable egoism. It's just that the thrill of noticing oneself makes all else minister to that surprising and exhilarating discovery of one's ego. Stages one and two correspond to the child stage in transactional analysis ("I'm OK, you're OK"). Still, one must not associate the six stages too closely with a person's age especially beyond levels one and two.

Next comes the *good boy/girl*. Abstract conceptualizing of rules is growing. But it is tied in with the need for approval from authority figures such as parents, teachers, and other adults. Being good is related to the approval and praise extracted from the authorities. It is learned that conformity to the wishes of authority gains praise, and this counts for what stands as good. "Be good, play nice" sounds just right. The status quo is good. Father and mother know best.

Moving on, the moral thinker comes to *law and order*. More abstracting takes place. The parental role is subsumed into law and or-

Kohlberg's Stages of Moral Thinking

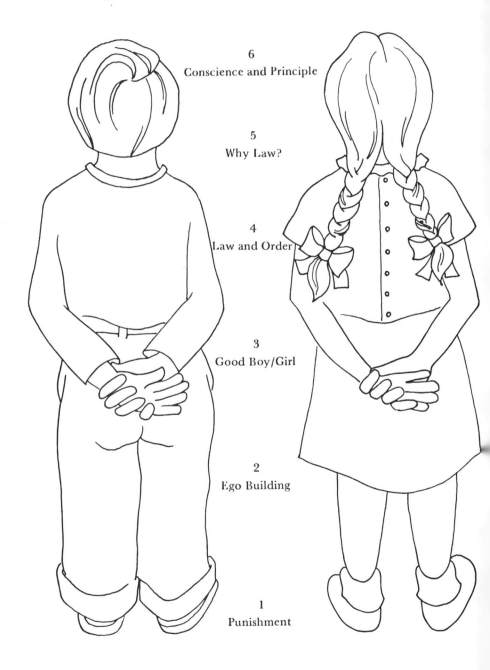

6
Conscience and Principle

5
Why Law?

4
Law and Order

3
Good Boy/Girl

2
Ego Building

1
Punishment

* After a drawing by Sr. Kathleen Marie Shields

der rules. One's sense of personal righteousness comes from conformity to law and order. This offers a moral criterion for judging others. Good people obey laws. Bad ones don't obey or conform. It is expected and desired that lawbreakers be punished. In one's own case, atonement, remorse, and guilt are party to one's own disobedience.

Treat others precisely as the law demands. Don't worry about acting impersonally. The law is uppermost. Moreover, it shields one from the weakness of compassion.

A fixation at this level of moral thinking leads to legalism. The person identifies with the abstract law and often lapses into a harsh and inhumane moralism. The shift from personal and parental authority to impersonal and legal, in its worse form, yields the classic stuff of which tyranny is made.

Beyond law and order lies the stage of *questioning the reasons for laws and rules.* Here the person investigates the origins of law. He comes to see that laws are made by people. They arise out of struggles to preserve human rights. Laws are not simply guidelines to measure one's personal goodness or badness; they are also the result of complex developments that should stir within us the passion to seek the civil liberties of others. In probing the rationale for laws, we become aware of different systems of laws and the assumptions upon which they are based.

This growing awareness of assumptions leads to Kohlberg's final stage, which is that of *conscience and principle.* For him this is the final moment of interiorizing. We now possess the capability of abstracting to universal principles upon which laws are based. These principles include the right to privacy, the freedom to speak out, the need for justice—principles such as those embodied in the Bill of Rights.

At this level people become aware that moral conflicts are often immensely complex. They see that moral dilemmas are not just a battle between good and evil, but sometimes, most painfully, between good and good. Conflicts between freedom and law, the rights of the individual and the rights of the community, the reverence due to parents, and the need to make one's own way in the world can provide a thousand case studies about tragic moral conflicts between one good and another.

These, then, are the six stages. Many religious educators point out the need to identify a stage that is related specifically to grace and faith, namely, that of martyrdom, a heroic witness to one's moral convictions. This is a correct observation. Kohlberg confines his own research to observable, rational phenomena. He makes no claim to speak of a consciousness that proceeds from the mysterious realm of religious faith. Neither does he deny or repudiate such a consciousness. He simply maintains that it is beyond the scope of his scientific competence.

Hence his typology is limited to what reason can discover about moral thinking. I see no intrinsic opposition between the rational and faith aspects. I will take up the question of the religious aspect further on in this chapter, and again in the next chapter (on spiritual education).

What is the value of the developmentalist vision of moral thinking? What does it offer to educators? How does it relate to the valuing processes discussed earlier?

The valuing processes arouse human consciousness to the existence of moral issues. The developmentalists tell us how people may come to make moral judgments about those issues, depending on the kind of consciousness they are capable of bringing to the matter. An educator's effectiveness largely depends on an appreciation of the present horizon of the student. How often the axiom is heard: "Begin where the students are in order to open them to newer horizons."

The valuing processes show the teachers the current content of their students' moral consciousness. The developmental model should enable teachers to note the kind of thinking their students bring to the content.

Simon proposes games for the valuing processes. Kohlberg's implementers suggest the use of case studies with attendant problem solving. The assumption is that the student's replies during the discussion about the case will reveal the stage of moral thinking he or she has arrived at. For example, if the student gives a law and order solution to the case, and does so consistently, the teacher may conclude that the student is at stage four. If so, then the teacher must, through probing questions in subsequent cases, provoke the student to go more deeply into the dilemma seeking for the reasons behind the laws cited to solve the cases.

I see three difficulties at this juncture: 1) the temptation to stereotype, 2) the failure to appreciate each student's inevitable complexity, and 3) misreading emotional outbursts for moral thinking.

Kohlberg is careful to point out that he is limiting his work just to the thinking capacities of people. His stages are not an indication of moral worth. Students favoring the ego building stage (even if they be twenty-five years of age) must not be considered morally worthless because their professor expects principled and conscienced people in his or her doctoral seminar.

Even if teachers realize this, they must still cope with the temptation to stereotype:

- "I'm plagued with twenty-three law and order types."
- "Bobby and Sally are goodie two shoes."
- "I never saw so many red-neck law and order individuals in one class."

The tendency to stereotype is a persistent human failing. I think this tendency is augmented by stage theories, especially when they are called "invariant" as Kohlberg does for his model. *Invariant* locks one into an inevitability in the process—"I shall have to climb this ladder of moral thinking without skipping a rung (though I could slip). And I shall stand on only one rung at a time."

The Kohlberg literature seems to favor this locking into stages. If so, then I can see stereotyping as not just a temptation, but even as a way of life. I like the ladder because climbing it implies groping for a goal. It is a fine motivational image. I dislike it when it unintentionally persuades teachers to ignore the complexity of each student, who is always more than any judgment made about him.

I have pondered a way out of this dilemma and offer this as a possible solution: "Dial a consciousness." The beauty of Kohlberg's six categories is not their value as rungs in a ladder so much as six different kinds of consciousness that a person may bring to a moral issue.

The injustice collector and self-punisher can sometimes make a startling appearance in an otherwise seemingly adult and mature person. That is exactly the teaching and the appeal of transactional analysis which demonstrates that the "child" in us never quite seems to die. Stroke seekers, good boys/girls, and law and order remain lively ghosts in even the maturest of people.

I neither approve of this nor am happy about it. I am simply affirming that even those who happily have stormed the summits of principle and conscience still carry with them the baggage of the "lower orders," and that the traces of immaturity will surface from time to time—usually unexpectedly and at the wrong time.

In any moral discussion occasioned by a case study, dial a consciousness. What I mean is, prepare to hear any one of the six categories brought to bear upon the issue regardless of the age or maturity of your audience. It's not that people are perverse; it's just that people will invariably resist any attempt to corner them. The more you "sincerely" want to categorize them so you can *help* them, the more they will shift into unpredictable categories. Most students can smell any effort to box them it, no matter how pure the intention, and they will effortlessly escape as surely as air drifts away from a closing fist.

Still, there is no question that a given social group will tend to respond in fairly predictable ways. The resistance arises when the leader attempts to nail down the consciousness and call for a maturer response. Curiously, the group then begins to let fly with variations of all the categories and—to continue the telephone image—short circuits the connection of the leader with the group.

I stated earlier that the educator will face three difficulties in using the Kohlberg stages, that of stereotyping and ignoring the complexity of students and confusing emotional with intellectual responses. I reply to the first two problems by asking you to dial a consciousness, that is, be prepared to hear any one of the six categories from anyone at anytime.

As to the third difficulty, you must be ready to note the persistent appearance of combat and catharsis in any discussion. Heated discussions may be very interesting, but they do have a tendency to generate more heat than light. This is especially common today when preoccupation with emotions and obsession with experiences make any effort to conduct a cool, rational discourse either quaint or else irrelevant.

The mood of the times smiles on the nonrational and, I am afraid, even on the irrational. I think formal education bears a responsibility to speak to both the intellectual and the affective dimensions. Hundreds of articles on education are filled with attacks on head trips, piling too much into the mind, and the dreadful aridity of intellectualism.

I agree with most of the critiques. I disagree with solutions that would make classrooms literal Etnas of emotional lava. There is no point in replacing rampant intellectualism with rampant emotionalism. Two wrongs never make a right. I see little value in being rampant about either type. Students have minds and students have hearts. A mindless teacher who just talks to the heart betrays his profession. A heartless teacher who just talks to the mind betrays his profession. Teachers must recall that they have a mind and a heart just as much as the students do. Both types of people need care and love.

To spot combat ("I need to win today") and catharsis ("I need to get this off my chest") is simply to note that you are dealing for the moment with an emotional event rather than an intellectual one. I don't say that combat and catharsis must be banished or that they are bad. I simply bring to your attention that they present a different dimension in the discussion from the Kohlberg categories, which refer to a thinking process more than to an emotional one.

Your skill as a discussion leader must be to see the difference, to allow for affective expression to the extent needed, but also to call for a rational expression as well. Any lively and enriching discussion is bound to be a mixture of both types.

Toward the end of this chapter I will give two examples of case studies with questions and a chart for selection. This concludes my coverage of the valuing processes and the Kohlberg model. The next section takes up the religious context for moral education. I will relate the contributions of the humane sciences herein discussed to the religious context and will provide a model for integrating the two elements.

The Religious Context

Valuing processes yield a content that arises from the lives of the students. Developmental stages (or ranges of awareness) speak of thinking in terms of laws, reasons for rules, and moral principles and consciences. Note that the developmentalists do not enunciate laws and principles so much as state that at the higher levels of mature thinking, moralists think in terms of law, their reasons, and the principles that govern them.

The Catholic religious context possesses a content in both senses discussed so far. Just as individual students verbalize their own value concerns, the community of faith articulates its value concerns—world hunger, justice for the underprivileged, sacredness of life, the need for peace, and the enduring demand for personal integrity.

Just as students are called to become persons of principle and conscience, so also the community of faith witnesses to a similar development. Moreover, the Church conserves a tradition of laws and principles that are the result of believers' interaction with God's insightful grace. The religious context of moral thinking and behavior is covenantal with its consequent moral stipulation. (Cf. the development of this concept in Chapter 2.)

At the beginning of this chapter I quote Socrates as claiming that virtue is in the final analysis a gift of the gods. The Catholic context claims no less. The acquisition of virtue, the achievement of a stunning moral life is a grace of God, a gift of our Lord Christ. This by no means excludes the human effort to become a virtuous and moral person. As Augustine says, "Pray as if all depended on God. Act as if all depended on you." Socrates told Meno about the need for dialogue and moral leadership. This is human effort. Yet even Socrates affirmed that, in the end, the result is a gift of the gods.

Religious tradition would say that, in its case, the climbers of the moral ladder (or dialers of moral awareness) do so as believers. Moreover, there is no need to reinvent the wheel. Catholics do not begin their maturing in morality in a vacuum. Millions of believers have gone before and have left a heritage of moral principles and insights that remain perennially valid.

Principles and Laws

Each generation may find a fresh language for speaking about these principles, but the reality to which they point remains the same: a timeless insight in a timely package. It is important to distinguish between principles and laws. Remember the Kohlberg distinctions: laws/reasons for laws/principles that guide the creation of laws.

A law may not be as perennially valid as a principle. Laws change. The Church advocates the virtuous principle that fast and abstinence are good for the soul. For many centuries the Church enacted precise laws about how to fast and abstain, and when to do it. Today the Church has changed those laws but has not changed the principles. The value of fast and abstinence remains; the responsibility reverts to the individual Catholic.

Principles and Situations

Furthermore, a host of new moral challenges has arisen in our post-industrial society that will require both the development of new moral solutions and pertinent rearticulation of the principles of our heritage. The "new morality" has drawn our attention to the importance of the psychosocial factors of the moral situation. In fact, the concentration has been so great in this regard that the term "situation ethics" has become commonplace.

I think we have enough perspective on this development now to see what happened. Prior to the advent of the new morality, we could have characterized moral education as a province of principle and law ethics. Teachers started with the principles and laws and then applied them to the situations. But a deep analysis of the situations was often missing. The new moralists devoted their energies to extensive probings of the contemporary moral dilemmas and all the psychological and social factors influencing moral behavior. But advertence to the heritage of classical moral principles was played down.

I believe we are in a position today to bring the two factors together. Principles and situations are both part of the moral education package. Rather than principle ethics or situation ethics, I submit that we have "principle-situation ethics." In this way we can preserve the cherished values implicit in both the objective order of principle and the subjective order of situation.

Fundamental and Deed Options

Critics of the older type of moral education lamented that too much time was devoted to sin lists. The period was one of "acts morality" in which deeds were catalogued according to the degree of their sinful-

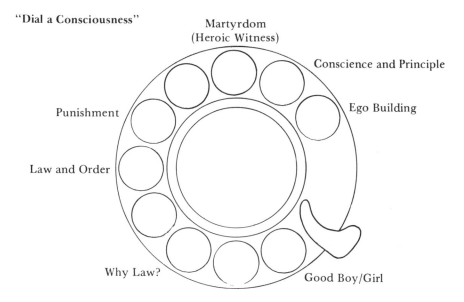

"Dial a Consciousness"

Martyrdom (Heroic Witness)

Conscience and Principle

Ego Building

Punishment

Law and Order

Why Law?

Good Boy/Girl

ness. While love and the call to the positive life of virtue were never ignored, they seemed to be submerged in what some called a guilt-producing attitude. Whether intended or not, God seemed more angry than forgiving and loving.

The reaction was to speak of the primacy of love in moral education. Jesus is the Good Shepherd, who as Risen Lord on Easter speaks the word of Peace/Shalom to the apostles huddled in fear. Moreover, attention shifted from acts morality to person morality. Look more at the person and the fundamental option he or she has made for Christ, than at the specific acts whereby he or she lives out that option.

Fundamental option looked to the subjective side of morality, the inner moral attitude of the person regarding Christ and the good life. Acts morality tended to dwell on the objective side of the case, citing the moral quality of a given deed. We now have the perspective to see exaggerations on both sides. If acts morality tended to ignore the subjective quality of the person's inner attitude to Christ, the fundamental option tended to obscure the moral quality of a specific act. Balancing this off today means that we need to ponder both the fundamental option of the person (where the Kohlberg range of consciousness is especially pertinent) as well as the degree of goodness and badness associated with individual acts.

Process of Making Moral Decisions

How is the religious educator to put all this together? How do you link principles with situations? How do you align principles with laws?   What are you to do with fundamental option and individual acts?   Lastly, how are you to integrate the helps from counseling psychology (valuing processes) and experimental psychology (developmental models) into the big picture?   What is the role of faith and grace in the process of decision making?

I think we are at a point in time where we can give some reasonable responses to this admittedly large question.   I now propose a method for approaching the problem.   I owe the nucleus of the idea to Rev. Leo Farley, professor of Moral Theology.   It is a model we have gone over in conversations and which I will proceed to build upon here.

Before I attempt to describe the model at any great length, I offer the following images as a way of including all the diverse elements so far discussed.

1. **The Sun**
   This is the image of our heritage as rays of light informing moral decision.

   No one can stare at the sun too long and expect to see. No one can look at the face of God and live.

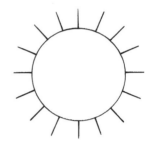

2. **The Prism**
   This is the image of the moral situation through which the light of principles is refracted.

   Just as an array of colors is seen by the sunlight refracted through the prism, so also the diverse "colors" of moral principles are seen in the moral situation.

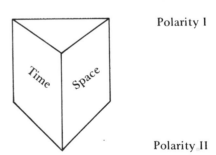

Polarity I

Time   Space

Polarity II

3. **The Mountain**
   This is the traditional image of prayer.
   While acts of reason will play a prominent part in solving unresolved moral dilemmas, faith expressed in prayer will also seek the gift of discernment.

4. **The Rainbow**
   This is the image of reconciliation, indicating that a covenantal, grace-filled solution
   has been found.

   Making a moral decision that
   fulfills the will of God and the
   best of human hopes is an
   event of reconciliation and a
   disclosure of the divine presence.

I will take each of these images in turn, and expand on their meaning and relationship to each other and to the act of moral decision.

The Sun   Principles are like the rays of the sun. Just as one does not
look directly at the sun, but rather at the objects lit up by the sun's
rays, so also one does not, in a sense, stare directly at a principle in a
pure state, but rather at the moral situations illumined by its rays.

When Moses approached the burning bush, God asked him to be less
concerned with the fascinating phenomenon and to be more concerned
with its meaning. No one looks into the face of God and lives. Even
in a solar eclipse one dares not look directly at the sun. The process
must be perceived in shadow.

What are some of these principles?

a. A discriminating judgment. The virtue of prudence.
b. A passion for justice. "I will not stop fighting for justice in this
   world so long as one person is treated unjustly."
c. Restraint. Every human activity requires a moderating force. The
   virtue of temperance.
d. The courage to be. "A boldness for the good and right insofar as
   God gives us the light."
e. The will to believe. We approach morality as believers in Christ,
   striving to judge life from the divine perspective.
f. Trust and surrender to the vast number of possibilities including
   the final victory of Christ.
g. A love that conquers all. The Spirit's gift of love that is the primary driving force toward the highest good.
h. The Ten Commandments. (Cf. Chapter 2, p. 45, for the Commandments as values.)
i. The transcendentals—the one, the good, the true, the beautiful.
   Moral life seeks:
   · reconciliation in the One;

· union with the highest good;
· a personal integrity that rings perfectly true;
· a splendor of character that reflects the beauty of the Lord.

These principles shed light on all moral behavior. I shall act with a discriminating judgment, ever in search of just solutions, moderating conflicting positions with grace and courage. I do so as an irrepressible believer, hoper, and lover eager to create the possibility of the ten values (Commandments) and motivated by the inspiration of the one, good, true, and beautiful.

These are not the only possible principles. I offer them here as a beginning for your own lists. I see them as gifts of God, tendencies and drives planted within our nature and brought to light and life with ever deeper maturity by living, thinking, praying, struggling, and rejoicing to run the great course of life.

The Prism The prism is precisely where principles and situations merge. Just as the rays of the sun are refracted into colors by the prism, so also the fundamental principles are refracted into specifics by the prism of time and space. The light of God is not seen directly on this earth. It is refracted "prismatically," and perceived within the patterns dictated by the history and culture of a given time and space.

I can only hope to perceive my world as a mid-twentieth century American raised in an Irish Catholic milieu and subsequently modified by a world war, the atomic bomb, TV, IBM, Vatican II, and the SST. I am neither a medievalist, an Elizabethan, nor an eighteenth-century rationalist. I may admire and imitate their perceptions, but I live with the world in which I find myself, and try to make the best of it. No time machine is available to lift me from my appointment with destiny in these receding years of the twentieth century.

I make this personal comment not by way of confession or autobiography, but rather to affirm that my own experience is probably similar to that of most of my readers and thereby to illustrate what I mean by "seeing principles through the prism of one's own history and geography."

It is this time and this space that provide the moral ground upon which the light of principles shines. This is one of the interactions with which we must deal. The other is the matter of polarities. You will note that I indicate Polarities I and II as part of the prism image. Making moral decisions will not just be a proper wedding of principles and situations. It will also involve weaving our way through the demands inevitably imposed by the polarities of life.

The greatest virtue is love. The greatest transcendental is the One.

But it "takes two to tango" (and tangle), and the quest for the One implies there is a multiple reaching for it. In other words, polar opposites abound in loving, in the adventure of seeking the One and in making moral decisions. I am not speaking of the irreconcilable poles of good and evil, but rather of poles that need reconciling if mature moral judgments are to be made.

What are some of these polarities?

- Freedom — Authority
- History — Future
- Thinking — Feeling
- Transcendence — Immanence
- Normative — Exceptional
- Individual — Community
- Personal Morality — Institutional Justice

Our skill as moralists is not to make a forced choice for one pole in preference to the other, but rather to weigh the demands that each pole makes and attempt to find a moral solution that honors the cherished values represented by each pole. I know the importance of personal freedom. I also appreciate the value of authority as a condition for an orderly society. My freedom must not be absolute, for then I would become totally self-centered. Authority must not be absolute, for then it would lapse into tyranny and totalitarianism.

If I think only of history, I am doomed to be an antiquarian. If my eyes never wander from the year 2000, I am a dismissible idealist, never in touch with reality's fullness.

Should I make thinking and abstracting the essence of all I do, I would atrophy into arid intellectualism. But were I to dissolve into unmitigated passion and emotion, I would be little more than a sentimentalist.

When I place all my expression of God in transcendent terms, I create a divinity who has no interest in the problems of people. When I seize nothing but expressions of the God of immanence, I tend to trivialize Him and lose a sense of the divine mystery.

If I am so stuck on the normative in life that I never allow for the exceptional, I shall never gain a new idea. (I will be too old far too soon!) When I dally only with the exceptional, I shall never know the values of stability and continuity.

Should I place all my money on the rights of the individual with no reference to community, I would create a selfish monster. But were I to endow the community with absolute rights, I would snuff out the beauty and uniqueness of each individual.

I might become so concerned about my personal morality that I would care little about the social injustices that plague so much of the earth. On the other hand, I might become so absorbed in public struggles against institutionalized injustice that I would forget my call to personal inwardness and spirituality and thus prejudice my very effectiveness in accomplishing social reform.

I hope this expansion about polarities is clear. Rarely does anyone come equipped with a complete balance of all these (and many more) polarities within one's life. Individuals tend to favor one pole or the other, depending on their upbringing, temperament, culture, history, psychological thresholds, and socioeconomic status. How one was raised both as a Catholic and as an American in a technological era has much to do with his or her value systems. The reasons are myriad.

I don't think it is important to know all the reasons. I believe it is critical, however, that one recognize polarities in moral discourse and not see them as necessarily bad. In a moral discussion, a rich diversity of views caused by polar preference presents the condition for a richer and truer solution to the dilemma. A group of discussants whose polar preference is authority is bound to arrive at a one-sided solution. Mix freedom and authority types, however, and you have a chance of coming closer to the truth.

Simon's valuing processes, forced choice and rank order, are excellent ways of surfacing the polarities present in the discussion. Case studies with attendant dialogues will do much to bring forth a wide number of awarenesses and preferences. Punishment seekers, ego builders, good boys/girls, law and order people, rationale seekers, and conscience and principle people will emerge in these discussions.

In the roil and mix of the *Prism*, principles, situations, polarities, high thinking, and hot feeling converge to force a moral dilemma to yield a solution, and lead to practical moral decision making and behavior.

The Mountain The noise of all this reasoning, feeling, and discussing deserves a reprieve. Intense involvement requires a time for withdrawal and prayer, especially when we are speaking of a community of believers. God gave us reason to discern the truth. God gave us faith to discern the truth. Reason and faith are friends and must work together.

The reasoning in the prism is not enough. There must also be some faith on the mountain. In the quiet of prayer and meditation we grow still and become hearers of the Word, listeners to Being. In this tense alertness before the Lord, we yearn, sigh, beg, and pray for the light that is "a lamp unto our feet." We replace the necessary busyness of reason with the necessary tranquility of faith and prayer. We beg to know the Lord's will.

We do not do this as one ignorant of the problem, insensitive to the many dimensions of the dilemma, uninstructed in all the data required for a prudential judgment. We come before the Lord as people who have done their homework, and, like Solomon, we implore the gift of wisdom. We want to do more than merely know the truth in a detached way. We wish to be at one with it, just as we desire to be at one with Christ.

Most of the happening in moral education takes place between the Prism and the Mountain. The sunlight of principles endures throughout it all. And every so often the fourth image surprisingly and joyfully appears.

The Rainbow If the Prism is like the Deluge with its intense involvement, teachings, learnings, reasonings, and experiencings, and the Mountain is like the Ark of faith and prayer that invites repose and respite, the final image of the Rainbow is the epiphany that makes it all worthwhile.

With God's help we can come to a solution. Just as rainbows appear after storms, so do reconciliation, fulfillment, and divine disclosure appear after the "storms" of moral efforts. We can come to know the truth and that truth does make us free. Our educational enterprise in moral searchings will not frustrate us in the end. When we knock sufficiently, the door will be opened. When we ask persistently enough, we shall be heard.

Our task in moral education, therefore, is not a useless passion. We are not a crazed Sisyphus doomed to push a big rock up a hill only to find the fates at the top will kick it back into the dark valley. That is the pessimistic position. Nor are we a blithe Pollyanna romantically romping with a pink parasol through wheat fields full of butterflies. This is a foolish optimism. We will have to struggle like Sisyphus and experience many kicks of fate. But we will catch that butterfly, the elusive beauty of God's will for us.

Thus in the end, the right moral decision—like virtue—is a grace, a gift of Christ, an Easter moment, a transfiguration of our present darkness into the ineffable light of the risen Lord.

The four images—Sun, Prism, Mountain, Rainbow—invite you to see one way of going about the matter of making moral decisions and of integrating the humane sciences of counseling and experimental psychology with the religious context, with its elements of principles, laws, situations, polarities, prayers, and expectations of the reconciling gift of God.

As you can see, most of the action goes on in the Prism, especially the educational approaches of valuing and case study suggested at the beginning of this chapter. You may also notice how much more deserves your attention.

a. The sense of sin and sins (fundamental option/acts morality).
b. The role of guilt.
c. The question of moral responsibility and accountability.
d. The divine judgment.
e. Careful nuancing of responsibility according to subjective states of maturity.
f. Sensitivity in balancing the objective degree of guilt according to an acts/morality point of view against the sliding scale of subjective guilt, related to the depth and maturity of one's fundamental option.
g. The omnipresence of the Divine Lord and forgiveness as illustrated by the story of the Prodigal Son (Prodigal Father?).

In other words, I cannot hope to cover every element of moral education in so short a chapter. I think my main job here was to build some bridges — between behavioral science and our religious heritage; between Principles and Laws; between Principles and Situations; between Fundamental option and acts of morality; between prayer and Reason; between personal effort and the grace of God; between the myriad of polarities ever present to cause us conflict and agony.

I have invented for you a big picture. I admit in advance that my process is a juggling act. I trust you will find it a challenge and an appeal, perhaps even a seductiveness to find in moral education one of the most adventurous and fascinating forms of religious education.

Since moralists from time immemorial have been intrigued by case studies as the principal peg upon which to hang their thinking, believing, and solving, let us round out this chapter with some case studies and a small model of how to get at them. Because my own bent is the world of literature and drama, I shall draw these studies from them rather than from a journalist's or theologian's notebook (or from my own life).

Case Studies

1. My first example is drawn from Richard Kim's The Martyred.

The Case
Time: June 1950
Place: South Korea

The north Koreans have just captured the city of Seoul. The communists have captured a dozen Protestant ministers and killed ten of them. The two surviving ministers return to their hometown of Pyongyang, where the drama unfolds.

Colonel Chang is the military leader of the town.

Captain Lee is his intelligence officer.

Chang is a pragmaticist; Lee, an idealist.

Chang sees the martyrdom of the ministers as a morale booster for the local population. Their death will inspire patriotism and fervor. Why not have a memorial service?

Chang summons the Reverend Mr. Shin, one of the survivors. The other one has committed suicide.

Shin raises two objections. The ministers did not wish to die for Christ. They went to their deaths as cowards, not as martyrs. Secondly, Shin confesses he has lost his faith. He is now an atheist.

Chang sees no problem. The people think they died as martyrs. Why disturb them?

Lee sees a great problem. How can you use a lie at the service of truth? What good is patriotism based upon deception?

Probe Questions

1. Chang is a practical man. He wants fervent defenders for South Korea. Do you agree that it is better to suppress the truth and use the "martyrdom" as an inspiration for the people's morale?
2. Lee is an idealist. He can't bear the thought of using a deception to arouse patriotism. What strengths and weaknesses do you see in his position?
3. Even if you agreed with Chang, would you use Mr. Shin, an atheist, to conduct the religious service? Would you, or would you not, plead that he was too weak or sick to preside?
4. Do you sense polarities operating here? (Idealism/realism)
5. Is there any middle ground?

The story ends with the service as Chang had planned. But he and the other planners of the service die before it comes to pass. Lee survives and stands near the memorial gathering. He hears the peasants humming songs of homage to their homeland. As they sing under the starry dome of night, Lee joins in their music and discovers within himself a hitherto unknown lightness of heart.

6. Has Lee sold out his ideals by joining in the singing? Has he compromised instead of balanced the tension between the ideal and the practical?

7. How would you feel if the president asked you to join in a televised memorial service for presumed (though not real) heroes who died for America, in order to boost your pride and patriotism?

8. Similarly, how would you react if the Holy Father asked you to take courage from the presumed heroic behavior of a group of Catholic missionaries, if in fact their behavior wasn't at all heroic, as is the case in this story?

9. How do you feel about pride in your country and your church?

10. How would you want patriotism and church loyalty stimulated and encouraged?

N.B. *I am not in any way implying that president or pope would ever use such an incident to promote loyalty and pride. I am merely trying to emphasize the values of pride and patriotism and the difficulties that may be faced in soliciting them. Remember that the case study is a fictional one and my questions applying it to church and state are equally hypothetical.*

2. My second example is drawn from the well-known Man of La Mancha.

The Case
Time: Sixteenth century
Place: Spain

La Mancha is a shameless idealist (as so many young people are).
To him a roadside inn is a castle.
In Aldonza he sees not a prostitute, but the Lady Dulcinea.
He dreams impossible dreams and reaches for an unreachable star.
Everyone tells him: "See life as it is."
He *has* seen life as it is. Over the fifty years of his life, he has witnessed cruelty, pain, misery, and hunger. He has looked at men die in battle by his side and under the lash in Africa. He has held dying men in his arms. They saw life as it is and died despairing. They whimpered a "Why?"—not about dying, but why they lived at all.
La Mancha says that when life seems crazy why is it so? Maybe being too practical is madness. That could be seeking treasure where there is only trash. Perhaps the greatest madness is seeing life as it is and not *as it should be.*
One day, La Mancha fights the knight of mirrors, *life as it is.* The realists defeat him. He becomes a shell of a man and waits to die. But to his deathbed comes Aldonza, now transfigured into the Lady

Dulcinea. She awakens in him the dream of life as it should be. She tells him how his dream transformed her own self-image.

If he is about to die, then let him do so with the knowledge that he was right. One should be idealistic; one should fight for life *as it ought to be* and not settle for it as it is.

Probe Questions

1. What would happen if life had only La Mancha types?
2. In *My Fair Lady*, Professor Higgins sees a potential lady in a dirty, foulmouthed flower seller on the street. Is his vision the same type as La Mancha has toward the lady of ill repute, Aldonza?
3. Do you think realists are attacked unfairly in this story?
4. Should most people be a blend of idealism and practicality?
5. Is La Mancha's fight with the knight of mirrors (realism) typical? In other words, La Mancha lost. Do idealists always lose in such confrontations with the real?
6. La Mancha actually succeeded in helping Aldonza become the Lady Dulcinea. Do you see a parallel in the way Christ was able to transform Mary Magdalene? If so, do you see any difference between the approach of Christ and that of La Mancha?
7. Do you find your own personal idealism being scoffed at? If so, by whom? How do you react?
8. Do you think you will become less idealistic as you grow older? Do you regret this? If so, how do you think you can forestall it?
9. Do you see a connection between idealism and spiritual insight and faith? What is that connection?
10. Why be an idealist? Why be a realist? Why be a blend of both?

Some comments Both of these case studies deal with idealism versus realism. In the story of *The Martyred*, a moral issue is at the center. Is it better to be a lying realist or a truthful idealist? Or are there shades of accommodation in between?

Man of La Mancha overstates the case for idealism presumably as a reaction against overstated realism. While the issue here is not moral in the overtly normal sense, still the conversion impact on Aldonza is enough to draw your attention to the value of idealism when pragmatists rule the roost.

In the first story you may find the law and order proponents strong in fighting for Lee, on grounds of the law of honesty and the principle of the right to know the truth. You may also find a few students who are not so "purist" in their approach, and who see some merit in Chang's realism. Of course, Lee's capitulation at the end muddies the waters, which is precisely the intent of the case—to point up the messiness of any deep moral situation and the ensuing difficulties of a clean resolution. Small wonder the image of the Rainbow is always a time of radical amazement and surprise! Even though we await the sound of the dim drums of Christ the conqueror and his occasional appearances, we never cease to marvel when it happens.

A Lesson Plan Outline

How should you go about these case studies?

I suggest giving everyone a sheet listing the four images, along with a talk about their meanings.

It would be best to give everyone a xeroxed copy of the case studies.

Let them read both of them and ponder the questions for awhile.

Ask them to make notes.

Allow your students ten to fifteen minutes for personal pondering.

Take up the questions one by one and ask for responses.

On the chalkboard write:

Principles	Laws	Polarities	Culture	K Categories

You could even add combat and catharsis, if they are not too threatening. Characterize your students' responses accordingly. Invite them to fight you and argue your characterization. Don't be too set in your ways or too definitive.

Take some time to pray and meditate about the matter.

On days when the Rainbow appears—and you all will know it—let there be a thanksgiving hymn, an alleluia (praise to Yahweh).

Keep reviewing the basics of Sun, Prism, Mountain, and Rainbow.

The chart on the next page may help you see the varying elements that should catch your eye as you go about selecting case studies. The eight categories along the side should serve as guidelines for your probe questions.

CHOOSING CASE STUDIES

Source (Check one)
News
Bible
Movies/TV
Plays
Novels
Personal Experience
Other

Situation	
Characters	
Conflict	
Issues	
Values	
Principles	
Polarities	
Relation to Students' Lives	

A Self-evaluation Questionnaire on Value and Moral Education*

1. Catholic education *is* value education.
   The questions become:

* Courtesy of Sr. Kathleen Marie Shields, C.S.J.

    a. How are our values spelled out in our philosophy, goals and objectives, organizational setting, programs, and curriculum?

    b. What values are reflected in the adult witness of our teachers? Our priests? Our parents? Our total parish community?

    c. What are we *doing now* in our educational setting and program that clearly indicates our values?

    d. What are we *not doing* that clearly indicates a negation of our values? A failure to communicate our values?

2. The process of valuing is related to all that we do in education. We do not "teach" values, but we do open children, youth, and adults to a process of learning to choose, cherish, and act upon fundamental basic Christian principles.

    a. Teacher education must include value education.

    b. Parent education must include value education.

    c. Childhood and youth education must include value education.

3. Helpful tools for teacher education (*all* teachers) include the following:*

    a. *The Qualities and Competencies of the Religion Teacher* (cf. especially Goal 4, pp. 14–15, and Goal 5, pp. 16–17).

    b. *Developing the Competencies of the Religion Teacher* (cf. especially Modules 3.2 and 4.1).

    c. *I Believe in God:* a basic book for in-service faculty on the value (virtue) of faith (cf. especially p. 11, pp. 26–29, and p. 37).

4. Parent programs in value education can be designed from Module 4.1 in *Developing the Competencies of the Religion Teacher.* The preassessment and postassessment scales will be most helpful. Learning experiences can be built around areas of need. Availability of audiovisual materials and paperbacks are important considerations too.

5. A highly effective adult education program could be planned cooperatively *by parents and teachers* for parents and teachers.

6. In looking at the present Catholic school curriculum, administrators and teachers should reflect on these questions:

    a. What values are we holding?

    b. How are these values evident in the attitudes and experiences of the child? The teaching-learning situation? The curriculum? The school atmosphere?

    c. How do the areas we teach reflect our values?

religion	ecology
social studies	health
science	other
physical education	

*All these books are available from NCEA.

  d. How does the *way we teach* give witness to our value system?
  e. How does the *way we relate* give witness to our value system?
    1) administrator-faculty clergy;
    2) teacher-child relationships;
    3) teacher-parent relationships;
    4) teacher-teacher and teacher-faculty relationships;
    5) student councils;
    6) parish board of education or education committee.
7. Value education is integrated education. Consider these questions:
  a. Are some of our values missing? (e.g., respect for life; call to simplicity; careful use of material goods, etc.)
  b. Do we need to reaffirm some of our values? (e.g., faith-life is expressed in communal worship; daily prayer is important; what happens to people in India *does* affect the way I live today.)
  c. Do we need to build in some minicourses to make certain that we are taking a look at justice? At peace? At our environment? Or, can this need be taken care of by a stronger emphasis in our present program?
  d. Can we *readily identify* our values from personal witness, from daily experiences, from curricular content, from school environment?
  e. If we cannot do so, is it because:
    1) the values are not there?
    2) we have not identified them?
    3) we have not taken time to reflect on them?
8. Are parents and teachers aware of the educational tools available for value clarification? Is a clear distinction made between the use of value clarification techniques and strategies and the lifelong process of valuing? How is value clarification helpful in value education? How is moral education an integral part of the valuing process?
9. Whose values are we talking about in a Catholic school community?
10. In the light of these questions, what do you need to do in the areas of:
teacher education?
parent education?
childhood education? (include school environment, witness, curriculum, neighborhood service, etc.)
adult education for the total parish community?
11. How do you plan to assess your needs cooperatively?
12. How do you plan to communicate where you are and where you hope to go?

Summary

Moral education is an extraordinarily complex affair. It involves the assistance of the humane sciences such as counseling psychology (the valuing processes) and experimental psychology (the developmental stages). It stands within a religious context of inherited principles, enduring polarities, fundamental options, acts of morality, prayer, faith, grace, and the Lord's gracious disclosure of his presence and will.

Its complexity need not be a frightening matter, however. Throughout the years the gradual introduction and review of the varying elements can be brought to your students' attention. And never forget to bring the abiding love and forgiving presence of Christ to each classroom meeting. Our dear Lord wants your students to know the joy of noble, idealistic, and moral living every bit as much as you do. You do not teach alone. His Word waits ever so excitingly in the center of your gathering, ready to heal and make grow.

Still, you have every right to know some discouragement. You will win out as Thornton Wilder so aptly put it, "By the skin of your teeth." In his play of that name, the central character, George Antrobus, having lived through many cataclysms and catastrophes, asserts:

> All I ask is the chance to build new worlds and God has always given us that. We've come a long way. We've learned. We're learning.

That's what's going on with you and your students. That is the perennial miracle of teaching and learning. Let no complexity deter you. Let no simplicity derail you. God is giving you and your students the chance to build new worlds.

Let it happen!

4

SPIRITUAL EDUCATION

There never was found in any age of the world, either philosopher or sect, or law or discipline which did so highly exalt the public good as the Christian faith.

Francis Bacon

Scene: A bookstore specializing in the occult*
Characters: Jill (owner of the bookstore)
                Jack (customer)

Jack: I want a book on the stars.

Jill: Were you born under a lucky one?

Jack: Perhaps. I'm a Sagittarius, but I want to have a better idea of how my life is shaped by the movement of the stars. I'm supposed to be an optimist according to my December star.

Jill: I happen to be a Gemini, the sign of the twins. It fits me well. I do feel at times like two people inside.

Jack: The two faces of Eve? Or two-faced? Or a split personality?

Jill: Beware the flippancy. The battle is often too big within me. I wonder who will win.

Jack: Why don't you take charge? Or groove more with the stars?

Jill: I try. Then I give up and play a game of patience with Tarot cards. Do you want me to tell your fortune?

Jack: No, I'll stay with the stars and rock music and meditation.

Jill: Is that your way to a high?

Jack: Sometimes. I can also trip with my horoscope so long as I block out the world with rock and the breathing exercises. Then I start feeling vibes from the skies.

Jill: "When the moon is in the seventh house and Jupiter aligns with Mars . . ."

Jack: ". . . Then peace will guide the planets and love will steer the stars."

Jill: This looks like the dawning of a sale. Here's a book for you. Are you getting into religion?

* From an article entitled "The Heart of the Matter," by Alfred McBride, *Hi Time*, Milwaukee, Feb. 20, 1976.

Jack: I may just do that. My girl is all full of God and Jesus talk. I look up
        and see stars.   She breaks into, "Praise Jesus!   I love you, Father!
        Spirit, stay! "

Jill: I feel I may lose this sale.

Jack: Not yet. I don't convince easily. Yet, she grooves on my own hungers
        to hear music from the heavens.

Jill: Stop. You're tripping on poetry. Hit the earth. How about a zodiac
        medal, one with Sagittarius on it?

Jack: Sold. I'll take the book, too.

Jill: How about one for your girl?

Jack: Okay. She's a Virgo. But she may be moving me to Trinity.

So much of religion ultimately is a response to spiritual hunger. And
that hunger is of the very bone and blood of each human being. God
makes us with an unrestricted inner drive toward Himself as the absolute fulfiller of every hope within the heart. God promises that He
will never cheat us. He will deliver what He has pledged.

The fictional dialogue with which I open this chapter reflects the
signals emitted by youth concerning their spiritual hunger. Many of
them, deprived of spiritual food from religion, have sought their inner
highs from drugs, sex, and hard rock. Then they have quietly turned
to parareligious experiences provided by the occult. Next has come
the excitement of the Jesus movement. Now, we are in the midst of a
fascinating combination of eastern meditation practices and Catholic
worship.

This is a favorable time for religious education. We can act as midwives in their moral growth within a community of believers. We
also should find a call to minister to their spiritual growth within that
same community. The chapter on moral education shows the need to
integrate the world of the developmentalists with religious tradition in
the moral sphere. In this chapter let us turn again to the subject of
growth and development and the need to relate it to the religious tradition in the spiritual sphere.

William Blake, the metaphysical poet, once wrote that growth is a
passage from innocence to complexity to organized innocence. Philosopher Paul Ricoeur speaks of it as a journey from first to second naivete. Jesus describes it as going from childhood to adult life and then
being born again as a little child.

The theme of growth is constant. One starts in the sweet simplicity
of the nursery and then plunges into the ever increasing maze of disorder and complexity that characterizes so much of life. But we need
not be imprisoned in the labyrinthine complexities of life. Beyond
them is the world of newly found simplicity.

Joyce Cary illustrated this theme with an anecdote. Once upon a time a four-year-old boy sat on a lawn watching a bird. Quietly he stared at the bird and enjoyed that simple communion. His mother looked out the kitchen door at him and exclaimed, "Oh Billy, what a beautiful robin that is you are looking at!" At that moment complexity started for Billy. Analysis began. He was introduced to the taxonomy of the bird population.

His education commences. Many, many years pass. Billy is docking a canoe at his camp. His own children are splashing noisily in the lake. A robin lands on the dock. Years fall away and Billy finds himself stopping and quietly meditating on this beautiful creature. Its "robin-ness" is still there, but that factor no longer stands in the way. Billy is born again. In the fullness of his maturity he relearns to commune, to know, to be at one with the subject of his contemplation. He is no longer the innocent. He is now Blake's organized innocent— not a naive child, but an adult in the peace of a second naivete.

This is the basic structure of growth, its inevitable beginning-middle-end. Present-day pioneers in developmental psychology are seeking to plot the inner demography of that voyage. They are distilling recognizable landmarks in the dense fog that is the typical climate of the marvelously supple complexity of the human psyche. Piaget, Erickson, Havighurst, and Kohlberg have given us a host of original insights into this field.

We have seen the value of the developmental model for moral education. I believe that a parallel model can be useful for spiritual education. Dr. James Fowler, an associate of Kohlberg, has begun to transfer the developmental insights to the area of faith-knowing. Kohlberg stayed scrupulously within the world of reason-knowing. Fowler affirms that there is such a thing as faith-knowing, and that it deserves the kind of scientific inquiry and trained scholarship that have been exercised on other forms of knowing and perception.

Growth in faith-knowing is one aspect of spiritual growth. Hence it deserves our attention here as one important phase in spiritual education. Developmental research rightly holds a deserved appeal for educators who want to pride themselves on meeting a student where he is and assisting him to mature and develop. Today's scope and sequence charts in every manner of curriculum reflect a respect for and a debt to the developmentalists.

What is faith-knowing? Is it knowing about religious content? Is it knowing about God? Is it knowing God in religious experience of an ecstatic form? Or knowing God in a less dramatic way?

The answer is YES to all of these questions. Teachers have generally settled for faith-knowing as either a knowledge of religious truth claims (creeds, dogmas, etc.) or as a religious experience, a spiritual high. But there is also a faith-knowing that understands how God, man, and the world are related. In this form of faith-knowing, the meaning of life never occurs apart from its relationship to God.

This form of faith-knowing does not exclude "truths and experiences," but its attention is on what the Bible calls covenant. At the Sinai covenant, the land (the world), the people, and God are bonded together. Christ's covenant on Good Friday and Easter binds people, the cosmos, and God together into an express relationship. Faith-knowing, as used here, is the capacity to bind together, in a covenant, the world, people, and God. It is a habit of mind that interprets life always in these terms.

Faith-knowing links creation to the ultimate and the transcendent. In order to appreciate this idea, think of a world where there would be no faith-knowing. Suppose no religious faith-knowing were going on? Actually, this is more than hypothetical, since it is fairly true of many people's lives and perceptions. The poet Yeats noted this phenomenon and commented on it in his work *The Second Coming:*

> *Things fall apart;*
> *The center cannot hold;*
> *Mere anarchy is loosed upon the world, . . .*
> *The best lack all conviction, while the worst*
> *Are full of passionate intensity.*

A world without the covenantal binding and healing that is characteristic of faith-knowing would lead to two anarchies: philosophical nihilism ("Everything is absurd and meaningless") and moral chaos ("I shall play my trumpet whenever and wherever I please regardless of what anyone thinks or feels").

With nothing to bind reasoning together, we lose the ground of human discourse. Like the central character of *Cool Hand Luke* we suffer a breakdown in communications.

With nothing to bind our moral thinking together, we lapse into moral anarchy. As the muscle-bound man of Albee's *American Dream* says, "I let people love me. I accept the syntax around me. I let people touch me and draw pleasure from my presence. *I can feel nothing.*" He is morally neutralized by a world without covenant.

Hence faith-knowing is more than a casual way of perceiving. It is central to achieving the dream of ideal interpersonal communication and moral integrity. Unless the faith-knowing is operative, the goal of moral education discussed in the previous chapter will be a useless passion.

Does faith-knowing have any reference to truth claims of religious experience? Yes. The truth claims, situated in the context of the community of believers, provoke the possibility of faith as knowing

Christ in religious experience. The experience of Christ liberates the faith-perception from being a mirage and a delusion.

Spiritual education tries to help people develop their capacity for faith-knowing. It assumes the context of Church, truths, experience. Just as moral education takes place within a range of awareness and stages, so also does spiritual education. Just as Kohlberg has a ladder, so also does Fowler. I like ladder images because they illustrate growth so well. They also possess a motivational pull. ("I bet you I can climb to the very top!")

Again, I must register some hesitancy about ladders, rungs, and stages. They lead the unwitting teacher to stereotype students, to ignore their complexity, to oversimplify the mystery of growth. I repeat my prescription as antidote, "Dial a faith-awareness," just as I called for dialing a moral consciousness. Be ready to expect any one of the awarenesses from anyone at any time.

With these safeguards in mind I wish to review Fowler's stages and apply them to spiritual education. The controlling assumption behind the stages of growth is that everyone possesses a radical drive to the infinite. This is a nonnegotiable item. You either accept this or you don't. Test yourself. Do you believe that you have within you the unrestricted hunger for the ultimate? Do you believe this of every person you meet? If you do, then you can both expect and enable the possibilities of growth. If you do not, then these stages are simply an accident, a trick of fate that has no inner substance behind it, and no God to found it or call it forth. This, then, is the basic assumption— the inner spiritual drive to "be beyond."

Out of this primordial sea of the preconceptual, prelogical, and preanalytical are born six states of faith-knowing and valuing. I will choose nontechnical language to describe them, since I believe the decoding will draw us more quickly into the reality that is the essence of our discussion.

1. The Poet

The first act of faith-knowing sees God, people, and the world as a unity. It is like an egg, whole and complete. The nursery rhyme "Humpty Dumpty" starts with an animated egg sitting on a wall. This is first perception. It is the naive appreciation typical of a child. To say that it is naive is not to put it down, but rather to assert that the complexity of life is not yet apparent. Like a poet whose gift is to see life in unified wholes, this faith-knower starts the journey with the taste of a dream that will only be realized at maturity.

2. The Reasoner

Complexity begins to set in. Differences are noted. People quarrel and disunite. The simple unity is gone. ("Humpty Dumpty had a great fall. . . ." The poet's egg has broken into analytic shell parts. How shall one hold it together? Better still, how shall I piece it together? The light of reason dawns and comes to the rescue. It offers its services to link God, people, and the world again.

Authority also renders its service. Parents and other adults who are trusted are sought out for answers and solutions. Of necessity the perceptions are quite literal. Nuances, overtones, and connotations await future development.

3. The Ecumenist

The pool of complexity widens. The faith-knower finds life compartmentalized into a multitude of worlds: family, school, leisure, politics, nations, religions, ideologies. The egg broke into more shells than anticipated. How are all these worlds held together? How does God fit into the picture?

Instinctively and mercifully, an ecumenical breadth aids the faith-knower to cope with the variety. The term *ecumenism* is not used here in its specialized religious sense (the dialogue between religions) alone; it is widened to respect the sheer diversity of life itself.

To manage all this the faith-knower comes to trust the public traditions of religion and the social/legal order. For the poet, the reasoner, and the ecumenist, the religious faith of the community functions as a support system. It is seen as an explaining and comforting authority, a celebrating group that through ritual and symbol reinforces nonverbally the sought-for unity now threatened by the increasing perception of life's complexity.

4. The Personalizer

"I want to do this on my own. I want to find my own way to covenant bind God, people, and the world." The faith-knower wants to put it altogether on his or her own. Reliance on authority and tradition gives way to the inner drive toward personal synthesis. The faith-knower and valuer realize the importance of developing a personalized management of life's varieties and dilemmas, for without it he or she will never really grow. Just as withdrawal from apron strings is necessary for intellectual and emotional maturity, the same is true for faith-knowing too.

Once the faith-knower has begun to create his or her own personal integration, a new kind of complexity can be perceived. This is the element of polarities (already discussed in Chapter 3). He or she discovers there are unavoidable conflicts ever present. How do I reconcile the demands of the individual versus the community? How do I bring together the particular and the universal, law and freedom, reason and poetry, subjectivity and objectivity?

The polarities cause tension and discomfort. One's reaction to the tension produces a religious crisis that could stunt further growth if it were badly handled. The kitchen may get too hot. The temptation is to run away—but run away to *what*?

Relativism

Deny the polarities. Pretend they don't exist. Declare that everything is "kind of true." Be genial. Take no stands. This is a benign neglect of the tensions. It is the grandeur of nonadvertence.

Absolutism

The absolutist chooses a fundamentalist approach to religion. One doesn't just deny the polarities; one banishes them. Thus one abolishes tensions and distinctions. Or one may select a more respectable form of fundamentalism, an uncritical retreat to traditionalism in religion. He or she effectively identifies with the dead faith of the living instead of authentic traditionalism, which is "the living faith of the dead." If, however, one refuses to fear the tensions that come from polarities, he or she is ready to move on.

5. The Tension Bearer

Now the faith-knower begins to understand Christ's call to the Cross. Far from being a passive responder to the tension, the faith-knower faces up to the polarities and struggles to keep the antitheses ever in mind. Slowly he or she perceives a new and unexpected balance appearing. One gains new respect for the symbols, rituals, traditions, and beliefs of religion, while at the same time noting the limits—the so-called scandal of particularity.

An example of this type of polarity is Christianity's claim that Jesus is messiah and son of God. There is a particularity about the belief.

Why?   Right now there are over two billion people in the world who don't believe it.   In fact, there are millions who actively disbelieve it. No amount of ecumenical twistings and turnings can evade an affirmation of Jesus in terms that defer to others' sensitivities to the point where one's own meaning evaporates.   You are either with him or against him.   Either he can save you or he can't.

Bearing the Cross, accepting the role of tension bearer, has received rich attention in religious literature.   Tillich says we need the "courage to be" in order to bear it.   Bonhoffer claims it demands "costly grace" to live with such tension.   To John of the Cross, it is a "night of the soul" that is both redeeming and purifying.

6. The Universalizer

This is the moment of becoming again as a little child.   We are Blake's organized innocents and Roceur's people of second naivete.   The complexity is not forgotten; it is integrated into the higher unity.   When Humpty Dumpty fell and cracked, the child wept that "all the king's horses and all the king's men could not put Humpty Dumpty back together again."

But the universalizer does put him back together again.   The faith-knower now rejoices in the grace of his or her labors.   The universal and particular relate.   The universalizer is a covenant person, a reconciler, a living testimony to the realized dream that began at the poet stage.   The dream comes true!

Such a person comes across as a simple, lucid interpreter of life.   It may be thought that such people are in short supply, but there are more of them than public opinion realizes.   This is because the universalizers tend to be self-effacing and unself-conscious in their virtue. Their presence is always a grace and an inspiration to all others to pursue the processes of faith-knowing and commitment.

These, then, are the six stages: Poet, Reasoner, Ecumenist, Personalizer, Tension Bearer, Universalizer.

I prefaced this material with the assumption about the inner drive that makes the growth possible.   There are several other assumptions to bring to the surface.

First, it is clear that only a person with faith will be a faith-knower. The steps will mean little to a reader who denies the possibility of religious faith.   The exposition is meant for a teacher and learner who agree on the possibility of religious faith.   Only then will all this talk about faith-knowing make sense.

Secondly, it is assumed that such faith is a grace and a gift of God. It thereby shows in a beautiful manner how God's grace shines

Faith-Knowing and Valuing

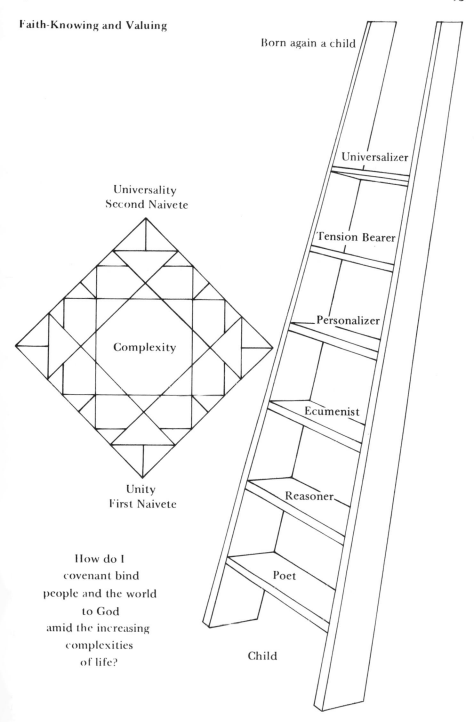

Born again a child

Universalizer

Universality
Second Naivete

Tension Bearer

Personalizer

Complexity

Ecumenist

Unity
First Naivete

Reasoner

How do I
covenant bind
people and the world
to God
amid the increasing
complexities
of life?

Poet

Child

through many levels of human maturing, as well as being a divine partner to the growth process.

Thirdly, valuing processes, techniques to uncover moral awareness, can now be transferred to the realm of spiritual education. In addition, of course, there are the aids from a specifically religious context such as prayer, meditation, study, and worship.

Fourthly, there are variables affecting the quality of each stage and the possibilities of growth. These are five in number: Authority, Criteria, Symbols/Concepts, Roles, and Challenges.

Authority

Authority wears many masks. Its best known one is that of the stern ruler, demanding accountability. Yet today its opposite is fairly popular, namely, the smiling, permissive person. There is also the lamentable authority that is indifferent, and the praiseworthy one that is creative. Responders, equally, come in different styles. See the craven, passive, obedient ones. Look at the contentious and rebellious ones. Glance at the insouciant ones; they never seem to notice authority. Catch the smiling, sly ones who dedicate themselves to subverting authority.

These variables affect growing and faith-knowing. Stop for a moment and think of all the mixes possible between four types of responders — surely enough to fill a transactional analyst's notebook.

Criteria

By what shall good and evil be measured? How shall our faith-knowing find direction? By many ways: parents, teachers, principles, laws, customs, traditions, upheavals, styles, books, philosophies, fashions, criminal witnesses, saintly testimonies, simplistic analyses, sophisticated observations — the list is painfully extensive.

In a fluid world the criteria keep shifting. And with social mobility shifting the people, the combination of the variables of criteria is almost infinite.

Symbols/Concepts

Formal education stresses concepts and analysis. Apart from literature and the arts, there is little formal education in symbolic language.

But outside of formal education, the story is quite different. Between religion and advertising alone the human psyche is flooded with communication that is largely symbolic. The "logos" of the big companies via TV and the mass media magazines, plus the Logos of the

Church via rituals and biblical pronouncements, assail the modern psyches, which in most cases are unprepared to handle well either the sacred or the secular symbols. The formal poets are rarely heard. The informal ones—especially the advertising ones—have, I blush to say, more influence than Shakespeare.

Faith-knowing must weave a path through the maze of concepts and symbols, with which it most frequently must cope.

Six Stages   Five Variables

The Labyrinth of Faith Knowing

Roles

Shifting roles provide another variable to affect faith-knowing. Consider the roles of child, parent, teacher, boss, worker (white and blue collar), player, lover, beloved, learner, middle manager, soloist, celebrator, mourner, counselor, counselee—and so on.

It is quite possible for one person to play almost all of these roles at one time or another, and even others not listed. The role influences the thinking—sometimes to the point where it controls the thinking. The role of leader may temporarily banish the consciousness of what is on the follower's mind. Growth in faith-knowing means that roles, while they must be assumed responsibly, cannot and should not retard inner development.

Challenges

A certain number of typical challenges recur again and again to test and affect the quality of faith-knowing: defeat, error, mistake, envy of another's success, discouragement at another's victory, criticism, advice, inspiration.

Responses to challenge are equally varied: fear, dismay, paralysis of will, withdrawal, overexactness, loss of freedom, joy at a challenge, gladness to solve a problem, the appeal of advice and the urge to act on it, the appeal of advice but the inclination to do nothing.

Faith-knowing needs challenge. Any kind of growing does. So much depends on the intensity of the challenge and the timidity or boldness of the responder.

So now we have six stages and five variables (which when multiplied by all the modifications given here add up to fifty or more subvariables, not counting the numerous extra shapings brought on by the different transactions).

Yes, the process is a web, a labyrinth—sometimes a Dante's Inferno. I deliberately stress this aspect here so that the simplicity of the model does not mislead anyone. Here is the simpler version:

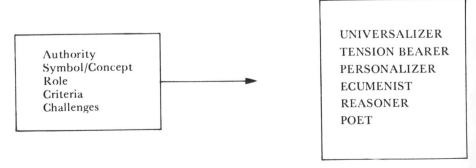

| Authority
Symbol/Concept
Role
Criteria
Challenges | → | UNIVERSALIZER
TENSION BEARER
PERSONALIZER
ECUMENIST
REASONER
POET |

But this purified typology, while fine for clarity, obscures the messiness and subtleties of real relationships. I see no harm in starting simply so long as the nuances are permitted to emerge. On the other hand, I would not want you to become so mired in the particularities that the Big Picture is eventually lost.

The great spiritual masters have always understood that direction to a goal demands clarity of vision, and that the journey there is through a morass of valleys and peaks, nights and days. Perhaps that is the origin of the axiom "God writes straight with crooked lines."

I have already suggested that a teaching method associated with this concept is the case study and dialogue. I offer two parables, a sample dialogue, and some analysis in terms of the stages and variables involved.

PARABLE I "Question 7"

Time: 1950
Place: East Germany

A fourteen-year-old boy, Hans, son of a Lutheran minister, is about to receive the sacrament of Confirmation. Part of the ceremony requires that he sign a statement that says, "I will be faithful to my Lord Jesus Christ until death." Filled with faith and youthful idealism, he gladly puts his name to that declaration and goes on to be confirmed.

The great dream in the family is that Hans become a concert pianist. There will be little hope for this unless he is accepted by the state conservatory. His application has been filed for almost a year. Finally, a reply arrives. The letter contains the conditions to be met for entry. A long questionnaire, as is usually the case, is enclosed.

Hans eagerly begins to fill out the answers until he is stopped short by Question 7: "Are you a believer in Christ and a member of the Church?" (No believing Christians will be accepted.) His framed Confirmation certificate hangs over his desk. He stares at the bold confidence of his signature.

If he wants a music career, he must deny his conscience.

To do so would shame his father, who would have to preach to a congregation that knows his son betrayed the faith.

Many tears. Much agonizing. Hans cannot bear the thought of giving up his music. At a family discussion Hans rationalizes his desire to go to the conservatory and deny his Confirmation oath. His parents express shock, dismay, anger. They plead for him to reconsider. But in the end they tell him it must be his own decision.

To Question 7 he replies, "I am not a believer."

He is accepted and goes to live at the conservatory. Months pass.

Meanwhile, his father quietly arranges for Hans to escape to freedom in the West where he can pursue his studies and regain his faith.

When his son comes home for vacation, he outlines the plan. The boy, who has been filled with remorse all along, seizes at the idea. He knows it might mean he will never see his family again, but it means freedom both to believe in Christ and to seek a career in music. He agrees. The plan works and Hans goes off to freedom in the West.

The East German authorities soon discover how it all happened. As they send police to arrest the pastor, he is preaching to the people about fidelity to Christ and the trial of the Cross. While the police lead him down the aisle to prison and certain death, the congregation rises and sings:

> Jesu, joy of man's desiring
> Lord, who bore our sorrows great
> Fill our hearts with grace and courage
> That we may live with bold resolve.

Sample Dialogue   (L) Leader   (P) Participant

L: Was it fair to ask a fourteen-year-old to make so serious a promise to God?

P: Yes, though he would need to be informed about the challenges he must face.

L: Do you think his parents were right to leave the decision up to him? Should they have used more authority?

P: No. If they considered him mature enough to make the Confirmation promise, they must also let him live with the decisions that flow from it.

L: Do you believe the state had the right to forbid him entry because of his religious beliefs?

P: No. The state should allow and encourage freedom of religious belief and not use it as a lever for discrimination.

L: How wise was the father in obtaining a secret escape for his son?

P: The father loved his son. He wanted his son to be both a pianist and a believer. Why shouldn't he find an alternate way?

L: But the son has failed Christ. He hasn't shown bravery. Why should he have his cake and eat it too?

P: God never ceases to hold out the possibility of forgiveness. The boy's father reflects the Lord's compassion.

L: Is the father's death worth all the trouble? Could he have waited a few years and encouraged the son to defect, then regain his faith? Then both would be alive.

P. _____

(You choose the answer.)

Reflections on the Dialogue

Clearly the dialogue barely suggests the number and kinds of questions and answers liable to come up on this topic. So much will depend on the age and experience of the leader and the participants. What are some of the stages and variables hinted at in the discussion?

Personalizer: The boy is urged to make his own decision.

Tension Bearer: The parents are torn between love for their son and devotion to Christ. The boy sees the tension and breaks it, at first, by choosing the state.

Authority: The boy stands facing the authority of his parents, the government, and Christ. He doesn't appear to be rebellious. He responds at the self-interest and reasoning stage, though his reasoning comes through as rationalizing.

Role: From the moment he signs the Confirmation document, he shifts from child to self-determining young man.

Criteria: He stands between commitment to Christ and commitment to his personal talents. The criterion of religious commitment declines as he senses the criterion of career assuming maximum importance.

Challenges: He faces challenges from Christ, parents, the state, and his own inner integrity.

Poet: His world is clearly blown apart. The covenant possibility in which God provides meaning to hold His world and people together evaporates.

PARABLE II   "But I Never Doubted"

I just finished my fiftieth birthday and my twenty-second anniversary as a priest. I was settling into the cozy conviction that life will not hold too many surprises for me and that I will face the ones that come with equanimity. Last Thursday quickly tested my complacency. I was invited to concelebrate at a youth Mass in a neighboring parish.

It was an interparish youth affair. Our own young people would be there along with a sprinkling of adults concerned about the youth programs either as teachers, counselors, or merely friends. A special "youth priest" had been invited, a man known for his skill in speaking of faith and religion in a manner calculated to appeal to the young. I enjoyed the prospect, almost like a grandfather glad to see the new generation restless to get into the race of life.

Everything started out well. The music and the mood suited the age dominance of the congregation. The wall-to-wall throng gave the church gathering the semblance of a rally. An excusable self-congratulatory note set the tone. ("How lucky we are to be here among so many others.") The organizers couldn't be happier. I scanned the congregation and was pleased to note a fine representative sample from my own parish.

Then came the sermon. The preacher, earnest and clearly dramatic, warmed up the group with praise and anecdotes and ritual predictions about how lucky the future will be to have such fervent religious folk to shape and guide moral and belief destinies. With that he launched into the main body of his talk.

His theme was about the role of doubt in the act of religious believing. I though of Tillich as I listened. The preacher evidently assessed that a youthful audience would be having many doubts about religion. Some may even have begun to drift away because they doubted so much. Then the preacher took too sharp a turn.

"I tell you. No one here can really say he or she has faith if they have never doubted about God's existence, the saving grace of Christ, or the claims of the Church! "

A series of sentences and stories rolled out to hammer home that strong and extraordinary position. I admired the eloquence even as I deplored the excess. I was ready to presume it to be nothing more than a harmless exaggeration. As the preacher finished, one was almost tempted to applaud, but church decorum and custom cooled the urge.

The program billed this as a dialogue sermon. Thus reactions were solicited from the audience. The doubting Thomases and Thomasinas testified, "How right you are, father. It was in the anguish of doubt that I found my Lord." It was then I noted a tall, gray-haired woman whose face was unlined, probably due to a lifelong serenity. A cloud darkened her. I could see her trembling all over. She was literally "quaking," which is what the original Quaker religionists used to do.

She quaked until she erupted and in a shaking voice exclaimed, "Father, I have literally never doubted my faith in all my sixty years. Are you telling me that I have lived under an illusion? That I truly have no faith at all, for I have never doubted? How many times I have read the biblical lines, 'I believe, Lord, help my unbelief.' In saying those lines from my heart I have always considered the unbelief not to be doubt, but to be an imperfection of my believing. I never doubted as Thomas did, but a thousand times I have spoken his words, "My Lord and my God." I have ever felt that the grace of Christ spoke to me for he blessed me for not having seen, yet having believed.

"Have all these years been a fantasy?"

Silence.

Moment of truth.

I felt like rising to her defense till I realized I was still at Eucharist, that this was no time to turn liturgy into a debate. Yet much was at stake.

Happily the chastened preacher had reserves of wisdom not so evident in his talk. "Forgive me, my friend. You have helped me to see deeper into the truth of believing and the mystery of faith. Your own luminous testimony of belief stands clear to all of us. Forgive me for my rashness."

She nodded her head quietly.

Sample Dialogue   (L) Leader   (P) Participant

L: Why did the preacher make such an issue of doubt in relation to faith?

P: Because doubt and skepticism about religion are so prominent today. People challenge us to doubt everything religious, from the miracles to the divinity of Christ, to his ability to exercise his saving power upon us.

L: Someone has said that when the young are taught to doubt everything they will wind up believing anything. Is this merely cynical or is there a grain of truth to it?

P: Everybody has to believe in something. Believing is part of living. Religious believing is a special type. If religious belief is taken away, some other kind of belief will come to take its place. So one doesn't believe in Jesus. Well, then they may turn to belief in witches, or money, or sex, or drugs. Absolute doubt would cause despair and suicide.

L: The preacher was trying to say that faith will be challenged, especially by doubts. The quaking woman of the story seemed never to have known such doubts. What kind of challenges would she have known? How did her faith come to grow?

P: Who knows? She had the blessed consolation of never knowing doubt. There are many other kinds of personal suffering that purify religious belief. Many of the mystics spoke of a sense of the loss of God. Yet even though they experienced the Lord's absence, they did not necessarily doubt his possible presence and existence. They seemed to know that a dark night was needed for a rich faith.

L: Would the author of the story have been out of place in publicly coming to the lady's defense? He says he held himself in check because he did not want to see the Eucharist become a debating ground. But suppose the preacher had not acknowledged his excess and asked forgiveness? What if the lady had been left with the tragic thought that she truly had no faith because she had never doubted?

P: The author was right about not debating the preacher. Fortunately, he didn't have to. If the preacher had unhappily reaffirmed his regrettable stand, then I think the author could at least have intervened with something like, "I think there is too much at stake here, a matter too personal and too deep to be dealt with in this kind of situation. May I ask that we continue our worship. Let us pray over the matter. If it is agreeable to both of you, I would like to take this matter up at greater length after Mass."

L: It's not easy to be so reflective at such times.

P: May the Lord be with you always.

Reflections on the Dialogue

You may recall that I characterized the stages and variables of faith-knowing as a web, a maze, a labyrinth. This parable and its sample discussion may give you some further appreciation of this aspect of treating something so sacred and deserving of reverence as the act of religious believing.

Universalizer: Ironically, the quaking lady, so assailed for believing without doubting, may well have been into the universalizing stage, the second naivete. Yet her simplicity and honesty made her willing to submit herself to one more test.

Authority: A preacher is granted a good deal of authority by the listeners. They come fairly well disposed to accept his interpretations. They may not always be treated to eloquence but their trust in the preacher's words is usually not betrayed.

Challenges: The preacher was honestly trying to speak to a challenge he assumed afflicted all of his audience, or at least the young ones. He knew that instability of their youth made them prone to be too impressed with the doubts raised by the skeptics and the unbelievers. Are they urged to doubt? Yes, many people lead them that way. But don't fear too much. Doubts are challenges that test the real metal of faith . . . And then the preacher teetered over the edge.

Symbols/Concepts: By building a whole talk around doubts the preacher confined the matter of faith to the realm of concepts. He seemed to make faith a matter of juggling arguments. But the writers on doubt, such as Tillich and Kierkegaard, were not thinking about doubt in concept terms so much as in a kind of inner despair, emptiness, and anguish about the Lord's love and concern. Truly this was something akin to the "dark night of the soul." How strange it is to reduce faith to concept battles in the midst of ritual, symbolic language, prayers, and the ineffable mystery of the Mass.

These two parables suggest ways for you to clarify the meaning of faith for yourselves and your students. I have selected stories about religious faith. It is also a good idea to compile a series of stories about human faith and trust. Show your students how much human faith enters into their everyday lives—how life can scarcely go on if there are not numerous acts of human trust and faith constantly experienced. Surveys of society today speak of the trust factor, the credi bility curve regarding politicians, businessmen, and other people in public life. Often the news is gloomy. If we can't trust each other, how can we go on?

I urge attention to trust at the human level, so that your students can appreciate the dynamics of faith as the religious level. I am not implying the two should be kept totally separate. I believe that the loss of religious faith accounts for the decline of the human trust factor and the failure of public officials to give evidence of a credible posture.

Up to this point I have spoken of a spiritual education that builds upon a model suggested by developmental psychology. You should also think of using parables and dialogue to spur faith-consciousness both as a human virtue and a spiritual one—as our Lord Jesus did so eloquently. The provisional models may be of some use to you.

Spiritual education must also include liturgy, which will be dealt with in the next chapter. For the present let us consider the continuing need for evangelization and prayer.

Evangelization

Evangelization is the key to spiritual education in terms of renewal agent. In the Bible evangelization is a call to faith in the ever-arriving kingdom of God. In the New Testament evangelization always begins with the believers. When Paul brought the gospel to Greece and Rome, he always preached to the Jewish brethren first, to those who believed in God. Only afterward did he turn to the pagan. Jesus was so strict about staying with his own people for the process of evangelization, that he practically refused to respond when outsiders came for light, as in the case of the Syro-Phoenician woman. ("I have come only for the house of Israel.")

Evangelization in spiritual education is a shot in the arm for faith. It is similar to what evangelical preachers do in crusades, revivals, missions, and parish renewals. It is a new call to faith, a summons to moral renewal. It's the sort of thing accomplished by a good retreat, which demands a radical rededication of the person to Christ. Good evangelization will be sensitive to the stages and variables present in the congregation as outlined earlier.

Good evangelization also takes into account obstacles that obscure the possibility of being heard. Just as a teacher must assess a class, so too an evangelist ought to assess the stumbling blocks that prevent him from reaching the people. While I use the title evangelist, I am not thinking exclusively in terms of a professional retreat master or a traveling preacher. The main concern is the teacher, who must assume an evangelical role from time to time. Whenever a teacher undertakes expressly to stir up faith in his or her students, there is a certain evangelical mood operating.

What are some of the obstacles to evangelization and how should one respond? Consider the following chart:

Evangelization

Obstacles	Responses
Nomads (social mobility)	Help form community of faith
Media (relativism in values)	Add value to the facts
Death of God	Personalize institutions
Cynical Questioners	Quest the face of the Lord
Atheism (reductive humanism)	Revive the will to believe
New Morality	Be a principled situationist
God Talk	Use thoughts that breathe, words that burn

Nomads

Americans are the most mobile people on earth. Twenty-five million move every year. This is equivalent to moving the entire population of California every year! The effect is to make us a nation of nomads. The constant moving splits up families, perpetually ends or changes friendships and widens our network of acquaintances. It makes it very difficult for people to feel the personal security and warmth of a community support system.

The ancient biblical people were nomads, but they brought their community with them wherever they went. Hence the ideals, spiritual goals, and beliefs were carried along. God marched with His people like a pillar of fire and cloud.

Some years ago the U. S. Government purchased a small southern town with the intention of erecting a military installation there. This meant that the whole population needed relocation. The last resident to move was ninety-year-old Sadie Collins. A reporter interviewed her as she sat sadly on her porch. "What's going through your mind, Sadie?" With a profound sigh, she exclaimed, "When you transplant an old plant, it dies."

In today's era of social mobility, with its endless transplanting, something of beauty seems to die every time a move happens. Especially is there an erosion of faith. What can we do about it? I believe that the Church must continually and consciously build a community of faith, for it can no longer assume that it will be there automatically.

We still employ the structure of the territorial parish, which is a good base of operations. The mobility of the population in the parish must call upon setting up processes such as I have described in Chapter 1. What once could be assumed, must now be deliberately created. *The caller to faith today is also a caller to faith community.*

Media

Most of today's high school seniors have seen an average of 25,000 hours of TV, which means they have spent more time before TV than before any teacher anywhere. Today's adults watch an average of three hours of TV a night. This means that Americans devote the equivalent of seven full weeks, twenty-four hours a day, almost two months a year before TV!

Besides this there is the jet plane that transfers millions all over the globe at maximum speeds. In 1830 no one in the world could travel over ten miles an hour. Now we can travel more than 600 miles an hour! What effect of the communications revolution poses a problem for spirituality and evangelization? Information overload with a consequent relativizing of values. In this media age a person in one day can count on absorbing more information than someone in 1776 could hope to encounter in an entire year!

The incessant hammering of information into our consciousness causes an overload that short circuits our capacity to reflect and assess the value and meaning of the data pouring in. The Bible states that the letter kills and the spirit gives life. That sacred writer today might put it this way: "The information overload numbs us so that the spirit of value and meaning fails to give life."

The evangelist calling for spiritual living must note that the listeners may hear only with half an ear, thinking this is just another version of the news, soap opera, western, talk show, or commercial. This is why spiritual and moral education means so much for moderns. It is dedicated to seeing facts in terms of values. The valuing processes are precisely systematic attacks on the stream of data, slowing them down a bit so that the spiritual and moral values implied may be judged and made applicable to personal life.

Death of God

The mid-sixties witnessed a curious movement called the "Death of God." What did it mean? Basically it was a criticism of a formal religion that snuffed out the experience of God. It was a painful message, clothed in an outlandish slogan. Yet some of it was true. The institutions and forms of the Church can sometimes become self-serving and hide the revelation of the Lord.

In one of the Easter stories, two women are on their way to the tomb. They ask themselves about the heaviness of the stone that bars the tomb. Will they be strong enough to move it and see Christ? Will someone come to help them? The women found that divine power had swept away the stone so that the glory of the risen Christ might be seen by all the world.

The apostles once asked Jesus, "Who will cleanse the Temple?" It was Jesus who purified the Temple so that the divine glory might shine through its transparency. The evangelist who calls listeners to faith must work to loosen the heaviness and opaqueness of institutional forms of religion so that he may point to the Lord whom he summons all to believe in.

Cynical Questioners

The growth of an educated populace has generated the fashion of questioning. There is nothing wrong with this so long as the questions remain a genuine search for truth.

What is odd, however, is that with libraries choking with information, studies piling on studies, and information managers abounding, there is another fashion regarding answers. ("I only ask questions. I am not an answer man. I don't know.")

Thus some educators encourage questioning for answers that presumably can't be found. The "I don't know" statement, which used to be either an embarrassment for a teacher or at least a statement of modesty, is now an art form for some. The trouble with this attitude is that it creates a cynical climate. It revs the students up with questions to which there are apparently no answers.

But even more deadly is the persistent use of the seemingly honest question that is in reality a veiled attack on the mysteries of religion. Such people cloak the question with research, dignify it with academic jargon, and quietly subvert the religious mystery out of existence. The combination of a questioning style that leads to cynicism or to the subversion of religious mystery is a genuine threat to spiritual education and the growth of faith.

Does this mean, then, that questions should not be used as an educational technique? Of course not. The processes that I have outlined in this book are full of questions. I have praised the use of dialogue and value seeking, which involves a lot of questioning. The critical aspect is to know how questions are being used. Sometimes they are used just for information. At other times they are meant to lead to self-discovery in the area of morals, values, and faith. Honest questions are really verbalizations of the inner quest of the heart. Persistent use of them leads one to ultimate questions about love, death, and God. When we can hear our students begin to utter ultimate questions with the conviction that they can be heard and answered, then we know the religious value of questioning that asks the Lord to respond.

Atheism

Overt atheism was once one of religion's major foes. Such militant atheism is not so fashionable at the moment. Why not? Possibly because the militancy of the believers is in decline. When there is no believer militancy, there is no theist militancy. Actually atheism is still flourishing, but it is using the "soft sell." Today's atheism is reductive humanism.

Building upon modern man's intense preoccupation with self, the reductive humanists come to our aid with all kinds of pseudopalliatives, some of which have a semireligious veneer. However, the package they come in is still anti-God. It may possess the comforting warmth and color of the human but inside there is the cold and forbidding despair of a world vision without God.

Humanists love to dwell on religious hypocrisy. Believers ought to beware of reductive humanist hypocrisy that often sounds friendly to religion, even talks a lot about Christ and meditation, but on closer look quite clearly sees Christ only as a man and meditation as little more than a technique to relieve stress.

Yes, a real believer ought to be humane. I think Christian humanism is the best blend of faith, with its concern and respect for the human. So many of the processes cited in this book are originated by humanists. It is the duty of the believer to integrate these processes with faith. The evangelical call to believe is not a repudiation of the human, but a fulfilling of it.

New Morality

In the chapter on moral education, I have already reviewed the meaning of the new morality and have suggested how to respond to it.

God Talk

The purpose of new theological talk has always been to make old truths come alive. It has often succeeded—and sometimes failed. A good deal of the new theological talk is just as analytical and jargon-laden as was the old. It seems to operate on the idea that 500 million Catholics are all regular participants in postdoctoral seminars in theology.

Some religious educators, evangelists, and preachers have been trying
to pass on this jargon, sometimes watered down, but always with the
idea that this enlightenment will spur a spiritual revival. Too much
of it is an overly abstract expression of the meaning of Christ. The
New Testament writers and Church fathers spared their people such
airy language. Augustine was one of the world's greatest theologians.
His approach to the gospel dominated the Church for a thousand years.
He spoke to the people in stories, metaphors, and examples.
He used thoughts that breathed and words that burned.

George Bernard Shaw once claimed that America and England are
two nations separated by a common language. I sometimes think the
same is true of Catholic teachers and people. Ireland's greatest poet,
Yeats, states that teachers should think like wise men but communicate in the language of the people.

If we are to call our students to grace and Christ, we must do so in a
God Talk that breathes and burns. It requires that we sense the
rhythm of popular speech and intuit the love that makes all language
sit up and sing.

Thus we have the seven obstacles facing the evangelical call to spiritual living: Nomads, Media, Death of God, Cynicism, Reductive Humanism, New Morality, Dry God Talk.

The seven responses are these:

· Communalize the nomads.
· Add value to facts.
· Personalize the institution.
· Take the cynicism out of questioning.
· Expose the reductive humanists.
· Be a principled situationist.
· Talk with a fire that has both light and heat.

Prayer

Ultimately, spiritual education will fail if there is no prayer. The
teachers must lead the way. They must be people of prayer. Daily
prayer is the guarantee that God will not be forgotten and that growth
in union with him remains an enduring possibility.

· Teach your students how to pray.
· Train them in prayer.
· Exhort them to pray.

This means a lot of things. It implies that students should know
formal prayers like the *Our Father* and the *Hail Mary*, among others.

Formal prayers of some kind should be said every day. Why? Because they help the human consciousness to think of God at least in some small way. For a while there was a reaction in some quarters against any formal prayer. This was due to an excessive use of formality that resulted in formalism. There was so much saying of formal prayers that God was forgotten and even disliked because of it.

This was followed by the age of spontaneous prayer (or no prayer at all). This is also something that should be encouraged daily where suitable. But it presents a problem. Spontaneous prayer somewhat relates to the mood of a moment. But moods come and go. What do you do if you don't feel like it? And suppose you don't feel like it for a year? Just as saying too many prayers causes formalism, an over-reliance on spontaneous prayer results in *informalism* and finally no praying at all. Spontaneity depends on the capacity of people to create on the spot. Let's face it, not many people are this creative. Anyone who has experienced a lot of spontaneity knows the banality that can sometimes occur.

Today's monasteries are restoring a purified type of formal prayer, morning and evening praise in psalms and hymns, readings, and canticles. These are consciousness raising sessions that open people to the gracious presence of the Lord. They are witnesses to the value of formally praising God each day. This doesn't mean that all Catholics should join in the divine office, it does mean that anyone interested in spiritual growth will speak to the Lord each day in holy words that echo the majesty and love of his presence.

There is also a need for meditative prayer in spiritual education and growth. The secular world has discovered meditation as a cure for stress. Our religious heritage has always known that meditation is the best way to nourish the fire of faith. We should take advantage of the meditation techniques so available today, especially those that favor personal relaxation and a letting go of concepts that dance before the mind. The use of mantras (biblical ones such as "Jesus, my Lord"), breathing exercises, alert sitting positions, listening techniques (such as Rogers's nondirective listening), zones of quiet, Za Zen (the system of the fourteenth-century Benedictine known as immersion in the Cloud of Unknowing), and many other similar types of entry into the world of meditation should be taught to our students.

The whole intent of such meditating is to help us to be *Hearers of the Word*. There is enough listening to self and other people. We should also listen to Christ. Today's meditation masters say that we should spend no less than one hour a day in this exercise—a half hour in the morning and another one at night. Maybe that challenge is too great; maybe not. At least it may get some meditation going every day. Our bibliography will indicate some direction in this matter.

Summary

In this chapter on spiritual education I have reviewed the developmentalist contribution to faith-knowing with its six stages of Poet, Reasoner, Ecumenist, Personalizer, Tension Bearer, and Universalizer — and the five variables: Authority, Criteria, Roles, Challenges, and Symbol/Concept. I have included some model parables and sample dialogues for classroom use. I have included the role of evangelization and the obstacles it faces, and finally the need for prayer and meditation. My hope is that our faith will grow.

> Epochs of faith are epochs of fruitfulness. Epochs of unbelief, however glittering, are barren of all permanent good.
>
> Goethe

Evaluation of Simon, Kohlberg, Fowler

In these last two chapters I have opened up some possibilities for moral and spiritual education as indicated by the contribution of Simon, Kohlberg, and Fowler. I did not advert to any limitations implied by their work or offer any critique, since I wanted you to concentrate on the full positive values being discussed.

Before proceeding to the next topic it would be well to spend a moment pointing out some aspects of these men's work that should help you to benefit better from them.

First, let us consider the value clarification techniques of Simon. These are excellent methods for getting value discussions going. The theory behind the success of the method is Rogerian, nonthreatening listening. Therefore it is easy for the students to talk up about their values. No one is going to jump all over them with "judgments."

Here, of course, is the "rub" and the limit. There is no other criterion for the rightness or wrongness of the act than the individual judgment of the clarifier of his own value. There is no place for communal evaluation or objective criteria and principles coming from a system of values held by a culture or a religion. Hence, in using the value clarification technique, there is still another dimension needed namely, that of how to make moral judgments in the light of community standards and the systems of values held up by a culture or religion. Use the value clarification technique with the knowledge that you will be delving further into the realm of moral judgments.

This brings us to the developmental models of Kohlberg and Fowler Keep this distinction in mind: their models — the stages and ladders of moral and faith development — are, at this point, hypothetical model more than empirically proven steps. It's true that Kohlberg has don some longitudinal studies. But his sample is still small and the members of his own profession would like to see a great deal more research before the stages can be said to be demonstrable by the canons of empirical methods.

Fowler's model is at an even earlier stage of empirical validity. It will take considerable testing and years of review to give his intriguing and impressive model the kind of empirical validity and reliability the assertions will require.

It is somewhat regrettable to have to make these statements about Kohlberg and Fowler, since they may be misunderstood as a caution to wait until all the empirical data is in. Not at all. Their models have already proven quite useful for educators who understand that a model is like a porcupine—it must be used with care. These last two chapters should demonstrate to you that I have great confidence in the models and their applicability to spiritual and moral education.

Why, then, do I insist on this aside about working models versus empirically proven data? Partly because many people are not aware of the difference and may go on to canonize a model as though it has been proven beyond a shadow of a doubt. The knowledge of the distinction will encourage a modesty of intention in the users of the models, and not as some would fear, deter them from using the models at all.

I like the valuing processes and hope they will be used. I trust that people will proceed with the task of helping students to make moral judgments and decisions.

5

LITURGY

Ritual will always mean throwing away something; destroying our corn and wine upon the altar of our gods.

G. K. Chesterton

We should worship as though the deity were present. If my mind is not engaged in my worship, it is as though I worshipped not.

Confucius

Catechesis, however, cannot ignore the fact that not a few men of our era strongly sense a remoteness and even absence of God. This fact, which is part of the process of secularization, surely constitutes a danger for the faith; but it also impels us to have a purer faith and to become more humble in the presence of the mystery of God.

With this perspective, it is possible also to understand the true nature of the worship which God demands and which glorifies him ... In the sacred liturgy, the faithful bring the fruits of every kind of act of charity, of justice, of peace, in order to make a humble offering of them to God, and to receive in turn the words of life and the graces they need to profess the truth in love, in communion with Christ, who offers his Body and Blood for mankind.

General Catechetical Directory, n. 48

One of the major roles of religious education is to help people participate more fully in liturgy. This participation implies both an intelligent grasp of the meaning of the various rituals and texts used and an ever-deepening attitude of reverent faith and awe in the presence of the sublime and wondrous Lord who is present at liturgy to commune with us in love and friendship.

What are some principles that should inform the religious educator's vision of liturgy? (I am using the word "liturgy" to include all Sacramental events as well as the liturgy of the Hours.) Of the many possible principles available, let us consider three:

1. Think of both God and people.
2. Appreciate the value of the art forms used.
3. Approach tensions creatively.

Think of both God and people

All liturgical events are a composite of the transcendent and the immanent, that is, divine and human elements. The transcendent side draws our attention to the divine presence and work. The immanent aspect turns our eyes to the human presence and its work. At liturgy God comes to us in the glory of His presence and the power of His grace. At worship people come before the Lord in awe and adoration with hearts open to the possibilities of personal enrichment.

Worship is often called either liturgy or sacrament, terms that possess a Greek origin and characterize the composite term under consideration here. Liturgy comes from the Greek words *laos* and *ergon*, meaning "people work." This is the element of immanence. Sacrament comes from the Latin word *Sacramentum*, meaning mystery — the element of transcendence.

Which factor deserves the primacy? In my opinion, transcendence. The fundamental dynamic at worship is divine presence that calls forth human reverence and awe. The second movement is that of divine grace responding to human need. The initial action, then, is God's coming to us, to which we respond with faith. The next action is the opening of our hearts to Him, to which He responds in grace and love.

The book of Leviticus sets just such a pace. At its heart is the *Shekinah*, the shrine of the Glory, which is the presence of the Lord. The very nature of this beauty and love invites awe and adoration from those privileged to experience it. Only then does the succeeding consciousness take place, namely, that of the personal expression of need and the offering from God of a grace and gift to our self-realization.

Our acts of awe and adoration will include both the inner attitude as well as offerings of charity, justice, and peace in union with Christ's supreme gift of himself. These acts are mingled with praise and thanks. Since the presence of the divine beauty will reflect our unfinished and imperfect state, we affirm our needs of at-one-ness, and go on to include other specifications that will enable us to realize our potential. With this we open ourselves in trust and surrender to the coming of the Lord and his grace.

When speaking of adoration, awe, and reverence, one should separate them from external forms that accrue from imperial and monarchical cultures. Some externals as we have known them are to a great extent ways of showing respect to emperors and kings. We do not live in an imperial or monarchical milieu. This means that we should, for the moment, work at the interior attitude of awe and adoration so that some appropriate exterior forms may emerge. Or at least we should put some life into the old forms that still abide.

In this first guideline I ask you to think of God and people. Those who stress only the transcendent may produce a liturgy that:

a. ignores the need to be relevant and vital,
b. fails to connect worship with Christian living,
c. may begin to make God seem both distant and capricious.

By emphasizing the majesty of God and the seriousness of the details of awe and reverence, the supertranscendentalist begins to lose sight of the needs of the people doing the worshipping. The liturgical movement and its consequent implementation by the Vatican Council was a response to just such a problem in the liturgy of an earlier time.

By being overly God-centered there is a second tendency to forget the justice and love needs of people in daily life. The act of worship should inspire the worshippers to go out and be visible witnesses of Christ to the world. A liturgy that has no connection with the moral behavior of the participants has missed its mark.

The liturgy that has ceased to advert to the quality of the attitudes of the people worshipping, and instead keeps drumming into them the sole consciousness of the God of majesty may be self-defeating. It could, unwittingly, make God seem a caricature, a divine martinet that needs our stroking in order to appease Him and ward off dangers.

The above are three possible shortcomings of a liturgy shorn of its immanent aspect.

Concentration on immanence, on the other hand, produces deficiencies such as:

a. worship is important only if someone gets something out of it,
b. worship is mainly a human fellowship gathering,
c. worship is secondary to the demands of social concern.

Those who look at the "people" side of liturgy will begin to worry about the intensity and quality of the experience the people are getting. Nervously, they will try to make these experiences ever more diverting in their desperate attempts to satiate never-ending appetites for a new spiritual experience. This is relevancy gone amok because of its pioneership in the "now" and its inadvertence to the need to go out of oneself in love and self-forgetfulness—a condition far more likely to mature and ennoble the worshipper.

The more the "people" side is stressed, to the detriment of consciousness of the divine presence, the more liturgy is reduced to a mere social gathering. No one denies that worship is, in part, a wonderful chance to meet people. We have already spoken of the importance of the community of faith, of which human fellowship is certainly a main component. But as sights are lowered to the point where God is not noticed, then the worship gathering is little more than a club whose main purpose for coming together has been forgotten.

Lastly, the overly-centered "people" approach will, in some cases, begin to politicize the group for all forms of social advocacy, and subtly downplay the spiritual values implied in worship. Then, what really counts is the people's capacity for social change. The act of adoration, praise, awe, wonder, and appreciation is incidental to the real intent of the gatherers.

These six extremes occur whenever either God or people is forgotten in the worship event. Hence we can see the importance of living by the principle of adverting always to both transcendence and immanence in liturgical training and practice.

Extremes

Transcendentalism: Irrelevancy...No advertence to life...Capricious God

Immanentism.....: I must get something out of it or else...The Club...
                       Social Action NOW...Worship?

Appreciate the value of art forms

The exaltation of worship and the expansion of the human heart are fundamentally invisible primordial events that naturally seek external and suitable forms. Our souls rise like incense to the Lord. We break out in praise and sing, "Great is His love, love without end."

The forms of worship are both technique and art. Everyone engaged in liturgy, both leaders and participants, must master some techniques such as singing, praying together, reading, "proceeding" (as with the gifts), and so on. All concerned should also be yearners for the gift of the art of participating. Art is a human grace that perfects the excellence of the technique. The forms, whether competent technique or privileged art, provoke the human person to seek the divine Shekinah/Glory and open his heart to the divine presence.

Once the question of art arises, then arguments about taste also emerge. And how distasteful many such struggles about taste can be. Commenting on this, the ancient Latins, good Mediterranean folk that they were, offered some sober wisdom: "De gustibus non est disputandum" ("Don't argue about taste"). Despite the Latins, arguments will go on because we cannot ignore the matter of taste entirely.

All I ask is, "Don't make taste a moral judgment." Beauty is in the eye of the beholder and there are all kinds of beholders at any worship gathering. Vatican II did not arbitrate taste. It did encourage a variety of cultural expressions, all the way from the jungle drums of the *Missa Luba* to the majestic sounds of a Haydn Mass, accompanied by a symphony orchestra—and perhaps, one day, to the remarkable synthesis of art forms present in something like the Bernstein *Mass*.

I would say that Benedictine simplicity and Franciscan lyricism measure the outer limits of proper taste. The overly simple is merely stark. The excessively lyrical is a hidden refuge for genteel self-indulgence. Tasteful liturgy will normally be a blend of simplicity and lyricism, one dominating the other depending on the cultural preference of the people involved.

What are the major art forms at the service of liturgy? Music, oratory, ritual, painting, ceramics, flower arranging, architecture, poetry, sculpture, designs for vestments, stained glass, furniture, and so on. Let us consider only music, oratory, and ritual here, mainly because it is impossible to treat everything.

Music, oratory, and ritual are fluid art forms. They will continue to change as life changes. As you train your students to plan liturgies and one day be on parish liturgy committees, drive this point home, so that twenty-five years from now they will be open to and willing to approve of fresh art forms that will most certainly be knocking at the door.

Music

· Use trumpets and organ to announce the mood of majesty and high festival.
· Employ flute and guitar to sing of simplicity and lower-key moments.
· Beat the drums when you want to march and have processions.
· Caress the violin for meditations.

How ingenious are the number and kind of instruments that can be used to praise God and gladden the heart! Psalm 150 calls for seven kinds of musical instruments to glorify God:

> *Praise him with the blast of the* trumpet,
> *praise him with* lyre *and* harp,
> *Praise him with* timbrel *and dance,*
> *praise him with* strings *and* pipe,
> *Praise him with* clanging cymbals!
>   Ps. 150:3–5

Six centuries before Christ, the Temple was already ringing with the enthusiastic harmonies of a variety of musical instruments, each one of which strikes a mood, an aspect of our desire to find every legitimate outlet to show our joy and sadness, our hopes and fears before the Lord.

What is the principle? The guideline? Pick the instrument to fit the mood, what one wants to say to God. All instruments are capable of beautiful sounds and can be used to glorify the God who inspired the original inventors who made them.

Next, there is the matter of congregational singing. For this, the Germans have two criteria: 1) pick a singable melody; 2) rattle the windows. (Unecumenically, this means, "Sing louder than Protestants.") These same principles are practiced at the Billy Graham rallies on TV. The hymns are tuneful. Everyone can sing them. The people sing with evident enthusiasm. I have always found that fervent singing does more to create a sense of fellowship than almost anything else.

I have long believed that one of the secret appeals of the old novenas and devotions lay partly in the simple lyrical melodies that most people could sing. This, of course, brings up the argument for taste. ("Do you mean that we should refill our churches with all that saccharine and sentimental stuff?") No, I don't, though I am not above some good, rousing sentimentality at times. However, there are dozens of fine, singable melodies that are clearly in good taste by any standards.

In choosing your music, you should stay in a voice range, where possible, from middle C to D above high C. This applies especially to the male members of the congregation, who will rarely be able to croak out even that permissible D, but at least could gamely try. You should also maintain a fairly even rhythm. A jerky pace dislocates the singing of a nonprofessional congregation. Rule out hymns that employ fancy jumps. That's fine for soloists, but a terror for group singing!

We will discuss soloists and choirs in a minute, but consider congregational singing a moment more. What kind of hymns fit the guidelines? Many of the melodies of the Bach chorales, such as "Now Thank We All Our God." "Amazing Grace" is a good example. Two warhorses from Benedictine days, though admittedly overworked, satisfy the requirements: the melody for the Latin "Tantum Ergo" and the "Holy God We Praise Thy Name." One does not need to use all the "old songs," whether Protestant or Catholic. These songs "work," though, because they are singable.

Happily there is a good deal of new music that is also singable. One should introduce new music and texts that help us worship in the best way. The only caution that must be pointed out is that some churches introduce so much new music so fast that none of it ever sticks to the ribs. People in charge of church music seem to forget that most Catholics spend little more than one hour a week at wor ship. This means they have very little time to learn new music, let alone get a feeling for it. Part of the charm of an effective song is that it gets into the blood and bones. That takes time. A new hymn, therefore, ought to be used often enough to achieve this familiarity that breeds affection.

Needless to say, one should gripe about churches that never introduce a new hymn. The staleness of their repertory dulls the edge of worship.

What about soloists and choirs? Yes, there is room for the meditative soloist in parts of the service such as the communion prayer reflection time. Yes, there is room for motets and other choral arrangements at specified places in the mass. It is all a matter of balance and planning.

Although a good deal has been said about the melodies, one must not ignore the lyrics. The hymn is a sung prayer. It is also a kind of sung theology. The lyrics of "Amazing Grace," in their simplicity, speak a thousand words of God talk, as do so many other hymns and psalms. Like anything else, some are better than others. All hymns cannot be masterpieces of religious thinking. They are like pieces in a puzzle. In teaching the music, consider the texts as well. Some of the wordings are out of current theological fashion. The phrasing may not be just right. Still, look for the faith-meaning that may be hiding within the text. Then your students will become accustomed to examining the texts and perhaps will come to appreciate Augustine's thought, "He who sings, prays twice."

Oratory

We live in a time of antioratory. Yet oratory has a long and honored tradition. Think of Demosthenes; think of Augustine—yes, and even think of Aquinas's famed catechetical sermons at Naples where he moved the people to tears.

The point of oratory is that it refuses to trivialize public speech. It calls for both good technique and art. Homilies are nothing but public speeches. Call them sermons, homilies, proclamation events, or what you will, you do not thereby absolve them from the discipline of speaking well.

Yes, let us be down to earth. There is no need to identify oratory with the Victorian style of flamboyant gestures and dramatic hushes. The microphone has liberated the speaker from the need to bellow. Movies and TV have freed the speaker from the apparent need to tear a passion to tatters. But, then, even Shakespeare advised against that practice long before TV!

Churchill, Roosevelt, Martin Luther King, and other gifted speakers of the mid- and late twentieth century have shown us that speaking is still an art form.   These men did not trivialize public utterance—neither should the homilist at worship.

The homilist should take time to learn and to appreciate the technical aspects of effective public speaking.   Enough said for that.   Let us also consider the content of the homily.   Liturgical guidelines specify that it take the sacred readings and explain their meaning in terms that relate to the lives of the listeners, in order to stir their faith that it may find expression both in the worship and in the Christian moral behavior expected of them outside the liturgy.

This is indeed a tall order!   Clearly, the guidelines indicate that homilies ought not to be courses on the Bible, occasions for the preacher to intimidate his audience or get something off his chest, or to give a lecture in theology.   Homilies may and should give evidence of Bible study, theological appreciation, and the depth of one's personal convictions.   In addition, they should give evidence of an appreciation of the religious and human needs of the listeners, who want to know how God can speak to their hearts.   The homilist is the delicate negotiator of that exchange.

The homilist should season the content with stories, parables, anecdotes, poetry, prayer, a sense of faith—and a profound feeling for the humanity involved.

Allied to the homily, and perhaps even more pertinent to your task as religious educator, is the question of reading the lessons at liturgy. You may be called upon to train readers from time to time.   Today's congregations are used to the good reading they hear from the national newscasters.   No matter how good-hearted they are, they are quietly critical, perhaps even offended by the quality of reading they hear at worship.

Train your readers.   Use the audiocassette with instant replay to help them in pronunciation, enunciation, and phrasing. *Slow them down.*   Most readers tend to rush the text, probably out of nervousness and a lack of appreciation of the rhythm of speaking and listening.

Ritual

Some of today's "informalists" seem to discount the value of ritual. Like the advocates of spontaneous excessive prayer, they counsel "natural movement."   The reason for their casualness is that they are reacting, rightly, against a ritual in which the participants seem like puppets going through stiff and meaningless gestures.   The solution, though, lies beyond a repudiation of all ritual.

Real ritual saves time and grooves the participants into purposeful gestures and movements. Anyone who has ever had to choreograph a wedding ceremony knows that a good deal of the tried and true is valued because it works well that way.

Just as so many Americans are tone-deaf when it comes to symbols in language, so also are they "body-deaf" when it comes to ritual. They simply do not get the point of it. I have occasionally recommended people to watch Zeni Riefenstahl's *Triumph of the Will*, her classic documentary film of the Nazi Nuremberg rallies of the mid-thirties. While I lament the cruelty, perversion, and evil of the Nazi experience, I must give a real devil his due.

The Nazi leadership understood ritual. The Nuremberg rallies were astonishing displays of archetypal ritual instincts. The parades, the flags, the cathedral pillars of searchlights, the martial songs, the processions to the graves of heroes, the oratory, and the sheer management of one million people at a "service" was an awesome use of ritual to galvanize motivation and inspiration. Certainly, I deplore the abuse of ritual in this case even as I am an unwilling admirer of its mastery.

American culture is not without its samples of secular ritual. Think of the opening ceremonies at the Rose Bowl or the Super Bowl. Perhaps even more awe-inspiring is the opening of the Olympics with the runner carrying the flame to light the great fire. Think of the Mardi Gras and the Mummers parade. Note the ritual surrounding the inauguration of a president, the burial of military heroes, and the revival (since the sixties) of the Senior Prom.

Clearly, rituals still abound. The genius of Catholicism is its retention of basic ritual for worship even as it allows mutations due to cultural change. Businessmen say, "Money talks." Worship says, "Ritual talks." Like a picture, a gesture is often worth a thousand words.

In the film *David and Lisa*, the plot hinges on how these two young people will break through their psychological isolation and love each other with ease. Lisa can only speak in doggerel lines. David refuses to be touched. The happy ending of that film has Lisa exclaiming, "I love you," and David reaching out his hand to let it be touched by her. They reach toward each other as God reaches out to Adam in the Creation scene as painted by Michelangelo on the ceiling of the Sistine Chapel. The ritual gesture says a lot about love and a new creation!

When training people in ritual, approach it both as a body language and as something to be done skillfully and well. Think of the walking that goes on. People become self-conscious when they do it in front of others. Suddenly, they stroll, amble, shuffle, paddle, march—they do everything but walk. Ritual movement requires attention, practice, and a fair amount of ego loss—a surrender to the dignity of the deed, to what scholars of comparative religion call the "hieratic stance."

Liturgy employs many rituals – processions; uplifted hands and eyes; folded hands; "Peace" gestures; silences; embraces; toasts; looks; bows. You learn to recognize good wine by its taste. You likewise learn to recognize good ritual by its sense of correctness.

We have considered at length the second principle, namely, the appreciation of art forms, especially music, oratory, and ritual. Help your students to respect both the technique and art implied by these forms.

Approach tensions creatively

Tension will always be part of life. In the chapter on spiritual education we discuss tension bearing as one of the major stages in the development of faith-knowing. This can be compared to the earlier religious language about self-denial and the carrying of one's cross. Liturgy gives us all a chance to be tension bearers because liturgy presents us with some truly gritty tensions. These tensions ought to be seen as chances to be creative, and not as depressing setbacks to worship. There are six tensions with which we must currently cope:

a. Elitists and Populists;
b. Children/Teens and Adults;
c. "Town and Gown";
d. Theory/Rite and Practice;
e. Worship and Spirituality;
f. Liturgy and Morality.

Elitists and Populists

Almost all phases of life involve tensions between the elitists and the populists in their midst. Rarely do they feel comfortable with each other. In liturgy and sacraments, where fellowship is an ideal, clashes between elitism and populism are far too plentiful and painful. The tensions are not completely avoidable. What is needed is a respect for the cherished values held by both types of people.

It was from the elitists that the liturgical renewal of our time took its strength and leadership. Our gratitude goes out to Dom Virgil Michel, Gerald Ellard, Reynold Hillenbrand, Martin Hellriegel, and H. A. Rheinhold, along with many others. Their struggle to make the mass the centerpiece of Eucharistic life generated the subsequent revi sion of all the rituals of the sacraments, so that today their symbols and ceremonies glow with a transparency that leads worshippers far more easily into their meaning.

Recall the efforts of yesteryear—the vernacular, new music, vestments, stained glass, art, architecture in which imitating the past gave way to original expression of our own tempo, active participation of the people, the addition of hundreds of new chapters of biblical readings so that over a three-year span, far more of the scripture is heard than in years past.

These contributions, along with many others, came from the elitist wing. The elitists deserve praise and thanks for their dogged fight to bring us a living worship.

On the other side is the populist dimension. Embodied here are most of our 50 million Catholics, worshipping in 20,000 parishes. Given the radicalness of the changes mentioned above, they have been accepted with remarkable resilience by the majority of the people, few of whom had received any extensive training in why the changes were taking place.

Surveys show that the populist wing has a few thoughts of its own about worship. Populists want better sermons. They desire a leadership that connects their morality with their faith more clearly. They ask for a leadership that will improve their spiritual literacy. They have accepted the new look of liturgy in music, rituals, art, and architecture. They like the letter; what they want now is the spirit, the vital link between the faith moment at worship and their moral behavior elsewhere.

Where do the points of the tension join? They touch on this very issue of faith and morality. Today's elitists, gifted with the capacity to lead and articulate, are currently a group in search of a cause. Populists are normally not given to speaking out. Their expression is more likely to be a rumble than a distinct voice. I hope the thoughtful elitist will join his or her voice with the inarticulate populist to bring to life this new phase of spiritual enlightenment that seems so characteristic of liturgical evolution today.

Children/Teens and Adults

Years ago it was common to have children's masses and religious rallies for teen-agers. The children's masses subsequently disappeared and youth rallies declined. Instead, the practice evolved of letting the children come with the parents so that the whole family could worship together. The call went out to give up the rallies, gather the teens in smaller groups, and use the various techniques of encounter to enliven their faith.

Today, we have special liturgies for children once again and the guitar masses for teens held in the late sixties are well-known. It looks as if our imagination is spent on the young with little left over for the adults. We all know the horror stories of subjecting adults to teen versions of liturgy. Mercifully that sort of thing seems to be past. But there is still a need to exercise our imaginations on adult liturgy. The previous discussion about music, oratory, and ritual basically had adults in mind.

At the same time one should applaud the arrival of liturgies for children that will help them to grow in their appreciation of worship. Let us be equally happy about efforts made to help teens find a suitable worship expression. What is needed at this point is a similar effort for the adult population. What principle can be invoked? Normative liturgy should be for adults. As far as possible it should have a multi-level appeal so that most participants can join in. Granting this idealism, the youth movement has shed a light on what needs to be done to soften the tension between youth and adult worship forms.

"Town and Gown"

This is a variation of the preceding discussion. By "Town" I mean normative adult liturgy in the parishes. By "Gown" I mean liturgies conducted for youth at high schools, retreats, and campus ministry centers. Quite often the liturgies conducted for youth are so sharply tuned to their needs at that level, that the young people are disappointed with worship when they return to their own parishes.

The high schools, retreat centers, and campus ministry parishes must recall that they are but transient structures in the life of the young. They bear a responsibility to assist young people in preparing for a lifelong worship, most of which will take place in parishes. Similarly, the parishes must realize that the new recruits arriving from the colleges and universities, as well as from the local high schools, come with comparatively "high mountaintop" experiences of worship. The parishes can reasonably expect that the young will learn to settle for experiences less dramatic, but the people in charge of parochial settings must sense a greater responsibility for enabling the young to participate at the local level.

The directors of liturgies in youth settings and the local parish clergy should get together and discuss their mutual needs. They should find ways to ease the transitions from one setting to the other. Both groups are bound by the common goal of helping students acquire a living consciousness and an active faith, nourished by a suitable worship experience. The mutual bond is the ground for a discourse that can provide a rational and comprehensive view of assisting our young people to acquire the skills, taste, and reverence for worship.

Theory/Rite and Practice

So much of life is a tension between theory and practice. We say that catechesis should be a combination of good theology and sound education. In liturgy this means good liturgical theory, with its knowledge of rites along with skillful practice of worship. Just as a well-rounded person needs to know the Why and the How of life in general, so does he or she need to understand liturgy.

Without question some people are more entranced by the Why of things; others, by the How. The two interests should ideally merge. Well-performed Liturgies of Reconciliation (the How) mean little if the participants don't know the rationale of the events. Knowledgeable experts of sacramental and ritual theory (the Why) help but little if they act aimlessly when it comes to conducting an Easter Vigil or Confirmation service.

It was mentioned above that we could well use a rational and comprehensive approach to these matters. This statement bears repeating. When we lack a systematic and rational plan, we ignore needs, we are blind to future consequences, and we decrease the quality of worship. When we have such a plan, its presence can do much to heal the unnecessary tensions that distract people from getting on with the business of celebrating their faith before God.

Worship and Spirituality

There is bound to be tension between personal devotion and communal liturgical celebration. The sober, ritualized format of liturgy, even, with its vast new variety and focal points for individual expression (e.g., Prayer of the Faithful, music choices, Communion Meditations), stands in contrast to the tempo and vibrations associated with "spirituality" activities. The latter refers to meditation, shared prayer, charismatic prayer, traditional devotions, and other mystical or semimystical (words used in positive meaning) approaches.

Here again the true tension bearer realizes the values of both elements. Spirituality enhances the quality of personal participation in worship. In turn, worship brings to spirituality our sense of oneness with the community of faith and an abiding appreciation of the role of celebration in life. Worship and spirituality are copartners in maintaining a continuing widening of horizons so that personal and communal needs are never forgotten.

Liturgy and Morality

The most enduring and largely accurate criticism of people who go to church regularly is that they are "Sunday Catholics." Satirists by the thousands can always be counted on to make fun of religious hypocrites who participate in liturgy on the holy day and gouge the public for the rest of the week. Not just these sneering critics, but all honest-minded people of any age lament this abiding sickness.

Read the sermons of the Old Testament prophets. Isaiah fumes against the worshippers of his day who spread out their palms piously, recite endless prayers, and send clouds of incense and animal sacrificial smoke up to God—yet ignore the poor, rob the widows, and crush others with all manner of injustices, hatreds, and betrayals. Jeremiah walked nude through the streets of Jerusalem to shock the worshippers into realizing their souls were as naked as his judgmental physical presence.

In the same tradition, Christ cleansed the Temple to remind the people it was supposed to be a center of prayer and not a den of commercial thieves. Times haven't changed too much in this regard. Spiritual illiterates still crowd around our altars. The spiritual illiterate is one who doesn't make a connection between faith in God and everyday moral choices, between worship in a sanctuary and the need to live out one's faith in the world by helping to establish justice and peace on earth.

Every act of worship, properly performed, involves the people in the reconciling death and resurrection of Jesus. This spiritual involvement at worship is meant to find a practical application in the personal and social moral life of the participants. A renewed liturgy is supposed to mean a renewed people. A renewed people is supposed to mean a generation of Catholics who astonish the world by a luminous witness to moral values and social concern. The fire is lit at the altar so that the light may shine into the world.

These, then, are the six tensions—Elitists and Populists; Children/Teens and Adults; "Town and Gown"; Theory/Rite and Practice; Worship and Spirituality; Liturgy and Morality. These tensions will never disappear. Our task is to bear them with grace and with a wit and quickness to see how they can be pressed into a creative Easter moment for our community of believers.

Accepting the punishment of these tensions is an act of purification, a dying only to be reborn, a Cross that has meaning because it leads to

reconciliation and redemption.   We do not face these tensions alone.
The costly grace of our Lord is available to us that we may sanely and
courageously forge our own path toward enlightenment.

Summary

I have suggested three main guidelines for understanding, teaching, and
participating in liturgy. 1) Think of both God and people, thereby preserving both the transcendent and immanent qualities of worship.
2) Appreciate the value of the art forms used, especially those of music, oratory, and ritual.   3) Approach tensions creatively, particularly
those that occur between elitist and populist approaches, youth versus
adults at worship, theory and practice, worship and spirituality, and
lastly, liturgy and morality.

You should study carefully the various documents that have come
out on the conducting of children's liturgies, the Rite of Reconciliation, the catechumenate, and above all, the guidelines of the *National
Catechetical Directory* on matters of liturgy. It should be clear to you
by now that the subject of liturgy is a vast one. I have only been able
to draw the broadest of strokes for your guidance.

To conclude this chapter, here are some suggestions on how to prepare your students for prayer services and liturgical celebrations, followed by a self-evaluation quiz that may draw your attention once
more to many of the items which have been discussed in this chapter.
Lastly, there is a meditation on Sabbath Observance.   There is widespread and legitimate concern about the decline in regular attendance
at Sunday mass, as well as a cultural destruction of the whole notion
of Sabbath.

The meditation I offer is directed at the restoration of a spiritual appreciation of the Sabbath.   The thoughts therein may help initiate
what is bound to be a most ambitious project, namely, to recover for
the community of believers a true sense of the Sabbath as well as the
worship occurring on that day.

Here are some guidelines for preparing your prayer service:

1. Select your environment
   Classroom
   Chapel
   Church
   Lounge
   Park
   Auditorium
   Other

2. Prepare the details
   Readings
   Bible
   Literature
   Poetry
   Spiritual writers
   News items
   Philosophers

Scientists
Other
Music
Homily thoughts
Banners, blowups, slides, films
Prayer forms to be considered
and practiced
Meditation
Shared prayer
Rosary
Cloud of Unknowing
technique
Zen awareness
Office chant
Meditative reading of Bible
Spontaneous testimony
Ignatian Method–discursive
prayer
Other

Musical instruments to be used
Organ
Guitar
Flute
Drums
Trumpets
Violins
Harp
Cello
Other
3. Establish the conclusion
Silence
Song
Resolution
Blessing
Procession
"Peace" gesture
Other

Following are some suggestions for preparing your liturgical celebration:

1. Pick a theme
A Passion for Justice
Growth in Love
Affirmation of Hope
Community Formation
Lasting Fidelity
Personal Moral Growth
Other
2. Prepare the details
Study sessions
Explore the theme in its biblical, doctrinal, and practical meaning
Readings
Music
Hymns
Psalms
Chants
Solos
Choral motets
Choir and people
arrangements
Banners, blowups, slides, films,
tapestries

Gifts
Relate them to the theme
Select the gift bearers
Homily ideas
Stories
Poems
News items
Bible quotations
Pertinent statistics
Quotations from well-known
people
Metaphors
Illustrations from parish and
student life
Personality sketches
Anecdotes from films and TV
Personal testimony
Dynamic words
Quotations from spiritual
writers
Quotations from novelists
Theological citations
Moral applications
Other

(The more the preparers can help the homilist with ideas, the more he is able to give a united and coherent voice to the spiritual expectations of the worshippers.)
    Prayers of the Faithful

Special gestures
    "Peace"
    Processions
    Other
Closing

Self-evaluation Guides for Liturgical Training (... or, "How do I know I'm doing right?")

OK   Other

____ ____ 1. I begin with liturgy as an act of worship.

____ ____ 2. I believe liturgy should be experienced as prayer.

____ ____ 3. I regard liturgy as communal prayer.

____ ____ 4. My students and I plan liturgy in a prayerful mood.

____ ____ 5. I insist we balance silence with oral and active portions.

____ ____ 6. I make sure my students appreciate the difference between and the relationship of Eucharist and Liturgy of Word.

____ ____ 7. I realize that liturgical themes should normally reflect the themes of the feasts and seasons.

____ ____ 8. In our planning of themes we always begin with the lectionary.

____ ____ 9. Frequently we are able to be involved with our celebrant in the preparation of his homilies.

____ ____ 10. We make sure that congregational response to the homily never take on the character of a debate, but rather be an expansion of faith testimony.

____ ____ 11. Clearly liturgy is an experience of shared faith.

____ ____ 12. Liturgy is an affirmation of faith, not a time to indulge in doubts and skepticism.

____ ____ 13. While the parish community is bound by a single hope and belief, it is made up of diverse age groups. Though the adult emphasis is normative, the younger groups deserve special attention as part of their maturing.

____ ____ 14. Youth masses must be conducted, not in the spirit of rivalry with adults, but with a view to developing adult faith as young people mature.

____ ____ 15. I know that the liturgy communicates through words, gestures, and symbols. I make sure my students can *read* the nonverbal talk of gestures and symbols.

____ ____ 16. In our planning sessions we stress the beauty of brevity.

____ ____ 17. Our readers are well trained.

____ ____ 18. We know the Eucharistic Prayer (Canon) belongs to the Celebrant. Hence, it is *not* meant to be chorally read.

____ ____ 19. We pick music that is tasteful and humanly attractive.

20. From time to time we use one or another of these rituals:
____   Processions with everyone involved (e.g., Palm Sunday)
____   Incensation of the lectionary
____   Candlelight service
____   Burning of the palms for the "Wednesday Ashes"
____   Carrying of the Paschal Candle in funeral processions
____   Outdoor ceremony for the Easter Vigil Paschal Fire
____   Parish baptismal celebration on Holy Innocents Day
____   Way of the Cross using contemporary signs of the Passion
____   Ceremonial planting of a new Christmas tree each year
____   Solemn signing of Confirmation pledge in presence of entire Parish
____   Corpus Christi parade through the streets of the parish area.

A Meditation on Sabbath Observance

The Sabbath concerns itself with time, for it is in time that we come to know and experience God. The Sabbath is ritualized time, in which the beyond is adverted to. The Sabbath is an invitation to taste the inwardness of God. The Sabbath is a corrective to the technological demon that deceives us into thinking that all of life is here, and that there is nothing beyond.

Technology absorbs us in the present world.

Sabbath discloses eternity to us.

Technology invites man to master the earth. The trouble is that the "busyness" this requires makes people subject to the earth instead of being its master. The successful managers of creation are finding that the good earth is turning to dust in their mouths. The victories over the earth are coming to resemble defeat.

First, Sabbath teaches us that civilization, good as it is, should not be seen as an end in itself. The builders at Babel were very civilized. But they ended up babbling in a total breakdown of communication. The Sabbath teaches that there is something beyond workdays, earth management, shopping, and civilization building.

Sabbath is a day on which we can have a respite from the vulgar groveling for yet more possessions. For one day at least, we bid goodbye to the gods of technology and turn our hearts to the real God. It is the day when we abandon momentarily the struggle for moneymaking. We call a truce with commerce. "Six days you may labor and do all your work, but the seventh day is a sabbath to the Lord your God." (Exod. 20:9) "If you hold back your foot on the sabbath from following your own pursuit on my holy day . . . If you honor it by not seeking your own interests, or speaking with malice, . . . then you light shall break forth like the dawn, I will make you ride on the heights of the earth." (Isa. 58:13-14)

No one argues that God wants us to work. Genesis teaches that God wants us to be managers of the earth and participate in the development of creation. But God also commands rest that we may sense the ultimate reason for creation, which is to lead us back to God.

Secondly, the Sabbath evokes the presence of eternity. The less we stop and think of eternity and Paradise, the less we reflect on our inborn drive and hunger for ultimate living there. It has been written that the Sabbath is the world to come experienced here in foretaste. Thus a seventh part of our lives could be experienced as Paradise anticipated were we to take Sabbath seriously. How can we hope to take Paradise/Heaven seriously in the future if we do not savor its foretaste here on the Sabbath?

Thirdly, the Sabbath is the communication of the holy. Philosophy quests for the good. Believers quest for the holy. The good is the slope of the mountain. The holy is the summit. If we look only at nature alone we shall remain infatuated with the natural. Sabbath calls us to lift our eyes beyond the hills to the world of the holy where the Creator of nature sends forth His love. God took six days to make the things of nature and to create man and woman. He spoke of all this as *good*. The seventh day he called *Holy*, for on that day man and woman could rest from work and look beyond creation to its source.

Fourthly, the Sabbath is an intuition into the processes of creation. Space speaks the broken language of things, while time is like a fiddler playing a melody to weave an inner unity through things. Space reveals the *products* of creation. Time unlocks the *process* of creation.

Things tend to block the vision of the Creator. The Sabbath, holy time, opens people to meet God.

Thus the Sabbath rescues us from total captivation with technology, invites us to a relaxation response in order to taste Paradise ahead of time, and inculcates a sense of the holy in order always to look beyond creation to the Creator. Lastly, it brings us to notice the divine presence within the processes of creation.

Early Christians called Sabbath the eighth day. Seven days were the image of earthly time. The Sabbath as an eighth day symbolized eternity. Sunday became the liturgical commemoration of the eighth day, a celebration of Easter and a foretaste of the life to come. They linked this eighth day imagery with the eight-sided Roman bathhouses that they converted into Baptistries.

We have said that Sabbath is a Paradise time. The old Baptistries were decorated with Paradise symbols. Paintings showed Jesus as the Good Shepherd, surrounded by his people in a lush Paradise setting of gardens and running streams. Often a deer was seen drinking at the waters. A snake would be wriggling from its mouth. Legendary science taught that when a deer ate a snake, it incurred an intolerable thirst. Hence the deer quenching its thirst in the baptismal waters of Paradise symbolized the candidate for Baptism quenching his thirst caused by having "swallowed the serpent of sin."

A materialistic, acquisitive culture does not favor Sabbath observance. Everybody must be going somewhere to do something. But as Shakespeare declares, most of this constant activity is "Much Ado About Nothing." The decline of Sabbath observance corresponds to the shallowness of contemporary living. People still talk about the need for a spiritual quality of life, but their Sabbath behavior mostly denies this need. The collapse of the Sabbath matches the collapse of spiritual values.

But the Lord is with us still, asking us to keep the Sabbath holy. Yes, Lord. We shall.

6

ADULT EDUCATION

A little learning is a dangerous thing
Therefore, drink deep brother of the Pierian spring
There shallow draughts intoxicate the mind
And drinking deeply sobers us again

Alexander Pope

In 1776 the average adult could count on a forty-year life span. Most adults died in their forties. Today most of them can anticipate thirty more years of life. After the second world war we spoke of the "baby boom." Today we speak of the "adult boom." This remarkable expansion of the adult population signals the need for understanding the educational needs of an adult population that basically did not exist in such immense numbers over so long a time period in any other era of history.

Of necessity the baby boom compelled us to be a child-centered people. The new exigencies of a burgeoning adult population require a modification of the absorption in children so that some attention will be given to adults as well. Clearly we must continue to educate and train our children in the best possible manner. Just as surely we need to educate and train adults in a systematic and intelligent way.

We should supplement the "shallow draughts" of child-centered education with the "deep draughts" of an adult-centered education. Not to do this supplementing leaves education at the intoxication level without allowing it to mature into sobering wisdom.

Earlier in this book we treated developmental stages in moral and spiritual thinking. We drew crucial distinctions that insisted on avoiding any stereotyping of persons by locking them into one or another stage. While those stages do apply to the full span of one's life, they do not specify even further distinctions one can make about an adult life span ranging from the twenties to the seventies.

It's easy to notice how the young grow. Over a period of twenty years their bodies shoot up, their voices change, their sweet childishness evolves from naiveté to know-it-allness, to rebellion, to the first tentative settlings of young adulthood. Stages of personal growth after age twenty are not so easily discernible. A twenty-year-old looks mentally and spiritually equipped to face life, yet often after two decades that same person wonders how he or she managed to cope.

While remembering our caution about categorizing people to the point where we lock them into our prejudgments, we can make some general statements about stages of personal growth in adulthood. Why should we bother to do this?

1. Adults deserve and need education as much as children do.
2. Adults continue to go through stages of development just as young people do.
3. Adults require an education that is sensitive to their stages of growth comparable to that of young people.

We speak here of development. We need to ask: development to what? To self-acceptance, wisdom, maturity, and mellowness in both a humane and religious context. With the humanists we search for the growth of wise people. With the community of faith we quest for holy people whose human wisdom reflects the depth of communion with God.

Granted this goal, what are some fairly reasonable steps of growth that can be identified? We shall list five of them and link them to specific decades of life. Linking the steps to specific age groups is a convenient generalization that allows for all sorts of variety while retaining some sense of an order in one's personal development.

Adult Growth
1. Twenties   Confidence
2. Thirties   Doubt
3. Forties   Urgency
4. Fifties   Self-Acceptance
5. Sixties   Wisdom/Holiness

Thanks be to God, people will always be people, meaning that they will resist being tagged by this model. Still, many will admit they do see themselves progressing somewhat along these lines. Holiness for sixty-year-olds means a maturity of faith life; it does *not* imply one must wait until sixty to be holy!

We will take each of the steps and comment on the general characteristics.

1. Twenties — Confidence
This is the decade for the buccaneers, the adventurers. They bid good bye to parental dominance. Almost all of them have chosen a marriage partner, a career, and their first major job. Very likely they are raising their first child. They brim with confidence and possess wha

is actually a "happy blindness," meaning that they are blissfully unaware of many pitfalls that could make them overly cautious too soon in life. They resolve to be competent both personally and professionally. They have the energy and vision to build a newer world. They fluctuate between allegiance to their own families and the network of new friends they have discovered. A surge of confidence marks their endeavors. For many people this period is the single most creative one of their lives.

2. Thirties — Doubt

The roaring twenties are over. The adults begin to concentrate on their children and the quality of their family life. They enjoy their social life, but they exhibit a new seriousness about the inner life of the family circle. The first seeds of self-doubt and nagging questions begin to sprout. Doubt impels them to wonder about the wisdom of all the life choices they have made.

"Why did I pick this mate after all?" "Why didn't my parents tell me life would be like this?" (In all probability they did.) "Why did I think this career and job would fulfill my dreams?" These carping questions arise from the realizations that inevitably must come after the honeymoon of the twenties. Every moon has its dark side, but it takes time to realize that fact. Everything in life is fraught with limits and unforeseen difficulties. Only the passage of time reveals this unpleasant news.

In most cases this age of doubt is not overwhelming. It serves as a sobering brake on the frantic pace of the earlier years and eventually discloses newer depths and unsuspected horizons. The doubters learn to become comfortable with complexity and begin to understand difficulty as an opening to opportunity.

3. Forties — Urgency

We might also term this the age of discomfort. Women face the end of possible pregnancies. Maybe they don't want to have any more babies, but the absoluteness of knowing that they can't induces a certain poignant sense of the finality of life. It's the first autumn leaf that points to the chill wind of aging and coming death.

Men note the decline of their personal strength and energies. They take account of their money and their careers. They believe they must make it to the top in a now-or-never type surge. The old adage "Life begins at forty" seems to mean that the first premonitions of one's own death must be fought by rebirth, new resolve, and another adventurous shot at the unrealized dreams.

Hence an urgency overtakes people in their forties, a drive to ward off the coming of death, even though, actuarially, they probably have as much as thirty years or more to live. They stand at midpoint between the promise of youth and the possibility of any decent realization in the near future.

They begin to speak of "old friends being the best ones." In fact, both friends and family assume a new importance. At the same time they find it easier to admit mistakes and to express regrets. They show the first hints of a becoming modesty that accounts for what is so attractive in maturing people.

This age of urgency exacts a negative toll on some people. Many marriages fall apart. Some men become "graying Don Juans." Some women wear themselves out trying to retain a girlishness that is nothing short of bizarre. These Don Juan strivings at seduction and girlish strainings at seductiveness are pathetic—even if understandable—outgrowths of the urgency to live gone awry.

4. Fifties—Self-Acceptance

Jesus once said we should love our neighbors the way we love ourselves. Another way of putting this is: accept your neighbor as you accept yourself. The implication is that neighbors won't be accepted if self isn't accepted. If ever this is going to happen in any stable and meaningful way, it should occur in the fifties.

An autumn leaf has fallen. Fledgling children have left the nest. Instead of being sources of anxiety as they were during the time of raising and educating, children now are young adults—easier to look at, relate to, and regard as sources of pride and satisfaction.

A half century has gone by and few resist the temptation to exclaim, "When I was young. . . ." Instinctively, people in their fifties become more meditative and reflective. For one thing they have five decades of life to reflect upon. The urgencies caused by ambition, with floods of energy to match, abate. These people seem to appreciate Kipling's line:

> If you can meet with triumph and disaster
> And treat these two imposters just the same.

The long-sought-for ideal of indulging in the simple things of life finally comes into reach. People in their fifties find they actually enjoy sharing joys, sorrows, victories, and failures with those close to them. Such sharing uncovers the human dimension of life so often obscured during their years of striving to reach out for the ring of glitter and glamor on the merry-go-round of life.

At long last, stability sets in. Having come to terms with life's limits, the peaks and valleys of high expectation and bitter disappointment level off. One can almost hear a huge sigh of relief about this, even if the sigh is tinged with bittersweet memories.

This is why such people come to be "set in their ways," and "old dogs not about to learn any more new tricks." Still, one must be cautious not to caricature this conservatism as the typical closed-mind mentality. Closed-mindedness is an affliction that has little to do with age so much as a character deficiency due to a need to experience unwarranted certainties. All extremists and radicals, whether of the liberal or conservative bent, exhibit closed-mindedness. Age does not seem to make much difference in this regard. Young people can be just as closed-minded as old ones can.

The conservatism of people in their fifties is far more a function of their hard-won realistic view of life than a cranky refusal to be open to new ideas. In fact, such people are quite supple in absorbing remarkable changes and making extraordinarily creative contributions to life. And history demonstrates in numerous ways that this talent can flourish exceptionally well as people grow older. Think of the daring creativity of Pope John launching the Vatican Council as he entered his eighties—and remember how he possessed an openness to the world rarely matched by any leader of any kind anywhere in living memory!

The result of the fifties is a sense of self-acceptance based on a realistic evaluation of half a century of living. This is why these people make such good counselors—their lives are like the mellow fire that welcomes one on a snowy day. They generally have learned one of life's hardest lessons and have earned the right to be supports for those still crunched by the struggle. These gifted people can be a treasure for the walking wounded—and happily they frequently are. These self-acceptors are a human resource little tapped as of yet. As awareness of their gift grows, so will the benefits abound.

5. Sixties—Wisdom/Holiness
An ancient German proverb states, "We grow too soon old, too late smart." To some extent that proverb reflects the times when death came early to people, when a forty-year life span was the most that could be expected. Possibly people in their sixties still think of the so-called suddenness of age and the presumed long postponed awakening to the really *real* of life.

In reality there is little reason for them to think that way. Even conceding that time is a tricky monster that tends to seem long or short depending on the circumstances, we can hardly say that a sixtieth birthday is an abrupt arrival. What's more, there are many early, distant warning signals. Some of these are painful; in economic matters, the rapidity of inflation strikes fear about survival. Some of the signals are positive, as talk increases about how to prepare for the aging years.

Laying aside for the moment the social problems allied with moving into one's sixties (financial security, health care, nursing homes, early senility, etc.), the stage of one's personal development is what is at issue here. Granted the ideal and stately progress through steps of development mentioned earlier, citizens in their sixties and beyond possess capacities for wisdom and holiness normally unachievable at previous ages of life. Although these sublime qualities can be achieved earlier, and sometimes are, usually they are not.

Shakespeare took a dimmer view of age, perhaps based on a view of old people having no way of maintaining vitality in a culture bereft of medical marvels and the wonders of technology. He observed their physical decline in shriveled shanks and mental loss in senility. He pictured them in second childhood, leaking and sniveling the way they once did as babies.

Preventive health care, the growth of interest in reasonable exercise, and the possibility of millions of retirees spending their last years in the healing climate of the sunbelt are factors that guarantee that these people in their sixties and seventies will be able to enjoy a heretofore impossible degree of inner vitality on a widespread scale. The dream of being a person of wisdom and holiness at an advanced age, a dream once confined to a privileged few, is now the present and foreseeable reality.

As this possibility expands in America there will most likely be a counterbalancing of an obsession with youth culture by the growth of a healthy veneration for age. We are all familiar with the proverbial respect for elders in Chinese culture. Anthropologists cite similar case studies from their research of tribal cultures. Such a shift in American sensibility is both deserved and healthy for the nation.

What is this wisdom? What is this holiness? A clue may be found in the Latin words for wisdom and the sacred: *sapientia* (wisdom); *sacer* (sacred). The Latin word for wisdom implies a taste for living. The wise person doesn't just know "about" life. He or she has tasted it deeply. He or she knows its bitterness and sweetness intimately and far better than most people. His or her wisdom entails both a discriminating judgment and, more importantly, a feel for what is genuine and life-affirming. He or she has mellowed as a self-acceptor. He or she positively shines as a life-affirmer. Therein lies the special beauty of the wise person because, as the very one who has the fewest years to look forward to, he or she can live them in the richest way and communicate this wisdom to anyone who cares to listen and follow.

The Latin word for holiness implies that the holy one is capable of consecrating the world around him or her, of making it holy. Thus the holy one possesses the capacity for revealing the religious depth of life around him or her, and performs this service in a simple, spontaneous, and unself-conscious witnessing. Far from being a moralistic preacher or imposing a sense of the holy in an artificial, offensive manner, the holy one has the grace of pointing to God in the midst of life so effortlessly that he or she comes across almost as an enchanter weaving a spell. The voice is soft, but the impact can be thunderous.

The witness of the sage and the holy one is invariably a subtle and genuinely sophisticated sally. Like the quiet shadings of light in a Flemish painting, these people evoke response by degrees rather than by the brash provocations of an alternate approach. Their very weakness is a blessing. Unable to shout—at least for very long—they are not given to berating. Conserving their physical strength by necessity, they do not indulge in boisterous intimidation to put across their insights. Maybe that is why the old sage and saint (Paul of Tarsus) was moved to say that the power of God is manifested through his weakness.

If these observations about life growth of people in their sixties and seventies (and beyond) be true, then we could well have in our midst a community of sages and saints yet to be heard from, a rich spiritual reservoir whose individual and collective voices could bless the nation and set a pace for living in our postindustrial society with a grace and ease that would make faith, trust, and love of God and each other a far easier task than our current life styles demand.

A person of beauty is a joy forever. Such a person is an inspiration to everyone at any time. Perhaps we have been looking in the wrong direction for the "beautiful people."

Adults, then, develop through stages of 1) Confidence, 2) Doubt, 3) Urgency, 4) Self-Acceptance, and 5) Wisdom/Holiness. This presentation has tied the categories to the succeeding decades of adult life, mainly for the sake of convenience and ease of discussion. Real life development flies in the face of orderly progression because of the person's inner pace, outer life style, origin, locale, upbringing, and enough other variables to keep researchers from running out of grant money to develop tests.

No matter. Adults go through steps somewhat like the above in time spans close enough to the ones mentioned to make the model a usable one. What does all this prove?

1. There is no such thing as a nondeveloping adult.
2. Educators should approach the topic of continuing education with some knowledge of the fact of personal development in adults. Just as youth come in many forms and packages, so do adults. Simply because the researchers have not done for adults what Piaget and Kohlberg have done for youth, doesn't mean that the findings can't apply to adults.
3. Better attention will be paid to continuing education when adults are treated as people in process and not as butterflies fully shaped at

age twenty-one. Failure to advert to this fact will simply reinforce the idea that only children change; adults merely grow old.

The sooner adults are seen as going through their own multileveled stages of growth, the more attractive adulthood is going to appear to the young who, willy-nilly, are going to be adults regardless of choice. We speak of offering the young adult models of faith, so that he or she can make some sense out of a tender, growing faith. But our first job is to hold up an attractive model of adulthood journeying toward goals in a series of voyages somewhat characterized by the steps mentioned.

The centuries-old popularity of the voyages of Ulysses presents a classical example of the case in point. To a child the story of Ulysses may seem just a charming adventure story. Unfortunately, that's also how it appears to most adults, that is, if they ever get around to reading the story. Yet the perennial and compelling meaning of the narrative is its clear evocation of the development and maturing of an adult who starts out as a bold voyager, is plagued by doubts, tortured with urgency to finish his task, mellowed by the years of testing, and finally comes home in full circle as the wise one.

So long as a stagnant model of adulthood is held up for the young, they shall never have much to look forward to. In fact, neither will adults themselves indulge in much excitement about the fifty-year drama they are asked to take a part in. They won't *see* the drama because the prevailing myth is that there *isn't* any.

Therefore, central to any efforts in continuing education is the need for the leaders to contemplate more deeply the meaning of adulthood today. Think of the possibilities and the consequent excitement. A teacher of youth counts on dealing with people in a sixteen-year life span at most. A teacher of adults can rely on an audience that plans to be around for half a century, an audience expressing itself in at least five challenging states of consciousness, an audience quite ready to take the "voyage of Ulysses."

Adults are taking and will take this voyage regardless of the myths about them, the inadvertence of educators, or the failure as yet of the behavioral sciences to look at adults with the depth they have taken toward children. I simply contend they will do it better and continuing educators will do their work better when this type of vision grabs the popular consciousness more effectively than at the current time.

Role and Person

No one contests the amazing growth of adult education both in secular society and the Church. The above remarks about stages of adult growth are meant to provide a perspective to the work that progresses in continuing education. Let us now consider the matter of Church-sponsored forms of continuing education.

Most of what passes as continuing education in the Church at the moment could be called "Role Education." Teachers are helping adults perform certain roles more effectively. Think of the thousands of Catholic adults who have volunteered to teach CCD. Almost all of them are given some minimal training in adult religious education. Basic courses in content and methods, in varying degrees, are made available to countless volunteers. They are taught how to perform their role of teacher with some competency.

Secondly, think of thousands more Catholic parents seeking help in raising their children. Secular society coaches them with parent effectiveness training. Christian education weighs in with variations of this type of training as well as with newly developed forms of family education. These programs assist adults in their role as parents.

Thirdly, a significant number of Catholic adults seek to make responsible sharing in Church leadership a reality. They delight in giving some substance to the call of Vatican II for a lively laity joining in building up the Body of Christ. Thus they come forward to join diocesan and parish councils, boards, and other representative bodies in the Church.

This group seeks training in how to make policy, how to see the difference between policy and practice, and how to be members of a decision-making team. Again, continuing education comes to the fore offering systematic guidance and training adults in their roles as participants in a decision-making process.

There are three roles: teaching, parenting, and deciding. Here are the most active fields in which Catholic continuing education currently finds itself expending its energies. Training people to perform their roles more effectively provides the simplest access to the task of continuing education. Depending on the consciousness of the students (cf. the five stages), the success of these endeavors relates to some degree on how well the adult facilitators are sensitive to the capacities of the learners.

Person Education

The majority of Catholic adults do not seek aid in enriching their roles in life, at least not directly. Most Catholics, at least subliminally, could use (as the rock song puts it), "a little help from their brothers and their sisters." They search for aid in areas of personal development because they know, even if no systematic model tells them, that they should be engaged in personal growth.

Such knowledge comes easily when the adults happen to be people fighting for survival, such as the poor and immigrants from other countries. Disadvantaged adults often beg for courses in how to speak and read English, especially the English on contracts, agreements, and medicine bottles. They plead for courses in how to look for jobs, find legal aid, take care of their health, get a loan with honest interest, cope with the school their children attend, deal with the children attending that school, shop within their means, budget for their shopping, find a decent place to live, negotiate a fair rent, and find electrical, plumbing, and roofing services within their slim means. If middle class adults moan about such problems, imagine how the poor, many of whom don't speak English very well, must let out sighs and groans that would be worthy of a Jeremiah!

These people need *person education* in its most basic form. Blessed is the continuing educator who hears and responds. Today's moral consciousness calls for eradicating the institutional injustices that curse our land, and this is a good thing. But in the meantime the victims cry out for simple education to cope with the injustices while the fighters are working to remove them. Both movements are pressing necessities.

However, it is not only the poor who need person education. The rest of the Catholic adults reach out for it too. Sooner or later they are all members of the fifty-year club, that half century of voyaging through many stages of personal growth. Out of the depths they cry both to the Lord and to the Church for guidance.

Correctly, they want their human potential realized. Just as surely, they desire their spiritual lives to grow to fulfillment. They ask for the bread of understanding. Let us not give them a stone. What should we give them? What should we do? I propose, in the following pages, twenty tips for continuing education that are mainly a reply to the demand for person education, though they will help people to fulfill their roles as well.

The tips are not arranged in any logical order. Some of them are directed especially to the priest as adult educator. Even though they are listed as "points," they should be seen as interrelated pieces of a puzzle. The suggestions assume all that has been said about adult stages of growth and the distinction between person and role.

Twenty Tips for Continuing Education

1. Community Worship

Nothing "teaches" religion better than a well conducted worship. A community gathered together in dignity, reverence, and faith provide the most beautiful display of instruction available to the Church. In fact, so effective was this format in the early Church that no other forum was needed for the continuing education of the adults. The current reform of the liturgy—both mass and sacraments—presents splendid opportunities for a total approach to the faith life of the people.

We have yet to realize the impact of a caring community gathered to worship the Lord in faith and love, open to His presence, grace, and power. That impact upon each participant can be the deepest and most effective way to minister to the *person* needs. The symbolic effect of ritual, the contagious joy of a believing support community, and the power of the proclaimed and explained Word can combine to set up the best of all possible conditions for the growth of a living, conscious, and active faith.

Counting holy days, this means that Catholics can anticipate fifty-eight "classes" a year conducted in an extraordinarily multidimensional communal atmosphere. Where else can such a climate of faith be so effectively mounted? What is more, the nuances echo and ring with 2,000 years of Jewish Passover and 2,000 more years of Christian Eucharist! Where else in the whole world does history converge and settle down so vitally, meaningfully, and spiritually?

But we need not stress this point too much further. We have already taken up the question of liturgy in another chapter, where some special thoughts and guidelines are offered.

2. Preacher Feedback

Precisely because of the persistent creativity needed, the one element of liturgy requiring a persevering effort is that of the homily. The homilist should be in touch with God and with his or her people. Clearly, most homilists pray and study to some degree. They do their best to get in touch with God. The major weakness of the majority of homilists seems to be their failure to get in touch with the people to whom they preach.

That is why some authorities suggest the practice of "Monday Evening Quarterback." Of course the selection of time depends on local needs. Monday evening is a bad time in the autumn, when there is plenty of actual quarterbacking going on on TV. But we all know of the "armchair quarterbacks" or "generals" who are always replaying and redirecting the games.

All good speakers today know they need good feedback. Life is too complicated for one person to assume that he or she knows the needs of people without ever asking them. In an earlier, simpler, stabler age, this may have been the case. Today it is not. The modern homilist must formally and systematically—not just casually—seek to know the needs of the people and how they react to the homilies.

Although many will reject this idea as out-of-hand, it is really not. This writer knows from personal experience in lecturing for over fifteen years in numberless auditoriums and churches how much he has gained from the hundreds of questions, comments, criticisms, and reactions received from all kinds of people. I know I have grown from experiencing the caring concern of such people. I know that my ability to speak to their needs, while still far from perfect, is meaningful because I have had the privilege of receiving their feedback.

Biblical studies point out that the preacher participates in the prophetic role of the Church. These studies also analyze prophecy as 1) announcing the authentic word of God, 2) articulating the unspoken faith aspirations of the people, and 3) foretelling the future acts of God. Homilists may reasonably beg off foretelling the future. Even the biblical prophets did not dwell too much on that aspect, despite their reputation. But homilists cannot retreat from the first two calls, namely, proclaiming God's word and giving voice to the unspoken faith outpourings of the people.

But how is a homilist going to be a spokesperson of the people's faith if he or she never hears what they have to say? How shall one gather up their many thoughts if one doesn't stop to listen to them, to get their feedback?

How is this to be done? Here is a possible strategy:

1) In your parish bulletin, print the readings (references), topic, and a brief outline of next week's homily. 2) Give the homily. 3) Announce some convenient time for a meeting when you will be present to receive feedback on your talk. Give the feedback sessions time to get off the ground. Don't fear devastating criticism. Most people come with good will and an appreciation of the difficulties of public speaking. They are on your side. You may be disappointed in the beginning at the smallness of the feedback crowd or at the superficiality of their remarks. The size of the crowd doesn't matter; it will wax and wane depending on the topic. The depth of their responses will grow as they attain confidence in speaking up, when they realize your ego is strong enough to take what they have to give.

You will soon discover that this is a superb form of continuing education because it is a form of adult sharing of a high order. The homilist grows as his or her awareness is stretched through feedback. The contributors grow as they find themselves expanding their capacities to make extensive, coherent, and intelligent statements about the deep issues of life and faith.

3. The Catholic "Watchtower"

Many of us are fascinated by the zeal of the Jehovah's Witnesses whose personal enthusiasm brings them to thousands of doors every year to spread their ideas. But what intrigues some people more is the literature they hand out—the "Watchtower." One is not overwhelmed by the content so much as by the method.

This method can be adapted by the Church for its own purposes. To be most effective, it should be tied into the local needs of the parish group as they emerge in homily and preacher feedback sessions. Suppose the people express a desire for a deeper understanding of the fundamental option in moral life. Find an article from a Catholic newspaper, magazine, or book that presents its message in an appealing and attractive way. Obtain permission for a reprint and distribute it to the people at liturgy. The use of the printed tract (or "Watchtower") should help reinforce what was said in the pulpit and discussed at the feedback sessions. It also fulfills another aspect of adult learning, namely, private study through personal reading.

The Catholic Newspaper A variation of this approach is drawing attention to articles in weekly Catholic newspapers. Many of them run a catechetical series entitled "Know Your Faith," a syndicated series of articles on faith matters published by the United States Catholic Conference's press department. It is not enough to be glad that the parishioners have the Catholic newspaper at home. Promotion is still the name of the game. This means that attention must be drawn to certain pertinent articles in the newspapers. Even the publishers of the two most renowned and widely read news magazines in the world— *Time* and *Newsweek*—promote articles each week via the other media.

4. The Lecture Mass

All liturgy schedules advert to problems of crowd movement, parking lot logistics, and other down-to-earth exigencies. This suggestion about a longer liturgy due to a longer homily is made in realization of the above difficulties. The possibility of adapting the idea depends on local capacities.

The idea of the lecture mass builds on the assumption that a series of in-depth homilies is occasionally needed. The kind of probing that this would call for would mean more time, perhaps a half hour for the homily. In times past the evening Lenten sermons fulfilled this need. But changes in people's use of nighttime, the rapid growth of crime in the streets, and all manner of other invasions have drastically reduced the popularity of the one-time Lenten talks.

What about a readaptation of the idea for the Sundays of Lent in the lecture mass? If the series might drift too far afield from the demands of the homily, let the talk be given prior to the mass. Naturally, the people would need to be alerted about the sudden extension of time at that particular liturgy. But it could turn out to be surprisingly popu-

lar. Six half-hour in-depth talks (followed by informal feedback at cof-
fee/donuts after liturgy) following a systematic theme that corresponds
to expressed needs of the people is more than a simple piece of the
puzzle that ministers to the adults in process.

5. Banners and Blowups

More than ever, in an image-conscious world, a picture is worth a
thousand words. Medieval decorators used tapestries to illustrate religious motifs. Today we possess the marvel of the camera and the simplicity of the handmade banner. Every teacher knows the power of
pointing to a picture or an image to bring home an idea. With liturgy
still as our base in this discussion, think of the use of banners and
photo blowups to illustrate the themes of the mass, the main points of
the sermon, and the concepts that the needs assessment have brought
to light.

The Campaign for Human Development employs this technique to
great effect. Every parish blossoms with posters of hungry children,
hollow-eyed adults, and hopeless hovels. These blowups reinforce the
appeal for funds the people hear from the pulpit. Why reserve this
technique for just one worthy cause? Why not apply the principles to
issues closer to home as well?

Every parish today has its reserve of camera buffs and banner
makers. For the camera experts provide a list of liturgical themes and
homily concepts that need pictorial illumination. One of the simplest
and most dramatic ways to start them thinking and working is to ask
them to compose a parish "Way of the Cross" for the Lenten themes.
Discretion should govern the final choices, since no one on the local
scene must be exposed to embarrassment.

Banner makers can come up with Bible texts, insightful quotes, and
challenging sayings to help fix in the memory the ideas for adult
thinking. It has often been said we need fifty-seven associations with
an idea before it begins to stick to the ribs. Banners and blowups are a
vital part of that series of associations.

6. Cassette Library

Americans may be the most literate people on earth but they can
hardly be called avid readers. Most Americans can read, but they normally restrict their reading to the newspapers, popular magazines, and
letters. Yes, a significant number do read serious books and professional literature. Far more do not. The nonreaders may be willing to
listen, but they may not read the reprint you handed out at liturgy.

Might they not listen to that same reprint were it read onto a blank cassette by a skilled reader (perhaps a drama student or teacher from the local community college)? The revolution in media has quietly turned Americans into skilled watchers and listeners of electronically produced information. There's more than one way to skin a cat! If the parishioners can't be reached through the printed page, then try the audio cassette and touch them through their ears. Think of the possibility of cassette sermons for your people in nursing homes, hospitals, and other shut-in situations.

Buy some blank cassettes. Bring in a good reader and ask him/her to put some articles and speeches on tape. Write up some outlines to go with the tapes so that the listeners can have some educational reinforcement should they so desire as they listen to the materials. Maintain a lending library. Promote the use of the tapes for pulpit announcements, blowup posters in the vestibule of the church, and systematic "word of mouth campaigns."

N.B. *It should be clearer by now that the parish church (and not just its school or community center) is itself a learning center. By no means is this meant to detract from the central function of the Church, which is liturgical celebration. Church buildings are not schools or learning centers in the primary sense—but in an auxiliary way they clearly possess an educational impact.*

7. Bible Days

The leaders in continuing education programs have little trouble finding a topic when the goal is role education. The topics for teaching religion and parenting are normally evident. What is one to do when the case is *person* education? There need be no difficulty here either when it is a matter of "Operation Bootstrap" for the disadvantaged. But what about the rest of the people? The Bible remains the most compelling topic of interest and study for person education.

This is more so today than ever. Americans are on the move. They are a rootless people. The Bible remains as the textbook of the roots of civilization and faith. No other book has done more to shape the values and identity of countless millions than the Bible. As a center of roots it is a shaper of culture and identity. As a center of faith it is a shaper of faith and values.

Continuing education will do Catholics an enormous favor by helping them to come to know the riches of the Bible. Launch the Bible study groups with a Bible Day. Think of the Bible Day as a kind of parish renewal day, a time for the parish to experience a revival of faith. Thus place the study of the Bible in the setting of the community of faith. The ecology of Bible study is the richness of the Church community.

Bring in a good speaker to give two or three talks about the book of the Bible to be studied. A good speaker need not necessarily be a scholar. Many a capable scholar is constitutionally unable to stir a group of people to appreciate the fruits of his work. A good speaker is like the middleman between the farmer and the customer—he delivers the goods. Without the middleman the farmer goes broke and the customer starves.

Tie the talks in with 1) Praying, 2) Singing, and 3) Honoring.

Praying Studying the Bible is more than an intellectual exercise, it is an enterprise of faith. Call the students of the scriptures to alert attention to the Spirit of God who hovers near the words and the hearts of the readers. Prayer is an opening to the voice of God speaking through the holy writ.

Singing Infuse the day with plenty of enthusiastic singing. Nothing creates a sense of community more than a rousing sing-along. The New Testament relates that the early Christians gathered with hearts gladdened by sing-alongs that included psalms, hymns, and spiritual canticles. They knew the psychology of community singing as the simplest way to create a group spirit.

Honoring The community spirit grows even more when love is shown by ceremonies of hospitality and recognition. There is a mistaken notion that in religious circles such events need not (and even should not) be held. ("People of faith don't need them!") Not true. People of faith are human like anyone else, just as Jesus was. Christ's incarnation was God's way of honoring and recognizing the human element in an incredible outburst of love and affection.

We can do no less.

· Welcome the newcomers and old friends back for a visit.
· Honor the Silver Wedding jubilarians with a white flower.
· Give the "Golden Rose" award to the Golden Wedding jubilarians.
· Ask the grade school and high school graduating classes to stand up for a bow.
· Give the Cardinal Newman Award (make it up) to your newest college graduates.
· Bestow the Aquinas medal on your newest master's degree recipients.
· Incorporate the name of your parish in an award for students who have received doctorates, law degrees, medicine degrees, etc.
· Select five families who deserve recognition and create a Family Life Award for them.

Acquire the *human touch.* Never walk with God so much that you lose the common touch. God didn't, for that is why He sent Jesus. We should not be above the master. Honoring people in a sincere and joyful way is one of the best cementers of community spirit available to a parish. Stress has been placed on recognizing the students, especially those with college and university degrees, because they often feel the most alienated from parishes after their years of study. Give them a sense of welcome. Take pride in "your sons and daughters—the doctors, lawyers, and so on."

Is this all part of continuing education? Yes! Even though it is nonacademic, it is an all-important climate setting for continuous progress in adulthood. It is the effort to create a firm and lasting community support system for the adults (and the youth) that will make continuing education meaningful and effective.

8. Bible Study Groups

In setting up Bible study groups remember that time is of the essence. This means, "something people don't have too much of." Bite off small pieces. Set up minicourses of six weeks—never more than eight. Have the study groups meet in homes. Limit the number of participants to about twelve to fifteen people. When there are less than twelve the number of ideas dwindles and the discussion falters. When there are more than fifteen the number of ideas multiplies to the point where some people have no chance of sharing due to the time limit involved.

Homes seem to be the best settings for study groups, but the school or parish center could be used as well. Start with the gospels, one at a time. Then branch out to Psalms, Genesis, or one of the books of the prophets. Provide each participant with a practical, readable study book to use at the sessions. Where it is economically feasible, see that each group has a Bible commentary for quick reference in looking up answers to questions. The parish leader in charge of the program (be that a priest, a member of a religious order, a coordinator, etc.) should train leaders for the groups. (Cf. point 11 further on about such training.) Set up both a feedback system and an answer bank for knotty questions the groups might encounter in their discussions.

9. Children's Texts

Relate the study of the children's religion texts to what has been said on role education, especially parenting. The radical change in religion texts disturbed many a parent when it first appeared. Angry meetings were held. Guidelines were written and criteria established. With the current subsiding of the clamor, the teachers no longer feel the need to involve the parents in the review of the texts. That's a pity, because parental involvement in the education of the young is necessary now more than ever. And one dimension of this involvement is keeping them abreast of the development in textbooks.

This involvement includes not only the parents, but the whole parish community. The parish bulletin could run a twelve-week series explaining the current texts in use and the purpose for using them. This could be supplemented by blowups illustrating the themes of the texts. With these bulletins and blowups on display in the church "gallery" accompanied by some further text explanations, the ideas could be even further disseminated.

Lastly, the teachers could be available at the door with handouts and a readiness to answer questions. Not all teachers need to do this all the time—but one week/one grade at a time. The more voluble and candid the communication, the more the whole community of faith is involved.

10. "Wheels and Bellboy"

When parishes were largely urban neighborhood affairs, it was possible to get out and walk to see the people. The growth of the suburban parish means that car and bellboy must substitute for the friendly walk (even in the cities). So much real adult education goes on at the face-to-face level. Most Catholics come to the parish only for Sunday liturgy or for special reasons.

The way to touch the people personnally is to return the compliment and go out to see them. The combination of car and bellboy gives a flexibility to "office hours." Offices become portable. The parish executive group need not be confined to the parish grounds for office hours. One sign of a vital parish life is a conspicuous rhythm of "people-going-to-center/center-going-to-people."

A variation of this aspect is the *parish traveling workshop*. Divide the parish into ten districts. Train ten groups of three people each as the "experts" to go out to the families in the varying districts to give courses. For example, let's assume we're dealing with a course on the Commandments. One person on the team develops the theme of covenant. The second person dwells on the values implied by each commandment. The third person conducts case studies related to each commandment.

Ask people with large family rooms in their homes to donate their space. Encourage wall-to-wall people crowding. By now the familiar theme of community should be cropping up again. The image is as much the message as that which the team brings. Outreach like this guarantees that the parish will begin to experience itself as a network of subgroups all bound by the One Body of the Eucharist into the One Body of the Church. More and more, as the strands of the outreach grow stronger, the sense of strong identity with Christ begins to mature. The gifts of the car and the phone are placed at the service of grace.

11. The Practice of Andragogy

Adult education expert Malcolm Knowles has coined the term *andragogy* to identify the style of continuing education. He built the word out of the Greek word *andros,* meaning adult. He contrasts it with pedagogy, which he says is the method for teaching children. He sees pedagogy as downward communication from adult to child. Andragogy is horizontal/lateral/face-to-face communication between adults.

In such people-to-people education every effort is made to see each adult as a sharer in the educational process. Every adult is an educational resource. Each one brings the gift of his or her life and experience to the learning situation. In the light of what has been mentioned earlier in this chapter about the stages of adult growth, this concept makes a great deal of sense.

At least five kinds of adults will be present at any one learning session: 1) Confident Adventurers, 2) Doubters, 3) The Urgent, 4) Self-Accepters, and 5) Sages and Saints. Here is a mixture that should never allow any gathering to grow dull! Knowles's genius is to give all these groups lots of elbow room and a maximum chance for self-expression. Using the numerous variations of group processes, Knowles suggests the endless variety of intercommunication that can exist among adult groups.

Climate Setting Knowles puts a particular stress on climate setting, that is, establishing a mood wherein the assembled adults will feel free enough to communicate with each other. As in so many cases of group activity the sense of threat caused by fear, ignorance, strangeness, or other factors must be removed if there is to be any free flow of communication.

Actually, the constant theme of community development brought out again and again in this book is precisely aimed at this climate setting. In a sense what is going on is the re-tribalizing of society. The old tribal system was a tight network of relationships in which personal ego strength was derived from the power of the community support. The new efforts at tribalization are meant to achieve the same goal without invoking the authoritarian use of a chieftan. Rather than imposing community from without, there is an invitation to develop community from within. We are not looking for a Maoist commune or a South Pacific island colony; we are reaching out for a Christian Community.

Knowles is strong on an interpersonal communication in an atmosphere of community. We need to add many other elements in systematic and rational aspects of education. The questions of input (Who does it? Who chooses it?), organization (Who picks the place to meet? Who orders the coffee?), and follow-through must still be part of the picture. For consideration of these aspects, refer to the chapter on "Teacher Talk."

It was mentioned earlier, in discussing Bible study groups, that something would be said about training the leaders of adult groups. The leaders should be aware of Knowles's well-taken point about the nature of how adult groups should be approached. Adults aren't children and should not be treated as such. They should be approached as people who have something to contribute that is every bit as valuable as the input brought by the experts, be they people or study books. Train the leaders to encourage the many types of adults to speak up and share their hopes, expectations, insights, fears, and cautions with the whole group. In addition the leaders should be familiar with the material covered in "Teacher Talk."

12. Conversion Experiences

Parishes have always provided the possibility of conversion experiences for the adults. That's what the old-time parish missions were all about. Fiery preachers came to condemn people for their sins, call them to confession, and purify them in the grace of Christ. That's what the old-style Ignatian, total silence retreats were all about. Alert the retreatants to their imperfect sinful states and then call them to repentance in Christ.

Conversion experiences for adults are still needed and they form a cornerstone for continuing education. The style may have changed, but the substance has not. People still need personal renewal and the call to spiritual growth. Well-known, new forms have arisen to meet this need. Cursillo's (highly emotional weekend retreats), charismatic movements, new style retreats, and updated forms of the Ignatian method are but four of the examples of mountaintop experiences available for Catholic adults today.

Even the parish missions are making a comeback. No longer full of fire and brimstone, but quite full of Christ's spirit and saving power, the contemporary parish renewals are directed every bit as much at stirring up the faith of the people as were the missions of old. Each time these conversion events occur, they provide continuing education with a new audience, for when people come down from the mountain they are going to need some guidance from the valley. Continuing education can offer some of the follow-through necessary in order for the excitement of the conversion to be channeled into the new wineskin of a revitalized life.

13. Audiovisual Library

Nowhere in the world will one see more breathtaking stained glass than in the cathedral at Chartres. When the sun shines through those windows it is as though God's rainbow is touching the floors of the cathedral and the hearts of the viewers. More importantly, those windows are a Living Bible. People of those times who could not read could see the story of salvation in living color and matchless art.

Today's "stained glass windows" are the visual media, the film in all its forms. Although there is also evolving a new artistry in actual stained glass and it is not meant to be excluded here, the attempt is to show how the old art form has been employed in film.

Almost all schools and centers have some sort of library of films, slides, and filmstrips, which detail the stories of the Bible, church history, and religious values and morality. This library appears to be a hidden treasure, however, since its use is confined largely to youth. Yet most of the resources could equally be enjoyed by the adults. Why not integrate the audiovisual library into the climate setting of continuing education?

What about the possibility of a film/filmstrip/slide festival prior to mass each Sunday for ten weeks? Most of the films are rarely more than twelve minutes in length. Link them to posters, explanations in the parish bulletin, mimeo handouts, and resource people giving introductions. Think of them as another form of "stained glass window."

14. The Choir

The rise of congregational singing resulted in a temporary decline in the use of church choirs. That period of decline is now over. Choirs are returning not as performing groups so much, but as members of the worshiping community assisting the enrichment of all the singing as well as providing meditation music and a sample of the repertoire of the great traditions of church music.

Many parishes budget an annual workshop for their choir. The members go to some college or music center and acquire some new information as well as a deeper enthusiasm for their work. Because of the nature of their work, choir members tend to become fairly knowl-

edgeable about the meaning of liturgy and the meaning of the words
they sing.

The result is that they are a fine resource for continuing education.
Could not the choir become a traveling workshop in the parish, giving
music/liturgy seminars in family rooms? Of course they could. (Cf.
point 10.) They could fan out into the subdistricts of the parish and
lead people in sing-alongs that include popular and patriotic songs as
well as the new hymns for liturgy. They could give some brief talks
on the meaning of the texts and the developments in liturgy. They
could easily call for adult sharing and they would obtain it. There is
perhaps no better way to stimulate parish singing than through such
miniseminars given by the church choir.

15. "Rosegarden" Ministry

The "sages" and "saints" living in nursing homes would like a piece of
all this action. The best ministers to such people are the teen-agers.
In the new education *chic* talk, this is called "intergenerational learning." Few groups seem to have a more instinctive liking for each
other than the teen-agers and the senior citizens in nursing homes.

Set up a tape-of-the-month club. The newly formed cassette library
(Cf. point 6) has the tapes. Bring along the study outlines. Are the
children wondering what to give the old folks for Christmas? Let
them give tape recorders. Give the oldsters a month to hear the tapes
several times while pondering the outlines. Have them form a circle
and hold a discussion. For the bedridden, pay a personal/educational
visit. These "gray panthers" have some powerful oracles for the
church community. Record some of their illuminating sayings.
Could they not be played back before or during liturgy? Enough said.

A variation of this ministry is the "Rosegarden" weekly lunch for
the elderly who are confined at home. Form car pools and bring them
to the parish community center. Use the same process of
tape/outlines/discussion. Their voices, to no one's surprise, will "rise
like incense to the Lord."

16. Diocesan Lecture Series

Hear the speakers.
  Read their books.
  There is one major value of bringing in outside speakers, especially
those who have written the books being used in the various courses
and study groups. Hearing the speaker tends to make the book come
alive. Another value is the "prophet with honor" syndrome. Local
prophets (that is, good speakers) are often without honor in their own
milieu. But bring in a stranger, a prophet with honor, who will say

exactly what local people have been saying for a long time, and he will be listened to and heard. Familiarity with local talent breeds deafness. Hence the arrival of an outside lecturer is a necessary counterpart to local efforts.

Because of the expense sometimes involved, it is usually absorbed by the diocesan education office, which sees to the invitations, fees, and the practical administration of the event. At the annual diocesan Christian Education Institute this concept is vastly expanded as a group of speakers is invited to come and share their thoughts with the local parishioners.

17. The "Climb on Old Ivy"

Local colleges and universities, with their newfound sense of community service, are fine resources for continuing education. They have professors with numerous specialities useful to the local programs. Many of these professors are only too glad to do some "moonlighting" at whatever the going rate per lecture hour is. In addition, the college library, its audiovisual facilities, and its own public lecture/fine arts series are all part of the concept of continuing education.

18. The Televising of the Message

The Church has yet to appreciate the Christian educational possibilities inherent in TV. Tentative efforts have been made to set up a national Catholic TV network. The growth possibility is there, but it will take much time, money, and effort to make this medium useful. One effective means could be the commercialization of the Video Disc, a simple and cheap way to put TV shows on records the way symphonies are put on them now. The convenience and the comparatively inexpensive packaging mean that church groups may soon find a way to develop programming that will be just as much used in the home as are the present commercial shows.

Only the convergence of money, time, and imagination will guarantee the effective use of TV in continuing education. Some groups have taken advantage of the hand-held camera, the Porta-Pak, to televise talks by local and visiting speakers, local programs, and annual institutes. The recorded material, in videotape form, is then distributed for local parish use.

19. Teachable Moments

This form of continuing education is well-known enough so that no special effort is needed here to expand on it. It is one of the most successful ways of involving adults in religious education. It builds upon what has been pointed out concerning role education—in this case, the matter of presenting properly when the young are about to make their First Confession, First Communion, and Confirmation.

20. Getting "Them" to Come

How often the question is raised, "This all sounds very nice, but how do you get people ("them") to come?" The question is based on a lack of awareness that "they" are already coming. Sixty percent of Catholics or more come to liturgy fifty-eight times a year. They *do* come! The attempt has been made to point out what can be done for them and with them while they are present. Liturgy is the highest and noblest form of continuing education, even though it should be emphasized that liturgy is first and foremost a celebration.

Secondly, the question could well be reversed: "How do you get the parish executive personnel to go out to the people?" Happily many of them do. But outreach is a critical part of assuring a successful continuing education program. The constant habit of gathering at the center and fanning out to the periphery is the only certain way to establish the network of community and sharing that will be the perfect climate setter for continuing education.

Summary

Twenty tips have been suggested for continuing education within the framework of the philosophy of adult stages mentioned at the beginning of this chapter. The stages are:

1. Confidence
2. Doubt
3. Urgency
4. Self-Acceptance
5. Wisdom/Holiness

The tips are:

1. Community Worship	11. The Practice of Andragogy
2. Preacher Feedback	12. Conversion Experiences
3. The Catholic "Watchtower"	13. Audiovisual Library
4. The Lecture Mass	14. The Choir
5. Banners and Blowups	15. "Rosegarden" Ministry
6. Cassette Library	16. Diocesan Lecture Series
7. Bible Days	17. The "Climb on Old Ivy"
8. Bible Study Groups	18. The Televising of the Message
9. Children's Texts	19. Teachable Moments
10. "Wheels and Bellboy"	20. Getting "Them" to Come

A Word About Diocesan Adult Education Programs

Some people lament there is so little adult education going on in the Church. There is a great deal occurring, but it is not always thought of as continuing education. This is especially true at the diocesan level. Almost every diocesan office lists at least twenty-six agencies that deal with continuing education in one way or another. It is important here to distinguish between school and education. School is one kind of systematic and formal approach to education. It is a defined institution, clearly seen. But the numerous other forms of education are not always so evident. The twenty tips just given about continuing education in a parish build upon the distinction between the school as one form of education and the numerous other forms cited.

Let us consider the twenty-five agencies of a diocese according to the model of Message, Community, and Service. Such a way of viewing diocesan educational ministries can lay the groundwork for noting how much adult education is going on and for moving toward a total view of education in the context of a cooperative ministry.

MESSAGE (7)	COMMUNITY (8)	SERVICE (10)
Seminaries	CYO	Charities
Campus Ministry	Liturgy	Family Life
Christian Education – CCD	Music	Hospitals/Prisons
Christian Education – Schools	Retreats	Spanish Apostolate
Continuing Education of Clergy	Board of Education	Communications: Newspaper TV
Special Education	Senates: Priests Sisters	Pastoral Council
Deacon Program	Associations: Pastors Associate Pastors Retired Priests Laity	Tribunal
	Interreligious Development (Ecumenism)	Personnel Vocations Missions

All these agencies are working to fulfill the three goals of proclaiming the message of Jesus, building community, and being of Christian service. They have been divided according to emphases, not because they are exclusively tied to the goal under which they are found. Remember that all of their labor finds ultimate fulfillment at the parish level where the people are. Every one of these twenty-five agencies (and some that have not been mentioned — the list is not exhaustive) is engaged in continuing education.

This is self-evident for the seven Message agencies that engage in teacher training, seminars for administrators, and enrichment programs for clergy.

It is not always so clear for the remaining eighteen agencies. Hence let us now consider each of those agencies and see how they are participating in the work of adult education.

Community Agencies

1. **CYO** Today the CYO is joining the efforts toward a total youth ministry in cooperation with the CCD, Schools and Retreat Movement. They work to train adults as youth leaders and help establish a faith community of adult models for youth.
2. **Liturgy** Liturgy commissions do more than supervise the implementation of institutional changes in worship. They are busy composing training outlines for the preparation of lectors, communion ministers, and anyone else who needs coaching in how to take leadership roles in liturgy.
3. **Music** Music commissions do indeed write guidelines for the kind of music appropriate for worship. In addition they conduct music seminars for choirs and musicians both at the diocesan and the local level. They serve as consultants to parishes and other diocesan agencies about music selection.
4. **Retreats** The group in charge of retreats is sometimes called, more broadly, the Spiritual Development Commission. All retreats for adults are a form of continuing education. Tip number 12 in the list above shows the significance of conversion experiences in the retreat movement and for continuing education.
5. **Boards of Education** These policy makers assist the adult educational administrators of a diocese (in both CCD and schools) to make decisions within a framework of common goals. Their own gatherings are continuing education experiences in themselves. They, too, offer training courses for the personnel elected to parish boards.
6. **Senates** In many ways, senate gatherings are adult education in its ideal form. There is input from position papers, committee re

ports, and speeches followed by lots of face-to-face sharing, debate, confrontation, and just plain interpersonal communication. A well wrought senate is a maximum exchange forum of adult educational resources.

7. **Associations** These various interest groups mainly conduct themselves in a manner similar to the senates. They generally assume an advocacy position that makes their exchanges more penetrating and educative than any other kind of adult grouping.

8. **Interreligious Development** Ecumenical seminars and dialogues conduct themselves in the best modern style of adult education. The depth approach to religious topics such as the one done by the Anglican-Roman dialogue on the Eucharist shows how trusting adults can illumine one another in a prayerful and intelligent way.

Service Agencies

1. **Charities** Charities offer all kinds of training materials and services for adults: a) literacy achievement; b) help with equivalency exams; c) assistance with affirmative action; d) Gabriel Richard leadership courses; e) Right to Life study guides and sermon outlines; f) Campaign for Human Development literature, etc.

2. **Family Life** The organization concerned with this aspect of church life oversees a number of programs for families: a) Pre-Cana; b) Cana; c) marriage encounter; d) marriage enrichment; e) family effectiveness training, etc.

3. **Hospitals/Prisons** Chaplains play a major role in these institutions. They refer to their work as a clinical pastoral ministry, which, if examined, would show much of the contemporary approaches avowed by continuing education. These people show their sensitivity to the new approaches to death and dying, to the puzzles of modern medical ethics, and to the rehabilitation of prisoners in an incontestable form of adult education.

4. **Spanish Apostolate** It has been said that as much as one-quarter of the American Church is Spanish speaking. Looked at this way, this is hardly a minority. But these people do have a minority status in our culture because they need the bilingual training that will help them operate effectively in the culture; and they need the cultural affirmation of their own traditions so that their identities may be saved both for their own sakes as well as for the Church at large. Language training of teachers and cultural affirmation are adult education endeavors.

5. **Communications** The Catholic newspaper is normally published with the educated adult in mind. TV, though, may appeal to both young and old. An added advantage of TV is that it helps new-

comers by putting on programs in ways of communicating best suited to TV.

6. **Pastoral Council** This adult group engages in mutual education in much the same way as the senates and associations mentioned above. Their gatherings are characterized by the same elements of reports, "rules of order," and lively exchange.

7. **Tribunal** The personnel at the tribunal do more than process the marriage cases that come their way. They provide counselors for saving marriages, they maintain a speakers' bureau to help parishes keep abreast of the latest marriage laws in the church, and they write summaries on marriage issues for the Catholic newspapers and media.

8. **Personnel** The personnel committee is in the business of needs assessments, that is, the gathering of adult data about adults. Their impact is upon the leadership groups of the diocese. They approach leadership distribution on a basis of perceived needs from data gathering, a dialogue with available personnel, and the resultant prudential (it is hoped) judgment.

9. **Vocations** The vocations office looks for candidates in the adult population. Their literature calls for college trained, comparatively settled people to consider the priesthood and the religious life. They operate with an adult mind set that appreciates the complexity of modern ministry and they conduct an education campaign that seeks out the mature.

10. **Missions** Almost all mission appeal is directed to the adult community, though there are youth missions as well. Preachers representing the foreign mission apostolate deal in adult themes of world consciousness, evangelization, and the humanization of the deprived especially in the developing nations.

What should these twenty-five agencies be doing? Exactly what they are doing. They are fulfilling adult goals of the Church in an adult manner. Could things be done any better? There is always a "Yes" to this question.

In 1776 the American colonies declared their independence.

In 1789 the American states met together and wrote the Articles of Confederation; that is, they federated, they declared the nature of their relationship as a nation to a federal government.

Could we have a model here for diocesan office agencies?

In 1976 they declare their Interdependence.

In 1989 they are able to write their articles of interdependence.

This would give the agencies a thirteen-year grace period to find out how to interrelate their efforts and share their resources for the greater good of the Church. No question but that the current separate efforts are giving glory to God. How much more they could do so as a unified group!

Many dioceses are creating an adult education agency. Such an agency could be a catalyst for the kind of vision outlined here. This catalyst could facilitate the interface of resources, could enable the evolution to a common consciousness and subsequent federation to serve better an extraordinary number of publics such as:

Teachers	Parents	Immigrants	Minorities
Prisoners	Sick	Clergy	Nuns
Deacons	Poor	Singers	Worshippers
Protestants	Jews	Elderly	Spiritually Hungry

This kind of cluster evokes the jet-age version of the Medieval Cathedral Community. In those days people used to speak of medieval harmony as a reflection of the "Music of the Spheres."

Adult educators: Are you ready for the music?

7

DELPHI TECHNIQUE AND FUTURES PLANNING

*The present is never our goal: the past and the present are our means:
the future alone is our goal. Thus we are never living, but we hope to
live; and looking forward always to be happy.*

Blaise Pascal

*My interest is in the future because I am going to spend the rest of my
life there.*

Charles Franklin Kettering

The theology of hope assures us we have a future in the final victory of
Christ. Intelligent planning is our human responsibility to help create
that future. It is the human underside of the virtue of hope. Jesus
tells us we have a future. Planning reminds us we have a stake in
making that future. What's more, everyone should be interested in
the future, since they will be spending most of their time there.

Christian educators are becoming increasingly aware of the need for
good planning. This consciousness accompanies the awareness of the
need for better organization of religious education programs and centers. Good organization calls for good management. Christ's parable
of the "unjust steward" is better characterized as the scenario of the
clever manager. Jesus holds up the example of a crooked steward, not
as one to be admired for his wayward morality, but to be imitated for
his imaginative cleverness in planning for his future.

As all managers know, decision making is central to organization.
In Christian education, because so many of the problems are new, the
act of decision making is exceptionally difficult. Planning deserves
more attention because it enriches the context of decision making.
Where there is no planning or informed decision making, the religious
education team is merely fulfilling Paschal's dictum, "Discoursing
simply to while away the hour."

Does this mean that no planning and decision making are going on
now? No, there is plenty of planning and deciding, but some of it is
past-oriented. Let us consider four forms of rear-view-mirror planning
and the reasoning that governs each form. In this regard we will look
at new possibilities for planning in the Delphi Technique and the Fu-

tures Planning approach. Although there are plenty of merits in the current planning systems, for the sake of argument let us advert only to the defects.

To begin with, there are four kinds of past-oriented planning:

Act as though the future will be just like the present

Are your classrooms too small? Make bigger ones. In the "soaring fifties" we planned this way. We built factorylike schools, mammoth convents, seminaries, and monasteries. Think of all the "For Sale" signs planted in the grass outside so many of these buildings.

Do you have only one slide projector? Get more audiovisual machines. Invest in a video cassette machine. There are tough choices to be made. Your group buys a Super 8 projector just as a video cartridge system arrives on the market. You make a quick switch to video cassette just as video discs become ready for commercial use.

Do you have just volunteer teachers? Hire a professional and give him or her a staff. Then leave the teacher to shed tears because no one thought to write up a job description, or bring up the matter of team ministry, or advert to the need for a community of faith. But then, why should anybody do these things? After all, the future will be just like the present (really meaning the past)!

"Oil the squeaky wheel"

This is planning based on outcry. Let us say you adopted the diocesan religion curriculum. Barely had you done this when the teachers came to you grousing that it's too limiting for their creativity. While you are nursing the headache they have given you, the phone begins to ring with parents' complaints that there is not enough content in the new curriculum.

So at your next planning meeting, you "oil the squeaky wheel" to subdue the unhappy noises. Happily you offer a variety of curricula (with lots more content sandwiched in), thus delighting your teachers with "options" and cooling the tempers of you content-hungry parents. Your choices may well have been superb, but you have established a perilous precedent when you narrow your future due to the scope of querulous voices. Your nervousness about jangling phones and tense staff meetings could reduce you to a passive responder and could start eroding your leadership possibilities.

Concentrate on the unhappy present and not the desirable future

Vatican II, the new theology, and the multitude of new teaching methods have created such an impact of change that a crisis of dissatisfaction is inevitable. So much change so quickly is bound to create a series of crises. Classical spiritual writers would call this a "holy dissatisfaction." Sometimes religious educators have resorted to crisis intervention as a way of life because of the turmoil. Seek a solution in terms of the present unhappiness. This has triggered some fancy innovation, and occasionally a good solution, but unfortunately it has reduced many educators to a "crisis" mentality.

When this is the governing attitude and when it is prolonged too much, it becomes self-defeating. Any leader doomed to stagger from crisis to crisis can only look forward to eventually slumping due to exhaustion from the battle. The CCD classes weren't working. So we started a Center and hired a professional. The crowds came. Smilingly, they strolled through the Center. As always, the initial enthusiasm began to wane. The crowds are now down. The professional quits and escapes to computer programming. Someone takes a felt pen and draws a frown button on the remaining piece of newsprint hanging lamely by one strip of masking tape.

Obviously one cannot definitely claim that Centers and professionals won't work. They will work when the planning for them is more rational, compassionate, and future-oriented.

"A fad in time saves nine"

Critics of Christian education delight in accusing the field of faddishness. They smirk about religious educators who were like the dean of a certain college, who came as he went, "with enthusiasm." It is an embarrassing criticism, and one not without some truth. Fad planning depends on false enthusiasm and the god of the moment. Visible fervor is supposed to carry the day. One should not worry that the fad may be a style that has little substance.

Yes, think of all those wonderful fads: Kerygma; Secular City; Death of God; Value Games; Folk Masses; Tech Weekends; Situation Ethics; Balloons; Jesus Freaks; "Smile" Buttons; Dialogue Sermons; Blue Jean Liturgies; Collages; T Groups; "I'm OK – You're OK"; Conflict Resolution; Serendipity; Yoga; Hare Krishna; Macrobiotic Diets, and on and on.

One certainly would not question the merits of many of the above movements. Some of them will escape the faddish "kiss of death" and become elements of lasting value for Christian education. But their goodness has, in too many cases, been deflated by the fad planners. Their contribution has often been marred by the thoughtless rushing from one enthusiasm to the next.

Fad planning has the unfortunate ability to destroy a good idea too soon, consigning it to the recycling center along with Pepsi cans, McDonald wrappers, and rusty Mickey Mouse watches. The unchanneled fervor and unsmiling desperation produce a marriage that ends up like the old Sarah Bernhardt play *Camille* and its more recent counterpart, *Love Story*.

We have looked only at the deficiencies of the above four forms of planning. Naturally, crisis intervention, enthusiasm, advertence to teacher and parent demands, and the values of tradition all possess positive aspects as well. The main attention here was on the kind of planning that took insufficient account of the future. Alvin Toffler has dramatized both the need for a future orientation and the "over-choice" that challenges sluggardly decision making.

Let us now consider two forms of planning that incorporate principles of management with skills that make the future the primary horizon. These are Delphi Technique and Futures Planning.

Delphi Technique

Start with the future and see how it affects the present.

The word *Delphi* is borrowed from an ancient Greek town where an oracle lived who presumably could predict the future. Here was an ancient form of Jean Dixon! The modern Delphi oracles inhabit "think tanks" such as RAND and the Hudson Institute. Perhaps the most famous of these oracles is Herman Kahn, known for helping us to "Think the Unthinkable" (the postatomic-holocaust world) and for giving us the "year 2000" as a mind-expanding date.

Popular versions of these oracles are the science fiction writers ranging all the way from Jules Verne's *20,000 Leagues under the Sea* to Arthur Clarke's and Stanley Kubrick's space odyssey *2001*. Comic book heroes Buck Rogers and Flash Gordon were earlier forms of this futures thinking theme.

The purpose of the Delphi Technique is to gain some expert opinion about the future. The talent of the Delphi community is to reveal what is most likely going to happen—or not happen. They try to present "surprise-free" predictions. Their special value for planners in Christian education—or in any endeavor—is to serve as reality checks on possible future developments. For example, if educators made plans based on the continuance of middle class populations dominating the suburbs in 1990, they might revise such plans if the Delphi predictors advised that the middle class will be back in the inner cities by that time.

How does the technique work?

1. Compose a number of predictions about the future.
2. Ask a group of experts about the likelihood of such predictions coming to pass.

The method the experts use to arrive at their predictions is detailed in a book entitled *Values and the Future* by Baier and Rescher, a Free Press paperback, division of Collier-Macmillan, New York, 1971. Read especially the essay by Olaf Hemler.

The futurists must rely on guesswork when it comes to predicting. But guesswork can, through a number of techniques, be made systematic, rational, and useful. The method draws upon the simple premise that when one is forced to make predictions, the best think to do is call upon the experts in the relevant fields and ask them to do what they can do best—make informed guesses. Like anyone else, they can be wrong due to any number of variables. Ten years before the energy crisis the experts were guessing there never would be one. Well, there *was* one! Delphi predicting is no panacea, but it is a reasonable way of trying to see what the future holds.

The "surprise-free" prediction means that, barring any major changes, the event will happen. Thus, excluding the unforeseen such as "acts of God," the prediction is certain. The Delphi experts make use of data gathering, statistical curves, and reliability measures. They also include the "probability die" (cast the dice) as the addition of the unknown negative factor that would mess up the prediction. The responses are weighted according to the competence of the expert, his/her previous success at predicting, his/her current sense of certainty on the point, and the use of simulation games.

Can Christian education make use of the Delphi Technique?

It could if there were a Delphi community available to do the predicting. There are enough knowledgeable people around. There is not yet the money or the interest that would make such a community a possibility.

If there were one, what would be an agenda for them to ponder? Here is a list of predictions for 1988 that they could mull over:

In 1988

1. There will be 10,000 Christian Education Centers, with hired professional staffs.
2. Two-thirds of the efforts of such staffs will be devoted to adult education.
3. Eighty percent of all learning input will be by disco-vision. Twenty percent will still read books, but the respected skill of that day will be the capacity to "read" images.
4. Many staffs will include Hindu and Buddhist meditation experts. Meditation will now be a required course.
5. After the completion of elementary school, the edu-credit card will be used for future education according to one's needs.

6. Ecumenical dialogue will be a major activity between Christianity and the oil-rich Moslem nations.
7. Spiritual enlightenment will be considered the principal goal of Christian education.
8. Peace and Prosperity studies will form a part of every curriculum.
9. The major topic in moral education will be death control.
10. Major Church documents will be written only after national consultations of the faithful.

These ten mythical predictions would be given to a Delphi Community if one existed, and their expert opinion would be sought. I won't presume to nominate the oracles for that august community, but I will give you a chance to fill in the blanks based on the ten predictions above.

Pick Your Delphi Group

	Name	Topic
1.	_____	Growth of Christian Education Centers
2.	_____	Expansion of adult education
3.	_____	Revolution in TV learning
4.	_____	Centrality of meditation
5.	_____	Edu-credit card use
6.	_____	Moslem-Christian dialogue
7.	_____	Goal of spiritual enlightenment
8.	_____	Peace and Prosperity studies
9.	_____	Death control
10.	_____	National Church consultations

The above may be a "dream list," but this kind of dreaming expands the mind to think about what the future can and should be like. It will take some time before such dreams come true, but that is precisely how so many "impossible" things come to pass.

While awaiting the appearance and growth of a Delphi Community, all is not lost. There is another method available right now to anyone who wants to take the trouble to use it. That method is Futures Planning.

Futures Planning

Start with the future and see how it affects the present.
Delphi looks to the *possible* future. *Can* it happen?
Futures Planning looks to the *desirable* future. How can I *make* it happen?

Futures Planning deals less with predictions and more with desirables. If Delphi existed, Futures Planning could measure its hopes against the reality checks offered by Delphi. That type of expertise does not exist at the moment, so one must get on without it. There are four steps to Futures Planning:

1. Take a dream trip.
2. Compose goal statements.
3. Identify future events three years from now.
4. Conduct a force field analysis.

1. Take a "dream trip"

Think ahead ten years. Write a story about what your Christian Education Center or school department will be like. Be as concrete and specific as you possibly can. Don't be vague. Nail down what you want, what you desire, what you would love to see. Dream wildly, but think concretely. Let each member of your staff write his/her own scenario. Make the individual stories the basis for a consensus scenario after comparing and sharing each of them.

Questions to guide your story writing

1. What will be your agenda for content?
2. Will you be media-centered?
3. Will you use an open classroom?
4. Will most of your meetings be in homes?
5. Will you have volunteer teachers?
6. Will you be training your volunteer teachers in competency education?
7. If you are media-centered, what will the teachers do?
8. Will anybody give lectures?
9. Will you be using serendipity, valuing processes, case studies?
10. Will you use T groups, sensitivity, Erhard Seminar techniques?
11. What will you be doing with books?
12. Will you give equal time to thinking and imagination?
13. What will your center or school look like?
    a. Rectangle   b. Circle   c. Open area   d. Closed areas
14. What will be the social concerns of the Church in those days?
15. How do you think Vatican II will be remembered then?
16. How do you think your programs will be affected by the *National Catechetical Directory?*
17. Will you employ grades?
18. How will you evaluate the progress of your students?
19. What will you be evaluating?

20. Will you employ some version of team teaching?
21. What will prayer and liturgy be like?
22. Where will meditation fit in?
23. Will you have what you think is a community of faith?
24. Will your program be interdisciplinary?
25. How will your program fit in with the tradition of the Church?
26. What role will the pastor play?
27. What will you be doing about budgeting?
28. If there is a school in the parish, how will school and CCD relate?
29. Will pluralism of religions and values still be a problem?
30. What will be the relationship of Church and State?

These questions are meant to direct your "dream trip" to specific issues ten years from now. Flesh all the matters out in careful detail. Appoint each member of the staff to write up individual "dream trips." Compare the stories. Push each other for clear expression. Despite the difficulties, insist on visible, tangible expression. Eventually, the staff should arrive at a consensus story that reflects a common vision of what it would be like to see ten years from now, the desirable future.

2. Compose Goal Statements

Once the story is clear, go through each of the concrete desirables and abstract from them a statement of the goal implicit in each event. For thirty desirables, there should be thirty goals. This process clarifies the dreams and helps to blow away the fuzziness. It is not easy, but it is well worth the time. The story is an implicit realization of unspoken goals in the back of one's mind.

Take time with all of this activity. Resist the impulse to rush. The tighter the expression of the goal, the better is its chance of realization. Remember to match the goal with the concrete details of the story.

What happens next?

A. List the goals in the order of importance.
B. Cream off the five top ones and move into step 3.

3. Identify future events three years from now

Posit this question: "What must be going on at the Center or school three years from now to fulfill the five top goals ten years from now? This is a reality check. What is desired ten years from now must already entail projects in motion three years from now to ensure their possible realization. So the scope is now somewhat narrowed to th next three years. What *in actuality* could be going on three years hence that would relate to the long-term goals? Be realistic. Settle on projects that have more than a ghost of a chance of realization. Most importantly, pick projects that the majority of the faith community can buy into and support.

Without the widespread involvement, agreement, and support of the community of faith, there is little chance for future success. This cannot be an elitist project that plunges ahead with no advertence to the expectations of the people at large. So many good projects have failed because the time was not taken to involve the people. People possess the encouraging strength needed to fulfill dreams. Bring them aboard! The opening chapter of this book is precisely based upon the philosophy and techniques reflecting such involvement.

Once the three-year plan is ready, proceed to the fourth step.

4. Conduct a force field analysis

Let us now return to the present situation. Take one of the projects planned for three years from now. Write it down at the top of the page. Underneath it, list at one side of the page all the forces that will favor that event occurring three years from now. List at the other side of the page all the forces that will restrain that event from achieving reality.

Why do this?

YOU CANNOT CONSCIOUSLY PRODUCE CHANGE UNLESS YOU KNOW THE FORCES THAT EITHER ENCOURAGE OR RESTRAIN YOUR DESIRED FUTURE.

Conscious influence on change assumes a knowledge of the positive and negative forces fostering and frustrating its achievement. Following is an example of such an analysis. Assume that ten years from now the goal is to have eighty percent of the youth participating thirty times a year in the religion program. The three-year project is to have fifty percent of the youth participating twenty times a year. List the positive forces (*Smile*) and the negative ones (*Frown*).

Smile	Frown
1. Excellent religion coordinator	No religion coordinator
2. Fiery parish assistant	The assistant was changed
3. Attractive programming	Programs irrelevant to needs
4. Sound budgeting	Unsound budgeting
5. Strong support from education board and committee	No boards or committees even exist
6. Plenty of personal contact with students	Teachers rarely relate personally with students
7. Regular recruitment program	Haphazard outreach for students

8. Parents are involved	Parents not even contacted
9. Community worship is vital	Liturgy is routine
10. Successful model programs are studied	Never bother to research other programs
11. Volunteer teachers growing more competent	Little training given to volunteers
12. Teacher morale is high	Teacher spirit is flagging
13. Feedback encouraged	No one's opinions asked
14. Faculty is a praying group	Faculty never asked about prayer
15. Faith goals stressed	No goals are clear
16. Content mastery is combined with "heart" education (the affective domain)	"Tell 'em and test 'em" is the main educational method

A sample analysis such as this is quite general. Each local Center or school must create an individualized analysis based on personal experiences.

One element that often crops up in such analysis is the "infinite restraining force." Frequently some person, tradition, or rule is viewed as so intransigent that the planning group throws up its hands in despair. Rigid, feisty, sometimes angry restraining forces do tend to block progress. Obviously, the planning group should make every reasonable, loving, Christian, and diplomatic attempt to leap this hurdle. When all else fails, use an "end run" (i.e., outflank your opponent)—or develop the faith that moves mountains.

Seriously, the strong opposition that one might face should not be dismissed nor should it cause a defeatist attitude. Take time to put the meaning across. New ideas are not as self-evident as the advocates think. One explanation is usually not enough. Brevity is not the soul of wit in this case. Even military officers today are advised to "Tell 'em why!" when they are about to lead their men into action.

When you want other people to listen to you, you must show them the courtesy of listening to them and really "hearing" their difficulties. It takes a lot of humility to be persuasive! Dostoevski wrote, "If people around you are spiteful and callous and will not hear you, fall down before them and beg their forgiveness; for in truth you are to blame for their not wanting to hear you." You may not want to take this advice literally, but you should be aware that adverse situations are sometimes caused by ourselves as well as by others.

The enthusiasm to be an advocate for the new idea can tend to make one overtalkative. Practice yielding. If the opposition interrupts you, let it. Kick the habit of insisting on getting your words in right away. That silence will usually mine some gold. Why fight to win the argument, if you lose the goodwill of others? Is it not a community of trust and faith that is to be sought? Those who communicate best are those who begin with the needs of the other, with the cherished values the other person is trying to preserve. Get to know the other person's point of view, for that is the key to successful persuasion and communication. When there is real communication there is a common ground and a shared possession of the value.

We have lingered awhile on this question of persuasion and communication because it is essential to productive Futures Planning. The widest possible involvement is needed, hence the demand for the fullest attention to the arts of persuasion. Learn how to listen, for good listening is like a magnet that pulls the people talking to you into your orbit. Nothing honors anyone more than the compliment of an interested and sympathetic listener.

Summary

The Christian virtue of hope calls for practical realization. One method of doing this is planning. Many current forms of planning are based on a rear-view-mirror mentality that starts with the past to see what to do about the present. This chapter has dealt with two alternative forms of planning based on the concept that one should start with the future and see how it affects the present.

The Delphi Technique is a method of obtaining expert opinion about the likelihood of future events.

Futures Planning is a method of creating the kind of future one would like to have.

If there were presently a Delphi community for Christian education, it would help the Futures Planners to work with some informed opinions serving as reality checks on their plans. Still, Futures Planners can go on with their work. They may pursue the task in the spirit of Tennyson's *Ulysses:* "Come, my friends, 'Tis not too late to seek a newer world."

8

TEACHER TALK

Those who educate children well are more to be honored even than their parents, for these only give them life, those the art of living well.

Aristotle

The teacher who is attempting to teach without inspiring the pupil with a desire to learn is hammering on cold iron.

Horace Mann

A community booster was congratulating the principal of a high school: "Permit me to congratulate you on the miracles you have performed at this school. Since you became principal, it has become a storehouse of knowledge."

"That is true," laughed the principal, "but I scarcely deserve the credit for that. It is simply that the freshmen bring so much knowledge in and the seniors take so little out."

Good teaching will always be a mystery and a problem. It is a mystery inasmuch as there is no absolutely certain way to be sure of one's effectiveness with students. The inner zone of freedom and personal mystery always remains beyond the capacity of outsiders to touch. Regardless of all the techniques, surveys, and program plannings, the process of education remains somewhat of a mystery.

This is what leads to the problem, namely, the continuing effort to induce the experience of learning amid tensions such as the personal freedom of the student and the demands of the society, the authority of the teacher and the participation of the student, discipline and cooperation, late bloomers and fast pacers, content and method, etc.

This chapter is not intended as a complete look at the teacher-learning situation, nor does it pretend to comment on all the aspects of mystery and problem which afflict education. Rather, the only intention is to give some common sense observations about teaching, be it religion or anything else.

Hence some effort is made to unravel the everyday meaning from the skein of educational jargon naturally found in a specialized field, in an attempt to dispel ambiguity and make the concept as serviceable as possible.

What Is Education?

John Dewey saw education as participation in the social consciousness of the race. The idea may seem obvious today but at the time he wrote, people were devoted to the idealism of the individual. Jack London declared we should live by the "law of the jungle." Darwin intoned that only the fittest should and would survive. Kipling's England bore the "white man's burden," and the sun never set on Britain's bright individualists ruling the empire.

Christian education today can be a participation in the social consciousness of the human race with a particular emphasis on the way in which religious consciousness informs perceptions and behavior. Obviously, this does not exclude the effort to help each student become an individual. The villain of the piece in Dewey's day was ruthlessness of the lone wolf. We should campaign against selfish individualism while championing a triumphant individuality.

Christian education is also the development of the power and sensibility of human intelligence. Education must work to produce a critical mind that delivers our students from a servitude to ideology and technology. Bel Kaufman, author of *Up the Down Staircase*, said that what disturbed her most in the inner city classroom was not the switchblade or the threat of disorder, but the alarmingly uncritical attitude of the students toward the class material.

Notice how the minds of students work. Insensible minds will easily swallow the slogans of the demagogue and the one-dimensional world of technology. The uncritical mind is a sucker for hucksters. Teachers should realize that students who possess natural sensibility will appear eccentric in a society of uncritical minds. Teachers should both tolerate and encourage this eccentricity. Why fear the "bum in residence?" (*Bum* here means the genuinely luminous person who has power to see and evaluate the worth of life.)

Too many teachers prize the *functional* person, the one who plays the role, who is ever so practical. Few teachers are comfortable with the dysfunctional person. To some extent their reactionary attitude is an outgrowth of the Puritan ethic, reinforced by a pioneer mentality and a nostalgia for early Americana.

It is the reason why the poet is patronized rather than having a patron. It lies behind the political resistance to an honest solution to the dilemmas of the disadvantaged and betrays a secret horror of the poor. It is full of a righteousness that is unwarranted and exhibits a piety that is questionable. It is far better to urge forth minds of sensibility that can be pearls of great price and be witnesses of an elegant freedom for which so many thirst today.

Peer adjustment Some teachers think that education means basically bringing everybody into line. They are trickier about their methods than in the past. No longer do they use the big stick to create uniformity. Now they do it by psychological manipulation. Appeals are made from the gods of mental health. Peers should adjust to one another. This concept is a trivialization of community and a sabotaging of the learning process.

Establishing phony fellowship patterns with peers is simply a new way to create the leaden conformity that crushes individuality and sensibility. The obituary for the famed Lutheran leader Franklin Clark Fry stated that he was less a shepherd sweetly leading the sheep than a rump-kicker of the lambs. Real shepherds know, of course, that poster art representation is false. Sheep frequently suffer from community adjustment overkill. Hence the shepherds must disperse them and make them go out on their own for food and air.

Teachers should act the same way toward students. They should liberate the students from fearfully looking over their shoulders to see whether or not they "are in line." Boys' knuckles were red in the old days because they had been soundly rapped. Today, I am sorry to say, they are often white with the tension of trying to be "normal" like the others.

Teachers should avoid the twin demons of individualism and conformity. They should prize individuality and sensibility. This requires the capacity to read the "body talk" as well as the "mind and heart talk" of the students. Take time to sense the thinking and feeling processes of each student. Reverence the personhood of the students. Yea, even see the Christ who appears before you!

Schools and Centers

School and centers can be a community of social heritage and faith. They can be the lifeline to the past history and culture of the country and the Church. In an age when roots are torn up so casually, these institutions may be the only remaining living "time machines" we have left. The cultural worth of the Church and the country need not be lost so long as the schools and centers stand.

While schools and centers play a role in preparing students for careers and for adult living, the learning center is itself a life experience. It is also a place to enter into and luxuriate in the discovery of the mind and its capacities. Education should be more than a *rite de passage*, an intellectual puberty rite that always looks to something else. It is a moment when students have the leisure to enjoy the use of their

intelligence. We scorn the drudgery of the Victorian schools. We
should be just as quick to scorn the current drudgery of the "computer
model" of education that stuffs zillions of facts into minds but seldom
pauses to let those minds mull, meditate, evaluate, and criticize what
is on the "input sheet."

Actually, the easier manner of an earlier age allowed students the
grace to stop and think about the material and maybe do their own
searching. But today's "rat-race" society is suspicious of an education
that is not in a hurry. The pace of the classroom should match the
frenzy of the freeway. The Greek word for school meant *leisure.* But
our education is a breathless, uncritical seizure of data. What should
be a balmy ambling becomes instead an Olympian race.

I once saw a cartoon of a snail that read, "What's the hurry?" I have
always enjoyed the fable of the turtle and the hare. It was the plod-
ding turtle, not the fleet hare, that won the race. Ben Franklin asserts
that "slow and steady wins the race." Perhaps the students who re-
sort to drugs that they call "speed" are aptly taking out their revenge
on an educational society that has fostered the illusion that the truly
educated are always out of breath.

Wouldn't it be a blessing if Christian education should take the leadership in helping students enjoy the wonderland of their own minds?
What a grace it would be to assist students to appreciate the slower,
natural pace of a quiet leisure and a sobriety of intention that achieves
real victories rather than the Pyrrhic ones so common today!

Content

A good deal of time has already been devoted in Chapter 2 to the origin of religious content. You may recall how religious experience was
related to basic teachings. The community of living believers was further brought out as the fundamental context for the content. What
this all comes down to is that intellectual content should seem to have
a connection with life experience, otherwise the content is disembodied like a ghost and will appear to have no vitality or meaning
to the students.

This is why there is so much talk about experience-based education.
It is also the reason for an emphasis on the so-called "affective domain" in learning. Truth is not just an object for the brain; it is also a
subject for the heart. Clearly, this is not an either-or situation.
Teachers cannot choose up sides between experience and content.
Both parts are needed. Experience provides motivation to learn content and find meaning in expressing it. Content, on the other hand, is

a distilled reflection on life and a standardized memory of experience as well as an effort to make meaning out of it.

This quest for meaning implies that a process of thinking is equally important for rendering content. If experience puts some life blood into the content, thinking processes put some soul and meaning into it. Content is more than a news report about an experience. It is more than facts about life. Content itself is subject to arrangement in logical thought patterns that result in meaning, judgments, evaluations, and decisions.

What, then, shall teachers advert to on the question of content? 1) Does the student have an experience of the content? 2) Is the student capable of thinking about the content? Has he acquired any capacity to use the muscles of his mind to think?

Content for Christian Education

Keeping in mind the above principles of content in the light of experience and thinking processes, we can see three areas of content for Christian educators.

Religious Content

This includes the Bible, Creeds, Church history, laws and moral principles of religious heritage, and contemporary religious thought. The chapter on basic teachings has already covered these topics.

Humanistic Content

Arts

You will note that Jesus did not confine himself to quoting the Bible in his teachings. He was not limited by the Torah and the Talmud (bible commentaries and theology) in his efforts to communicate the Gospel. The parables of Christ drew from the life experience of the people—tax collectors, lilies of the field, vineyards, wedding practices, and so on. In other words, he used "humanistic content" as well as strictly religious material for education.

It was the same way with Saint Paul. When Saint Paul preached to the humanist Athenians, he approached them with their favorite images. He walked through Athens, explored its moods, and attempted to get the feel of the people. He listened to their poets and their philosophers as they tried to expound the meaning of life. He examined their gods to see where they placed their ultimate concerns. When he was ready to preach to them he came as one who appreciated their human interests. He even quoted from their poets: "In him we live and move and have our being, as some of your own poets have put it, 'for we too are his offspring.' " (Acts 17:28)

Paul's other sermons are also full of humanist allusions. He cites in particular examples from sports such as racing, boxing, and wrestling. Just as Jesus used agrarian images to enliven his message, Paul employed an abundance of urban anecdotes to achieve the same purpose.

Christian educators should be ready to use the arts of literature, history, biography, painting, music, sculpture, and drama to bring life to their message. These outbursts of the human spirit are ultimately caused by God who imparts the creative gift in the first place. Not only are they illustrative of the Gospel message, they are also speaking of values that require discussion. Some of the values point toward God and others do not. Help students to see the difference between the two types.

Sciences
a) *Behavioral Sciences*
Psychology and sociology can be most helpful today to the Christian educator. *Counseling psychology* aids the teacher to set up the atmosphere of trust which frees both student and teacher to enter the adventure of learning. It assists the teacher to be alert to emotional blocks that keep the student from entering into the learning situation. It sensitizes the teacher to appreciate the network of relationships that affect the individual performance of each student. How much more effective group discussions are today, due to the insights given by clinical psychology in the area of group dynamics.

Developmental Psychology This has done so much to nail down more systematically the level of awareness and thinking of students at different times in their lives. Think of Piaget's complex analysis of early childhood. Think of Kohlberg's useful model for moral thinking and Fowler's similar pursuit in the area of faith thinking. Recall Erickson's classical outlining of the "ages of man" and the series of identity crises that attend stage developments. All educators are supposed to begin where the student is in order to help him or her move onward. The developmentalists give us useful models to detect these stages and hence be more effective in relating material to the student's readiness.

Sociology While psychology helps us see the student as an individual person, sociology aids us to perceive the context within which that individual operates. Sociological studies make us realize that everyone works in a context, and that the context does much to influence the learning and moral behavior of the individual. For example, sociology points out the impact of high social mobility and the communications revolution on the emotional stability and value consciousness of people. If people move a lot, their emotional stability is almost continually placed under strain. If people try to gobble up enormous amount of facts due to the communications revolution, their ability to make sound moral judgments and evaluations is paralyzed. Psychology provides the "text" (student). Sociology provides the "context" (community). It should be self-evident how important these two fine co-workers are for Christian education.

b) *Educational Theory*
Christian educators benefit from the thinking of such educational giants as Montessori, Dewey, Jungmann, Pestalozzi, Goldbrunner, Holt, Bruner, and Ashton-Warner, to name a few. Educational theorists tend to be romantic, classical, or developmental. There is a grain of truth to be found in each type of philosophy. All three types should be heeded, pondered, and then integrated into a full teaching approach.

The Romanticist The Romanticist thinks of the student as a plant. All the knowledge is inside, just as all the life of the plant is inside the seed. The task of the teacher is to create the right environment, the good soil out of which the student will grow. Spread the sunlight of invitational love and the inner truth will blossom. Human beings are noble savages who should not be corrupted by being stuffed with civilization's lost dreams. Instead, clear away the jungle and the savage plant will bloom. The educational method for the Romanticist is *discovery*. Create an environment of something to discover, and the student will find it, own it, and know it.

What is the value of the Romanticist? He or she appreciates the individuality of the student, the special talent and gift that lie within. He is aware of the student as a person to be honored, cherished, and reverenced. The Romanticist appreciates the enormous value of self-startership and experience in learning.

Where does the Romanticist go wrong? If he trivializes the work, there develops a lapse into mere permissiveness, a discounting of the history of culture and inherited wisdom, and a poor mouthing of civilization because he can see only its faults and not its values.

The Classicist The Classicist sees the student as a computer. The student is an empty head into which information is to be stuffed. The data to be put into that head is the history of the culture both past and present and all available useful information from the contemporary world needed in order to prepare one for life. The Classicist tends to use the *lecture* method because it is the most efficient and fastest way of imparting information.

What is the value of the Classicist? He or she appreciates the capacity of the human mind to absorb data. He/she is impressed with the power of memory and the power of knowledge. This type of teacher is, correctly, a keeper of the flame, a watchman of the history of culture and the hard-won wisdom of the past.

Where does the Classicist go wrong? He or she tends to ignore the individuality of the student. Such a teacher is loathe to involve the student in the learning process, other than by hearing and taking tests. The emphasis on information absorption puts too great an attention on the memory and results in little appreciation of the power of thinking. The teacher curbs the capacity of the students to make their own judgments and substitutes her own instead.

The Developmentalist   The Developmentalist sees the young student as a poet-wonderer alive to the possibilities of life. He or she sees the older student as the philosopher-questioner alive to the paradoxes of life. This type of teacher approaches the very young as a coadventurer, encouraging their idealism and sharing in their discoveries. He is probably field-trip-oriented, but unlike the Romantic presents his own experiences as well.

With the older students the teacher is like Plato, asking and challenging them to clarify their thoughts. He encourages their questions and moves them to ask ultimate ones. The teacher is not much given to lecturing, nor does he possess a romantic view of students. There is a distinct recognition of their limitations and their inexperience.

What is the value of the Developmentalist? He or she clearly touches students at the deepest level of education. By keeping alive their sense of wonder, such a teacher assists the students to retain a total view of life and not to lapse into categorizing that cuts life into too many pieces. By pushing them to be ultimate questioners, the teacher shows them how to cope with life's paradoxes, how to analyze its mysteries without destroying the sense of mystery, and how to be critical without being carping.

Where does the Developmentalist go wrong? She can go wrong by creating a false distaste for the specialist, a superficial knowledge of history, or too great an impatience with facts. Such a teacher could also be creating a mere "wool gatherer" and not a person balanced between the ideal and the real. And like any teacher, she may miss the special beauty of an individual student.

The grain of truth in each of these approaches to educational theory is this:

Romanticist:	The student is a person with inner riches.
	Help the student to be a self-starter and discoverer.
Classicist:	The student is inevitably an historical person.
	Help the student appreciate cultural transmission.
Developmentalist:	The young student is a poet/wonderer.
	The older student is a philosopher/questioner.
	Share the adventure of the younger one.
	Challenge and question the older one.

Take these three insights and "methods" and make them the major goals of your own educational theory. The integration of the insights is always a personal matter. That integration will, I believe, help you avoid the pitfalls of permissiveness, the forgetfulness of basics, and the inadvertence to your poets and philosophers.

c) *Administrative Theory*
Christian educators not only teach in classrooms, they also must run schools, centers, and departments. This means that they require the acquisition of skills such as:

1. How to manage.
2. How to budget and plan. (Cf. Chapter 7)
3. How to establish a job description.
4. How to run a meeting. You know how often a meeting is called and there is so little preparation for it. The items for discussion are in a state of disarray. The participants are not helped to stick to the subject. Hidden agendas are permitted to surface and take over, and so on.
5. How to relate to parish boards of education and the education and liturgy committees of parish councils.
6. How to write a philosophy of the school or center with some clear goals and practical ways to achieve them.
7. How to acquire a passion for detail. Without question detail is annoying and tedious, but no good administrator can avoid it. On the other hand, the best administrator balances the Big Picture with a nitty-gritty approach.
8. How to assess needs. (The process section of Chapter 1 is an approach to this skill.)

When it comes to being a Christian administrator, the theme of religious leadership should be uppermost. The curse of administrators is that they seem to lapse into mere secularity, running the school, center, or department much the same as a business person manages a store. They even use the expression, "minding the store." But the Christian administrator is engaging in a religious ministry and ought not to forget this high goal no matter how many details bog him/her down. Following are some reflections for Christian administration.

Religious Leadership

Distinguish faith community from organization. Organization is the rational arrangement and ordering of policies and procedures in the school. Community is that mysterious spirit of concordance of heart and mind which we pray will occur in our organization. To over-simplify this distinction: Man makes organizations. God makes community. Reason organizes. Prayer begs for community.

Both elements are needed. The biblical Samuel agonizes as he sees the era of Judges come to an end and the age of the kingdom start. The world of the Judges was one of faith community, a nomadic free-spirited life. God moves Samuel to institute the kingdom through Saul. Why? The community of Judges, without an organizational base, was doomed to dissolve.

Let us state this in our own terms: The work of organization is an institutional prayer for the coming of community. It is the condition for the possibility of community's arrival. The advent of community is a miracle and grace to which we respond with thanksgiving. We organize. We pray. We receive. We thank.

Don't forget the human touch. You are more than a secular administrator. You are a religious leader. Your model is the Good Shepherd. He takes time to know people. He allows himself to be known—to be vulnerable. As leader you walk ahead of your faculty and students, showing them direction and purpose. But as Idaho shepherds will tell you, there is a walking behind as well, for at times there is a "rump-kicking" aspect of leadership. You must provoke your people to responsible behavior.

The human touch means that you must remain an earth person. Know your people's names, their birthdays, and perhaps some of their hopes and fears. Go to their wakes, their hospital beds, their weddings, or what have you. Solicit invitations to visit their classes when they are putting their best foot forward. Let them know you would like to see them at their best.

Listen to them when they talk to you. Treat them with full attention. Restrain yourself from looking over their shoulder to your next duty and appointment. Hear and encourage their questions. Heschel asserts that religion begins in wonder. This wonder grows out of passionate questioning that is the external form of the interior questing of all hearts for the ultimate.

Take time from your administrative duties to pray, read, and think. Read inspirational stories about secondary school leadership — for example, *The Rector of Justin* by Louis Auchincloss and *To Serve Them All My Days* by John Delderfield. Balance the one-dimensional abstractions of your professional reading with the multidimensional form of literature. Be a person of humane letters.

Take advantage of humanistic sciences. Social psychology offers you an abundance of techniques for community development.

a. *Flanders Analysis* tells you how you rate on a scale of one to ten in your speech patterns. Are you autocratic or democratic? The scale value refers to self-insight. This scale can give you an honest appreciation of your mode of speech. If you thought you were Jefferson but found out you were Nero, you can at least be more candid about your approaches in conversation. You may never completely get over being Nero, but you can learn to temper your approach with some self-deprecating humor.

b. *Transactional Analysis.* When are you acting as parent, adult, or child in given situations? What effect are your actions having on morale and growth in your school?

c. *Value Clarification.* This intriguing technique, used so well with youngsters, might benefit you and your faculty too. (E.g., rank order: light, dollar bill, rose, Bible, gun.)

d. *Kohlberg's Six Stages.* These are useful categories — not absolute, of course, but interesting pointers. Is your moral thinking mostly conventional, or postconventional?

e. *Systems Analysis.* Your school is a learning system. Everything is interrelated for good or ill. Find out what that interrelationship is in your school.

These suggestions are only *pro forma* hints. Although one may not enjoy gaming with human personality and relation, the approaches may be of some use.

Develop a philosophy and theology of education. Relate this point to the observations about thinking, praying, and reading. Your development should not be a hurried one. It should grow slowly as plants do. It ought to have an organic quality. You can grow in your development two ways.

First, you can grow inductively. Look at what you are doing in your schools. The performance illustrates an implicit philosophy. Also see *Giving Form to the Vision*, an NCEA document on implementing the bishops' pastoral letter *To Teach As Jesus Did*.

After you see what you have done, you can make some abstract statements that point the way to your philosophy. You are not at the level of philosophy with such statements, but you are on the way. At least you can see the difference between what you conclude and what your official philosophy says.

Second, you can grow deductively. This method is an expressly *a priori* approach. It takes its starting point from the reflections of saints and thinkers. For example, consider Saint Luke's story of faith community in Acts. Cf. especially Acts 4:31: "And they came together, and they prayed together. And the walls of the room shook. And they were all filled with the Holy Spirit, and they spoke thereafter the word of God with boldness."

You would do well to meditate on Lonergan's chapter on religion in his book *Method in Theology*. I have drawn some thoughts from him along this line in an article, "Religious Experience: Public Utterance and Dogma Development," in the *American Ecclesiastical Review*, March 1974. I wrote a more technical article on the same subject in *Momentum*, May 1972. This article is entitled "What Is Religious Education?" The *Sunday Visitor* column "Wine and Gall" nominated me "Establishment Pentecostal of the Year" for that gobbledygook presentation.

It may be hoped that the inductive and deductive will meet somewhere in the future and touch a spark of the soul (*scintilla animae*) from which could come some workable philosophy/theology of Catholic education for our time. Again, the melding should be a patient project, slowly built, and carefully assimilated.

Get a guru. Alfred North Whitehead has asserted that every school should allow for exposure to greatness: "Education must involve exposure to greatness if it is to leave its mark." Jerome Bruner speaks of such a person as a "dysfunctional man." In Eastern Europe a century ago, members of the Jewish ghettos were proud of their scholar. They did not call him the competent educator or the professional administrator. They merely exclaimed, "There goes our beautiful man."

Could this be what Newman spoke of in his idea of a gentleman. Perhaps we need aboard our ship, if we can find him or her, a poet in residence, an official bum, a pied piper, a naturally likeable person, a gifted cruise director. Possibly this person will not always be likeable for he may have some painful criticisms to make. The person will be "beautiful" because he or she will be able to entice or criticize while being free from the organization process and at the same time retaining the role of *amicus curiae* (friend of the court).

As kings once had their jesters, maybe schools should have their gurus, exempt from the tedium but responsible for delighting, tweaking, inspiring, and scolding—for consciousness raising, in the current argot.

I don't know how seriously I can push this last point, but if even science today searches for the "odd man hypothesis", perhaps we could benefit by an official odd person in our midst.

The Parish Community

In practical terms the truly fundamental unit in Christian education is the parish community. Here are the trenches where the action takes place. The diocesan structure may supervise and guide, but it is in the parish community where Christian education will take place. Strangely enough, something so obvious is often forgotten, and the results are not always pleasant.

Educational units, be they schools or centers, have a way of assuming a life of their own. This growth is not done maliciously, but mostly out of a sense of dogged determination to do all the needed work, with the unfortunate result that the context of the educational endeavor—namely, the parish structure—is forgotten. One unpleasant result can be a Mexican standoff between the religious leader of the educational task and the pastor and his board and council. Similar standoffs appear in conflicts over liturgy and different expectations about Catholic beliefs and practices as articulated by the parish and by the educators.

It's not the merits of the expectations that deserve attention and criticism so much as the regrettable forgetfulness of education about its context. This is why the opening chapter, about the community of faith, is devoted so largely to parish involvement. Let us return to a favorite theme: *The Community Of Faith That Was Once Assumed Must Be Created Consciously.*

Advertence to the context does not solve all problems, but it does eliminate some unnecessary ones and gives everyone involved a clearer sense of purpose and responsibility. Like the early Church, we must recover the Eucharistic vision of One Bread, One Body, and One Church.

The Charter for Christian Education

Teachers and administrators must include in their plans the goals implied by the guidelines of recent documents on Christian education. I have already alluded to these earlier, but once again let us consider the context of teacher/administrator training and evaluation.

The General Catechetical Directory. This Church international set of guidelines stresses that we are in the business of helping students acquire a living, conscious, and active faith through the light of instruction. The *faith* spoken about here is both the act of believing and committing oneself to Christ, as well as the act of knowing the truths of faith. The *instruction* should be understood in the light of the three attitudes about teaching theory (Romanticist, Classicist, Developmentalist) mentioned earlier.

Basic Teachings. The chapter on Basic Teachings gives my own explanation of this document, emphasizing the origin, context, and language of the teachings and their relationship to faith and moral behavior.

"To Teach As Jesus Did." This well-known pastoral letter of the American bishops on Christian education established clearly the goals of 1) Announcing the authentic Gospel of Christ, 2) Forming a community of love around the Eucharistic Table, 3) Developing lives of social concern and service to the world, and 4) Building structures that service both the community at worship and its search for justice and peace.

The National Catechetical Directory. This adaptation of the GCD for the United States Catholic Church establishes a number of important guidelines for Christian education. For example:

1. Appreciate the meaning of revelation and faith response.
2. Develop a consciousness of Church as the standing context of Christian education.
3. Learn how liturgy is the Church's supreme celebration of recognizing and experiencing Christ's Easter presence in an atmosphere of faith, hope, love, and concern for others.
4. Ponder and practice the connection between faith and moral behavior both at a social and at a personal level.
5. Delineate the major aspects of the ministry of the Christian educator from the double viewpoints of training and mission.
6. Conduct a Christian education that is sensitive to the current ad-

vances in educational theory, especially as enhanced by the behavioral sciences.

7. Create administrative structures that will truly serve the cause of Christian education. Recognize the abundance of resources that bring vitality to the teaching situation.

Why do we need a charter? Because Christian educators should know where they are going. People should not assume they know what they are doing, especially when so much has changed so fast. One need scarcely point out how much confusion so many people have labored under in the last fifteen years. Thousands of talks have been given about the need for change and about the values of change. The change itself seems to present no problem. There aren't very many people around who need this kind of sensitizing. But where do we go? That's the reason for the charter.

It is hoped that Catholic colleges and graduate schools of education will incorporate the charter into their thinking as they prepare teachers and administrators for schools and centers. Hopefully, dioceses will be equally sensitive in this matter as they conduct their own programs.

Methods

The explosion of teaching methods has generated some mystic jargon that sometimes hides the methods from the teacher, as well as from the student. It is important to disentangle the morass of jargon from reality so that Christian educators can use the many fine methods available for catechesis. Technically speaking, not all the following suggestions are considered strictly methods, but let us think of the term broadly. Again, Catholic colleges and graduate departments of education should help prospective Christian educators and administrators to adapt these methods for use in catechesis. Here are ten of these "methods," with some comments.

1. Affective Domain

This is merely a fancy term for emotional life. We all know that everybody has emotions, but somehow the conceptual bias in education tends to treat it as a "brain to brain" process, leaving the class full of lonely hearts. There should be "heart to heart" communication too. Minds and hearts ought not to be separated on grounds of objectivity. Emotions should never be allowed to blackmail the mind, nor should the mind be permitted to be repressive of emotions.

Here is where personalist philosophy comes to the rescue. It tells us that we should approach the other as a person, not as a ghost in a machine (a disembodied mind) or as a forest fire (a disembodied heart). Treat the other as a full person who has both intelligence and feeling and is in search of integration and fulfillment.

Christian educators are always going to be talking about loving God and people. Won't this love require heart? The Church is ever struggling to motivate people to a behavior consistent with their faith. Is not one element of motivation dealing with feeling? Motivation comes from a Latin word (*movere*) meaning "to move." So does emotion. Leave out the affective domain, and you will produce a community of ghosts. Ignore the intelligence, and you will produce flaming fanatics. Deal with *persons*, however, and you will produce believing disciples.

2. "Back to Basics" (Memorizing)

The fire alarms that signal low reading scores, inability to count, and blank stares when people are asked to recite the Ten Commandments are prompting a "Back to Basics" movement. The teaching method implied in all this is *memorizing*. The very thought of memorizing is enough to make progressive educators froth at the mouth. Their fears are well grounded—who can forget the useless drudgery of hours, even years, of equating memorizing with education?

However, it looks as if we are presently at the other end of the spectrum, where nothing is memorized other than outlines in order to pass exams. But the fact of the matter is that God gave us a memory and we need to use it and train it. In a sense we know what we remember. Currently, there have been some studies about *eidetic* memory (photographic). The findings are that a small proportion of the very young are born with this talent, but most of them lose it by the time they grow up.

The majority of us are not fortunate enough to have been born with eidetic memory, let alone have the misfortune of losing it. But all of us generally have good memories when we are young. Old-fashioned memorizing took advantage of that youthful talent and helped keep memories supple until the capacity to use logic and engage in wider experiences was able to replace it.

Not only does there seem to be no harm in *moderate* memorizing as a teaching method (especially for retaining some basic ideas), but there can be some positive value to it. To be able to say some prayers and fundamental religious ideas and principles by heart is a blessing, not a tyranny. How charmed many of us are today by hearing someone recite lines of poetry by heart, even into their old age. Things of beauty are indeed a joy forever—if they can be recalled. We forget more than ninety percent of all we hear (and maybe we should). We probably can recall ninety percent of what we memorize, provided the memory work is not overdone.

What about the meaning of the material? Naturally, memorization should always be accompanied by explanation, experience, and logic.

3. Behavior Modification (Habit Training)

Behavior modification is a clever updating of the old method of habit training. In old-fashioned character education, the teacher tried to get the students to practice good behavior by forming their exterior acts along the lines of good habits. Then, as now, the idea was: "Change the outside and the inside will follow suit." This is all very similar to Dale Carnegie's well-known advice for getting a good start for your day no matter how you feel. After breakfast, square your shoulders, hold your head high, put a smile on your face, and whistle a happy tune as you walk to work.

It is also the sort of method practiced by Ben Franklin with his self-improvement diaries. Remember that behavior modification means the changing of one's behavior from a bad type to a good one. The method is exterior rather than interior. Instead of beginning with a logical statement and moving to a behavioral conclusion, you begin with a command, imposed by self or others, and simply force yourself to go along.

What is critical to the method is positive motivation. You can use a carrot or a stick to move a jackass. Behavior mod lingo says, "Use the carrot." B. F. Skinner, its modern proponent, calls this method positive reinforcement. When a military chaplain complained to Ben Franklin about the low attendance of the troops at religious services, he received a behavior mod reply. Franklin advised him to provide the soldiers with a glass of rum after prayers, even if this might seem beneath his dignity. Franklin noted that, thereafter, prayers were never better attended—how much better this motivation was than a few days in jail for missing chapel!

Franklin wanted to reach a point in his life where he would never commit any faults. Like a good modern self-manager, he made a list of thirteen virtues he wanted to acquire along with an explanation of the types of conduct designated. For Temperance, he wrote, "Eat not unto dullnesss. Drink not to elevation." Moreover, he kept a notebook with a page devoted to each of the virtues, seven columns for each day of the week and a letter grading system in order for him to see how he was doing. He admitted he never achieved his ideals perfectly, but he claimed this method made him a better and happier man. The system did not make him stuffy or moralistic either. In his seventy-ninth year he still complained of how hard it was to overcome pride, the worst of his faults. But if he overcame that, he might be tempted to be proud of his humility.

Used in the Franklin sense, the behavior mod system of Skinner can be a useful educational method that keeps the teacher alert to being positive in reinforcing behavior, aware of the value of outer behavior on inner attitudes, and sensitive to a climate that is favorable to the growth of faith. Here is where liturgy and the context of the community of faith are, for some, an unnoticed source of "social engineering" without the crass malice and disrespect for freedom implied by the term.

4. Behavioral Objectives

Once you know your goals, how will you achieve them? One way is to reduce them to more manageable bits. What specifics of knowledge content do you want your students to know? How much thinking capacity do you expect them to exert? What behaviors do you want? This method asks you to be clear about your aims and to establish ranges of achievement on scales. You are required to think through, perhaps more than you normally have, the hopes you have for your students. It means the painful writing out of such expectations as concretely as possible. The justification for it is that this procedure will take the fuzziness out of your thinking and reveal to yourself what you are looking for in your students.

This performance based approach to teaching becomes especially useful in training teachers toward continual self-improvement. This is the so-called Competency education. A Christian educator should possess certain qualities and competencies to fulfill his mission. The qualities are mysterious, nonnegotiable items, not easily measurable. They include faith, holiness, depth of commitment to the Gospel, and union with Christ.

The competencies are partially measurable. The National Conference of Directors of Religious Education of the National Catholic Educational Association has developed an excellent instrument on this matter. It is entitled, *The Qualities and Competencies of the Religion Teacher*. The opening section describes the qualities needed. The remainder of the book is an evaluation tool designed to help teachers improve seventeen possible competencies needed to achieve five major goals. The rating scales range from good to better to best and the sub-descriptions help the teacher to tell how to do the rating. The following sample sheet gives you an idea of how to go about the activity.

Competency 1

The teacher demonstrates the competency to carry out a variety of goal-directed learning experiences.

_____ Provides an attractive physical and congenial social climate conducive to good learning

_____ Is able to carry out learning experiences which are suggested in the teacher's manual

_____ Keeps parents and clergy informed of the learning materials and techniques

_____ Structures classroom activities in such a way as to give alternatives to students

_____ Develops responsibility in students for maintaining a physical and social climate conducive to learning

_____ Modifies or develops learning activities that meet student needs more effectively than preplanned textbook exercises

_____ Encourages students to independent and self-directed study

_____ Takes advantage of opportunities in which parents and clergy may assist in the teaching process

_____ Has knowledge of current educational innovations and experimentations

_____ Establishes a climate of respect for individual freedom and a sense of responsibility

_____ Develops and utilizes a wide variety of activities to meet special learning needs, including programs of independent study

_____ Directs activities so that students assist each other in the performance of individual and cooperative learning activities

_____ Takes initiative and provides opportunities and means whereby parents and clergy may join in the teaching process

_____ Occasionally conducts controlled experimentation projects

| 1 | 2 | 3 | 4 | 5 | 6 | 7 | 8 | 9 |

Competency 5

The teacher demonstrates the competency to evaluate student learning progress in relation to program goals.

_____ Recognizes the need of evaluation for program improvement and personal growth. Does not feel threatened by evaluation

_____ Has an understanding of the basic principles of psychological testing and measurement

_____ Understands the use and validity of appropriate evaluation instruments and techniques, such as teacher-made and standardized tests, rating scales, and observations

_____ Communicates results of evaluation to students, parents, and other proper reference groups

_____ Uses a variety of evaluative devices to assess student needs and achievement in both the affective and cognitive domain

_____ Provides for the students' involvement in the evaluation of their learning

_____ Utilizes parental, faculty, and clergy input in the ongoing evaluation

_____ Structures and utilizes an ongoing program of evaluation to identify student needs and redesign of objectives

_____ Structures activities to promote student self-evaluation and feedback

_____ Shows initiative in redesigning program to meet identified student needs

_____ Incorporates concerns of parents and clergy in modification of program design

| 1 | 2 | 3 | 4 | 5 | 6 | 7 | 8 | 9 |

5. Programmed Learning

This, along with all forms of computer-aided instruction, is simply a method of imparting content that, with its stop-start mechanical ability, assures that the student takes in the content with some degree of comprehension. Clearly it is no substitute for contact with a person. But then again, neither is reading books. That's why we call book-worms "bookish." At some point in time they have to meet people. The most one can say for programmed learning in religion is that, as in any other discipline, it is a self-help that may put something across to the student where other methods have failed. It must be considered as part of a larger picture.

6. Lecture Method

Obviously, this needs no explanation, since it is still, despite all criticism, the most widely used form of communication in all of education. Everyone knows its strengths and its weaknesses. I have pointed them out earlier in this chapter when talking about the Classicist theory of education.

7. Individualized Instruction

At Oxford and Cambridge Universities they call this tutoring. It's what coaches do on football fields, mothers do at home, and directors do in theaters and film studios. It is one of the most effective forms of all education, and probably the least used by the majority of educators other than sports and drama coaches. It's really not fair to be so critical about how little this method is used, since the sheer size of most classes prohibits the use of this *Best Method*. So rare is it, that it must be confined to an aristocratic few.

Some adaptations have been made through learning activity packages and individually guided instruction. These adaptations have been handled with surprising success when the teachers have been willing to prepare above and beyond the call of duty. Needless to say, this personal approach to education does much to help students appreciate the faith and caring concern of the teacher so that when Christ is spoken of, the feeling exists that Lord is also present.

8. Inductive Teaching/Learning

Practically all modern forms of teaching approaches emanate from some form of inductive learning. Most textbooks are filled with materials that operate from the viewpoint of inquiry-discovery. Input is given, but every effort is made to help the student engage in some form of self-startership. Socrates is the "saint" under whose patronage this type of learning developed. His method of questioning and searching serves as the underlying theory for its support. Dialogue and quest are the environment for its procedure.

In the chapters on spiritual and moral education, this type of procedure is recommended for moral and faith development. The lists of activities found in most texts are adjuncts of the inductive approach. For example:

a. Reading
b. Homework
c. Value clarification
d. Field trips
e. Case studies
f. Audiovisuals
g. Opinion polls
h. Creative prayer
i. Posters
j. Banners
k. Camera blowups
l. Skits
m. Musicals
n. Diaries
o. Home movies
p. Home TV taping
q. Role playing
r. Group discussions

These and many other activities are among the numerous ways that inductive teaching/learning has become a rich and valued development for all education as well as for Christian education. They help to create confidence in the class as well as a spirit of self-startership in the students.

9. Montessori Method

Used mostly with preschool and primary age children, this method is based on the principle that children should be treated as children, not as small adults. It is a total approach to children in which outer structures and the inner person are carefully wedded. Emphasis is on skill building and helping the students to perceive the basic structures that will help them later appreciate the intellectual abstractions they will be learning. In the hands of skilled teachers, it is probably one of the finest approaches to children in use today. One of the problems it faces is the educational gap that occurs when the child enters a non-Montessori environment. The pain is normally minimal. The greater complaint is that the student gradually loses the sense of wonder and self-containment taught by the Montessori method, unless teachers in the new environment happen to know how to continue and foster it (or unless parents find a way to do so.)

10. Team Teaching

This is not a method, strictly speaking, but an oft-tried approach that rarely seems to work. Team teaching is probably a prime example of a characteristic of our times, the "age of great ideas that aren't working." The real reason team teaching rarely works is that most teachers are simply not interested in other teachers' disciplines. What a splendid chance this type of approach could afford for religion, literature, history, drama, and music to join hands! This sort of thing has been tried and almost always has been found wanting. Somehow the various biorhythms don't merge.

The best we can hope for is that a "renaissance" type person moves to the chair of religion. Such a person would have the whole "team" inside him or her and would possess the gift of uniting the vision of many arts and sciences. A rare accomplishment? Yes. A possible one? Yes. Do we see it often? Sorry.

Summary

Teacher Talk, as we see, takes us through many byroads, such as:

1. What is education?
   A system that introduces religious and social consciousness while respecting the individuality and sensibility of the student.
2. What is a school and Center?
   A community of faith and social heritage; the one last refuge in a hurrying world where there can be leisure for learning.
3. What is the content for Christian education?
   Something that grows out of experience and is subject to thinking. This includes:
   A. *Religious content:* Bible, Creeds, Doctrines, Moral principles, etc.
   B. *Humanistic content:*
      Arts: literature, biography, history, etc.
      Sciences: clinical and experimental psychology, sociology
      Educational Theory: 1) Romanticist, 2) Classicist, 3) Developmentalist
      Administrative Theory: How to be a religious leader.
4. What about Parish Community?
   Absolutely central for Christian education. It is the essential context in most cases for catechesis.
5. Why do we need a charter for Christian education?
   Because Christian educators should know where they are going. The GCD, Basic Teachings, "To Teach As Jesus Did," and the NCD are the substantial elements of the charter.
6. What major methods can Christian educators use?
   Affective Domain
   "Back to Basics"

Behavior Modification
Behavioral Objectives
Programmed Learning
Inductive Teaching/Learning
Montessori Method
Team Teaching
Lecture Method
Individualized Instruction

All teachers know there is even yet more to discuss, but there should be enough to ponder at the moment. Let us conclude with these words from Abraham Heschel:

Religious education must recognize the dialectic of the human situation, pay attention to both the individual and the people, to discipline and spontaneity, to principle and example, to the pattern and the poetry, to inwardness and outwardness, to ideas and events, to cultivate intellectual piety as well as ritual observance, stillness as well as discipline, the importance of patience as a way of listening, rejection of complacency and conceit, the vital necessity of inner growth, the building of responsibility, the active involvement in aiding our fellow men, as well as a sense of authenticity.*

*Rev. Alfred McBride, O.Praem., *Heschel: Religious Educator* (Denville, N.J.: Dimension Books, 1973), p. 140.

9

PARENTS ARE "THE PEOPLE" TOO*

Insanity is hereditary. You can get it from your children.
Sam Levenson

Aside from such wry comments as this, it's hard to say anything consistently useful about parenthood. You can't consider parents without considering the children they're parents of. And the question of childhood in turn is one of the most baffling under the sun. Parents and children taken together are families, a very strange and awkward sociological entity.

We tend to think—especially in our nostalgic periods—that families and children were less complicated in the past. But that may simply be because most people in former times didn't feel compelled to spend their days in scrutinizing and figuring everything out. In fact, recent evidence suggests that before 1800 the idea of families as we understand them didn't even exist. It begins to appear that our notions of close-knit, loving families belong to fairly recent history, perhaps the last two or three hundred years at most.

In any case, during the past several generations, ordinary people seemed to take a lot more for granted than we do. Whether something was so or not, most people mutually agreed to accept a particular version of what was so. Little aphorisms helped to maintain the structure and perhaps the illusion. "Children should be seen and not heard" preserved decorum and allowed parents to get their work done. But "not heard" not only meant not being noisy, it also meant "not listened to." Children's concerns were not taken as seriously as they are now.

The images we used to get from the Catholic press and from parochial schools likewise suggested that there were neat and orderly processes to be followed. Some of these clichés were silly; some were cruel in their shallowness. For example, "Happy, healthy parents will produce happy, healthy children." But what if parents *aren't* happy or healthy? Apparently it's a moral obligation to be so, and it's their

---

* This chapter was written by Janet M. Bennett of Boonton, N.J.

own fault if they're not. And what of those physically and emotionally handicapped children whose difficulties arise from causes we can't
as yet identify or control? By implication, nevertheless, parents were
made to see themselves as guilty of some deficiency at home.

Such statements are logically flawed, as is the following: "If you
truly love one another, all problems will work out," which I found in a
pamphlet on marital difficulties. Such statements confuse the solution with the problem, and hold people responsible for the very things
they need help with. Instead of guidance and reassurance there are
only guilt and frustration. To admit to having a problem in this context is the same thing as admitting to doing something wrong. So in
the past people hid their problems. Many, still under the influence of
the old platitudes, still hide their problems.

Aside from the guilt-inducing moralisms of these pious preachings,
there is the guilt induced by sweeping inaccuracy: "Communication
gaps don't start suddenly in the teen years," asserts an article heavy on
parental responsibility. When they do—as they often do even in the
best-adjusted family—parents search their consciences to find out
where they've failed. Communication gaps *do* occur—and maybe they
should—as the young person begins to separate himself or herself from
total immersion in and dependency on parents. Youngsters need privacy, just as they did in grammar school when they were obsessed
with having their own things and their own places to keep them, often
with elaborate lock systems. At nine and ten years of age, this obsession is regarded as cute and tolerable, because childish pursuits are
considered harmless. But in the teen years these demands to be left
alone and a reluctance to confide can be threatening to parents, who
have been trained to sniff out wrongdoing, suspect bad thoughts and
bad deeds everywhere, and nip all kinds of things in the bud. Certainly parents are not helped much when they hear from church people
that a taciturn teenager is a sign of parental mismanagement.

Today we should be able to acknowledge that some things aren't always our fault. Behaving ourselves doesn't always confer happiness or
success. Difficult children can be the product of genetic aberration,
unsatisfactory medical treatment (such as brain injury at delivery), or
dimly-understood complexities within the family and community.
Difficulties with children, indeed, can be quite ordinary and normal
facts of life. As for marriage itself, it not only doesn't guarantee happiness to its right-thinking participants, but it often is itself the occasion for unhappiness for one or both partners. It's apparent that the
stresses and perplexities of ordinary contemporary existence make life
far more complicated than just a matter of identifying a set of rules
and making up your mind to follow them.

Bertrand Russell once said, "The chief defect of fathers is that they want their children to be a credit to them." Erich Fromm suggests that it's this very element that distinguishes the mother's and father's roles: the father's love makes demands and the mother's love is unconditional. Current thinking, under feminist pressure, might question such a distinction on philosophical grounds. But in practice, this defect is in any case not confined to fathers.

Many people, mothers and fathers alike, have been taught and still believe that it is their *duty* to raise creditable children. Many parents — at least those whose children are receiving religious instruction — suffer from *over*-responsibility rather than from the underconscientiousness they're readily accused of in Sunday sermons, magazine articles, and school bulletins. Parents feel — and are made to feel — guilty and uneasy about themselves and their children. Nowadays few people can hide behind brave codes of behavior that they declare are working even when they're not. In the end, responsibility is equated with a duty to worry. Parents feel that if they're not worrying they're not doing their job.

This accusatory undercurrent is often not intended or conscious. But there is a long tradition of public-spirited communication that produces such pronouncements as: "It's *your* community — support it!" "Only *you* can prevent forest fires." "It's working — but only if *you* help." Even the proliferation of joy-talk, balloons and banners, and the self-fulfillment, learn-to-relax, achieve-your-potential efforts still mean it's up to the individual to get going and do all these things himself or herself. As enthusiasm for such liberating attitudes increases, so does the intensity of the reporting of popular evils, with grim lectures urging involvement of "Concerned parents" or "Citizens united for. . . ."

I remember once being struck by a saying: "Irritability is the vice of the virtuous." This seemed especially true of me and of other parents I knew. I felt we were under too much pressure to do everything and be perfect. We were holding ourselves responsible for not only our own behavior but also for that of our children — and even the world — and it was an impossible strain.

I obviously don't advocate irresponsibility or extreme laissez-faire. But I am bothered about the way "responsible parenthood" so often becomes a way of life dedicated to ritual worrying.

Since teachers and parents are closely connected in their efforts with children — and since many teachers, especially in parish religion programs, are parents — I'd like to offer a few observations and opinions that have occurred to me along the way during twenty-five years of experiencing my own family. I certainly don't want to present any new Arthur Murray dance plan, suggesting that my childraising has been ultimately successful and that by following my recommendations yours might be successful as well. Mainly I want to argue for doing less rather than more, for slowing down rather than escalating our jittery striving for parental success.

My children are, at this writing, twenty-five, twenty-two, twenty, and fifteen. The youngest is retarded; the condition is mongolism. This fact has been very useful in considering questions of parenthood. So many things I suspected to be true in dealing with the other children have been proved and clarified in our experience with the one who is handicapped. The imperatives of finding a satisfactory life for this one have led us to reject institutional folklore in favor of meanings that will hold up under scrutiny. Increasingly the opinions of the older children have been added to the process, as they comment on the next in line as each passes through a particular stage, or as they now view the way they themselves were treated.

Who Are Parents?

A major difficulty in talking about parents is that they are not an identifiable group at all. Yet all kinds of orders and recommendations are issued from a million sources addressed to the species *Parent*, as though there is a common identity and character.

In every area of life there seems to exist a need to identify people in group categories—as audience or market, as political party or society, as parish or congregation. Differences are ignored in the interest of getting a handle on as many individuals at once as possible.

In a newspaper column at the time of the Patty Hearst kidnapping, Russell Baker pointed out that "The People" is a mythical entity, serving whatever purpose may be wished. Revolutionaries invoke The People as the rationale for their programs; television companies too claim that their programs are what The People want. Medicine and education dispense their wares according to a *norm*, which is as mythical—but just as convenient—a notion as The People.

"Parents" are likely to be another mythical group. Their definition and identity depend on the purpose they serve, whether it's audience, market, or whatever.

Parents are similar primarily because they have children. And for the most part, though this may manifest itself in a variety of ways, most parents are concerned about their children and want them to do well. (It appears that in the period between 1500 and 1800, even this could not be stated with certainty. Then it was possible that a man might not even know how many children his wife had had; he might be more concerned about the welfare of his livestock than about his wife or offspring.)

Beyond this there are all kinds of differences. Family personalities can vary widely. There are some people who enjoy a large extended family and boisterous enthusiasm, with lots of shouting, hugging, kissing, even fighting. But others prefer a certain distance and a psychic rather than physical intimacy and demonstrativeness. Ethnic inheritance and geography—who you are and where you come from—can play a large part We generalize about New Englanders as opposed to midwesterners—but is an Italian from Boston's North End the same kind of New Englander as a Cabot, or a Kennedy?—or an Iowa farmer the same kind of midwesterner as someone who comes from Chicago's Greek Town? There are Californians and Texans and Floridians—and Chicanos and blacks and Chinese—and there are parents among them all.

Time (and variables of time) is most significant. For instance: How old were the parents when the children were born—and how old will they be when the children are teenage? How many years separate the children—or is this an only child? Which place in the family does each child hold—and which sex holds which place? (E.g., the oldest child is often the greatest achiever and bears the greatest burdens, but the only boy in a family of girls may be loaded with parental expectation.) Is the youngest child spoiled by the rest of the family, or is this one left to grow up with less attention while the mother goes to work to pay for college or orthodontist bills? If this child gets less attention, does this lead to frustration—or to greater self-reliance?

The times too are vital—both the times in which the parents developed their own personalities and the times in which the children reach each successive stage. Even within the same cultural mix, each parent may be the product of different influences—for instance, a child of the Depression era who grew up and married someone who came from the wartime boom years. Each set of era-induced attitudes interacts with those of each of the offspring. And those of the offspring interact with each other. A recession economy in the 1970s may mean that unlike older children who went to college and backpacked around Europe, younger ones may not get to college, or at least not without a lot of struggle.

One aspect of this matter of variability is discussed by Anne Roiphe:

A mother I know once told me that she divided all the people she knew into two categories. First, there were those who believed that everything in the world would work out well, that problems could be worked through and that, if you behaved virtuously, good things would happen to you. Then, there were those who believed that tragedy was imminent, that nothing turned out the way it was planned, and being good had nothing to do with what happened to you in life—disaster was random, reasonless, and likely. As she looked over her two lists, my friend discovered that all the trusters, those with shining eyes and faith in the future, had young children, either beginning school, or in diapers, or in the womb, while those in the second, grimmer category all had teenagers or older children.[1]

This is a dichotomy I also have thought about and defined. But I happen to think it generally works just the opposite way. In my experience it's the younger parents who seem more anxious and worried about what evils will befall their children, and who are quite preoccupied with figuring out ways to prevent bad things from happening. The drug-and-dropout phenomenon is the most likely cause of their fears, just as the Lindbergh kidnapping frightened parents in the 1930s. A lot of youngsters were over-monitored in those days, and I think a lot of them now are being handled specifically in terms of ways to prevent future freakouts.

Today's older parents, by no means completely carefree and overjoyed about life, nevertheless seem to have been mellowed and broadened (often by the quite abrasive happenings they've lived through) to a point where they see that much is still possible in situations they once would have seen as disastrous. They've learned that the worst they could imagine can be lived through and learned from. They've passed all the "bargain-barriers" they once set up ("I'd just die if one of my kids got pneumonia"; "I don't care what he thinks, just so he stays in school"). These older parents don't set arbitrary limits quite so freely, nor do they give up so easily. They're quite aware of how much they've changed from the rather prim and righteous parents they used to be. Some, to be sure, are a little worn and puzzled, but many parents themselves have been freed by the process of keeping close to their children, in spite of innumerable breaks with convention.

Whichever view you take, it's clear that just living through a number of years has its effects. The process itself makes things happen that are impossible to know or advise about ahead of time.

What Are the Problems?

There are many people nowadays—and Anne Roiphe in the article quoted is one of them—who see the rather chaotic developments of recent years as perpetual, continuing, and inevitable problems. Whatever has been introduced into our consciousness—or our offspring's consciousness—is sure to remain and we might as well get used to it. Now that we know about drugs, we have to face that reality; now that

1. Anne Roiphe, "Teenage Affairs," *The New York Times Magazine*, October 5, 1975.

we've seen liberalized sexual behavior, we have to acknowledge and accept it.

I just don't think human behavior is all that predictable. Nor are social currents to be counted on. Biologist Rene Dubos suggests that, though we worry about the danger and complexity of contemporary society, modern people have more going for them than they may think. Our rapid communication means that the public becomes aware of problems and issues very quickly and very quickly takes steps to accommodate to them. Dubos says, "The future is never an extrapolation of the past." In world affairs, whether social or technological, "Trend is not destiny."

I believe that trend is not destiny in our young people's affairs either. It's apparent that widespread awareness of drug hazards has caused some changes in at least the *kinds* of chemicals young people are involved with. Certainly no one should celebrate the increase in alcohol usage as opposed to other drugs (alcohol, to young people, is now seen as "the high without the hassle") but it's clear that the change itself resulted from observation and experience. Similarly, there appears to be at least a more aware handling of the phenomenon of living together, as the data on this experience became available to successive groups of young people. The disenchantment or disillusionment of some cohabitants has been reported on, just as bad drug trips and potential genetic damage have also become known.

Further, the change in political atmosphere—the Vietnam war and the draft—dampened the impetus for public rebellion, or at least altered its methods. A slowing economy gradually shifted the emphasis from the pretend-poverty style of the 1960s to a quite realistic concern about jobs and costs.

Parents don't need to be obsessively concerned with each new problem—no matter how grave it may be—that comes up the pike. We're so afraid of being accused of having our heads in the sand that we're guilty of the opposite mistake: the don't-think-of-elephant error. The more we fret and worry out loud, and educate-against by way of guidance-related filmstrips, films, and curriculum packages, the more graphically and dramatically we keep our fear-subjects in front of the children. We draw blueprints based on Sunday supplements and TV specials. In effect we offer models; we imply that this is what we expect.

There is not just the danger that we may be perpetuating more difficulties than we're preventing or curing. The perversity of life and of children themselves often means that by the time we arrive at the stage we're apprehensive about, there are new and different problems, requiring a different approach and different information. And again we're right back there with old answers to old questions.

Each crop of children is likely to be different, responding to their own time period, but also responding to the experience of those who have preceded them. We have to trust our ability to handle things at the time, in tune with the time and the child as he or she is.

One job of the growing child is differentiation—developing in a way that makes him separate and different from his parents. But it seems more and more obvious, as children are given more and more opportunity to develop as individuals, that they have the second task of being different from their brothers and sisters. In both instances, this complicated undertaking—differentiation—usually is done in a way that nevertheless tries to preserve the basic characteristics and expectations of the family. It's a nearly impossible job—to be different and the same all at once. In fact, the enormity of the effort may be one of the very reasons young people are irritable and overtired so much of the time. Nevertheless, the script for young people nowadays dictates that they alter in some ways the pattern set for them by previous generations of young people as well as the one held up to them by their parents.

Parents of several children are usually aware of the individuality of these children—their dispositions, their eating habits, their athletic or artistic ability, and their intellectual differences. But it helps to keep this individuality in mind also when it comes to considering how they will respond to the unpredictable currents of today's high-powered life. Here too it's important that we don't unwittingly set youngsters up for something they are neither interested in nor ready for just because their older brother or sister "went through this stage" at the same age. Nor should we accept too readily a media version of which behaviors are to be expected when. (In this regard, school textbooks are as much media villains as the television shows and movies they so often criticize.)

Children differ not only as individuals but also as members of a time-group. As with wine, there are vintage years in children. Sometimes it appears in retrospect that a particular year was a good year or a bad year for children because of the climate and growing conditions that prevailed.

I caution parents not to be overwhelmed by fears about what will happen as their children grow, nor to try overmuch to tailor their children's upbringing according to data drawn from today's newspaper headlines. This is not to say that there are not scary situations around us. But it's draining and debilitating to worry about problems that may not even be the right ones. Such preoccupation takes time and energy from the factor that's probably the best insurance anyway, the ordinary day-to-day care and concern for our own children.

There *are* some basic truths that still apply to child-raising: truth telling, politeness, and what a dear old friend of mine calls "loving-kindness." No matter what the current style of problem, these tenets are still the best base form which to handle difficulties as they develop.

It's true that new understandings are generally making themselves felt—and these include the ideas and experiences of the children themselves to a greater degree than formerly. There are now more pieces in the total puzzle. But this fact should only make for a more sensitive and refined view of what the basic truths mean in any given case. It does not at all mean that the basic truths no longer apply, or that they've been replaced by hitherto-unknown psychological theorems that we must all study and learn.

The idealized view of the successful family, whether promoted by church or social worker or *Ladies Home Journal*, is probably unreachable—and we might, if we reached it, find it unattractive. The morbid view of the addict, the runaway, or the promiscuous teenager offered by the citizens' committee or the issue-happy textbook is likely, at the very least, to be overcomprehensive and conclusive. Trying desperately to attain the ideal while trying desperately at the same time to escape the pitfalls can quite plainly drive both parent and child crazy.

It's just this kind of tension that can inhibit stable family development and quite possibly precipitate the kind of unpleasant behavioral reactions we all hope to avoid.

Experts and Education

In trying to establish some kind of reliable framework for family life, we're conscious of experts and their advice everywhere we turn. Whether we follow them or disagree with them, we know they're there. Education in particular is riddled with expert-itis, increasingly drawn from psychological theory.

Education, like medicine, needs a Hippocratic Oath, with emphasis on the admonition not to give the patient any deadly thing. In both medicine and education, giving deadly things seems commonplace considering the passion for innovation and attention-getting experimentation and for what film critic Susan Rice calls "cashing in on hot issues." Some procedures, some medications are seen initially to be worthwhile and successful, but after a time they turn out to be hazardous, even lethal. Even when not demonstrably dangerous, many things are unnecessary and expensive. Because of all this, writers like Ivan Illich believe the entire educational enterprise is malignant and should be done away with.

In medicine, there are regulations and testing that claim to protect the public, but these are often slow to take effect and subject to political pressures. In education, only a few people seem concerned with public protection (though their numbers are increasing); these individuals are seen either as out-of-touch reactionaries given to censorship, or as wrong-headed radicals bent on libertine behavior and left-wing politics. Neither group is thought to have much to say to "the real world."

In the time I've spent dealing with schools, teaching, religious education, and children, I've found an alarming preponderance of attitudes, situations, approaches, and materials that surely do more harm than good. All these elements presented and promoted by experts—educational and psychological researchers—who doubtless frequently work from the best of intentions and whose arguments are couched in language both reasonable and wholesome. But unfortunately, just as in medical research, many projects and curriculum innovations arise out of competition for funding, for job status, or for publishing contracts. And they often draw from contemporary fads, fears, and gossip rather than from solid study of or real feeling for either subject matter or child. Even the recent "Back to basics" cry is sure to be mined by educational faddists and political opportunists jockeying for position.

Thinking about the tensions of expert-itis reminds me of my father's advice when I was learning to drive. He told me that when I drove at night I shouldn't look into the headlights of approaching cars but rather at the edge of the road. The point was to keep my car on the road, and though the other cars couldn't be ignored, paying too much attention to them by watching their headlights would almost certainly pull me off course. Like approaching cars, experts come and go, and you can't escape a certain passing relationship with them. But if you spend too much time considering them, you're likely to lose sight of your main concern.

More and more I find people holding mental conversations with experts, or talking over problems and decisions on the phone using sentences that begin, "They say we should..." or, "I worry about being one of those parents they talk about who...." With the opinions of syndicated columnists, lecturers, or talk-show guests always in their ears, parents may let their thought processes talk them into positions quite contrary to what their native common sense really tells them.

Thinking, talking, and digesting the advice of experts can also substitute for acting. I once heard a theologian say, "Well, I can't just postpone acting until all the data is in because it's never going to be completely in. I have to reflect, but I do have to make a decision sometime, and at any time it's going to be a less than complete decision." Some parents are simply paralyzed by the proliferation of expert advice. Others work out their confusion in local committees or action groups, while remaining unable to solve their dilemmas back home.

There is, unfortunately, a climate that has led us down the garden path into believing in the great power of information, and in the great moral imperative of "being informed," "being aware," "keeping up with new research," and that siren-song, the development of "communication techniques." Things *aren't* always made clearer for parents by more reading, more studying, and more explaining. Occasionally it might help to pose a question in terms of: "What would my grandmother have done?" After all, psychologists and educators don't *invent* human behavior, they only attempt to describe, define, and interpret it. And psychologists and educators from differing schools of thought quarrel among themselves about what it all means.

Analysis or instinct, argument or action, head or gut—which is needed—and when? No matter what combination we end up with, at least we needn't be conned into believing that the Right Way is always and only found at the end of the Right amount of reading and reasoning. Sometimes instincts have a built-in problem-solving power of a high degree of reliability.

A Basic Attitude

The difficulty in being a parent is not just that there are too many experts and too many points of view. There is the encroachment on the parent's territory, the undermining of the parent's confidence, the substitution of an expert/consultant attitude for the native parent attitude.

Among writers who have commented on this is Dolores Curran:

> I've found it isn't considered fair game, even today, for a Catholic parent to be honest with nonparents, except in the most sophisticated catechetical company. . . . It's unfair for the parents to point out that, theology notwithstanding, the child described by the Church or the bishop or the director of religious education is foreign to him. It's unfair for the parent to object openly to the Church's use of him as a scapegoat for almost every parish failure. It's unfair for the parent to point out that he is exactly where the Church has led him. It's unfair to point out that there is no parent apathy but that there is distrust of programs designed by nonparents for parents in the Church.[2]

Mrs. Curran identifies this malady as it exists in church circles. But it exists in similar form outside the church too. It isn't only priests

2. Dolores Curran, "Has the Church Failed Parents," *America*, September 30, 1972.

and church structures that behave this way. It's anyone who claims to be an expert or a "professional," anyone who sees parents as some kind of classifiable species, with the same characteristics, ready consumers of expert opinion.

True, those individuals who want to call the shots in many religion programs frequently are not parents. But I'm not quite sure it's only this factor that makes the difference. Sissela Bok, professor of medical ethics at Harvard (and wife of Harvard's president), makes a distinction—applicable to any field of endeavor—between a "maternal and caring attitude" and a "paternalistic and coercive attitude." She defines paternalism as the coercion of others for what is held to be their best interest or improvement, based on a claim of better information or greater foresight. She says, "Clearly, such claims are justified in some instances. But just as clearly, if they go uncontested, they can result in actions which are unnecessary, humiliating, and at times, destructive."[3]

The point is, I don't believe that it's the fact of being a *nonparent* that is entirely the problem Dolores Curran points to, or the problem I mean when I object to "experts." Rather, it's the fact that so many of these nonparents lack any possibility of having or acquiring a parent attitude. Furthermore, I don't believe that a parent-attitude is something only parents can have. There are many single women who are as maternal and caring as any mother or grandmother. There are many priests whose pastoral concern could be defined as maternal as well as in the conventional father-language. Given Mrs. Bok's distinction, I think it is the paternalistic attitude that is the problem, paternalism that is characteristic of many of the nonparents in religious education, but also characteristic of a large proportion of the experts in medicine, education, psychology, sociology, and other fields who push their opinions on parents.

More than this, I think that parents, by their dependency on and intimidation by experts, are more and more forsaking their natural identity as parents and adopting the "paternalistic and coercive" pattern of thought and action. Whether permissive or restrictive, the way parents respond to their children represents a decision. This decision, conditioned by either professional dogmatism or professional confusion, can enforce a climate that may be unnatural for both child and parent.

The influence of expert opinion on parents is in a way the contemporary, educated parent's version of an older influence, the concern for what the neighbors will think. This familiar problem still persists, of course; it too has the potential for coercion. What the neighbors—

3. Sissela Bok, "The Harm in Doing Good," *The Radcliffe Quarterly*, August 1972.

relatives—may think certainly cannot be rejected out of hand. The judgment of the community or family is a strong and necessary adhesive for social stability. But it cannot always be the primary norm in handling children. An overconcern for appearances risks losing sight of what this child is like, and what this child needs. I suspect most children ultimately are conservative and conformist, and will eventually subscribe to social conventions provided they are not strong-armed into them.

Worrying about appearances—keeping up a good front—doesn't just involve questions of dress, conduct, choice of companions, and the like. In some families it means channeling feelings and emotional responses into patterns dictated by social propriety. Insisting that youngsters always be cheerful, that they never show their irritation, anger, or frustration—this is a noble notion, but given today's pressures from school and society, it may clamp too tight a lid on children who need a safety valve at least at home.

The phrase "Caring attitude" is not altogether a good one. It has become a catchphrase of sorts for the feminist movement, another of many vague utopian slogans that, subtly and sophisically, encourages us to believe that we can substitute feelings for behavior. Because the whole question of phrasing is so basic, however, it is hard to find a phrase that will not suffer similar limitations. What "caring attitude" does *not* mean is a dreamy, sweet, sentimental hovering, or a free-floating, uncritical tolerance. Jonathan Kozol, in *Free Schools*, talks of the value of a teacher who "Comes right out, in full view of the children, with all of the richness, humor, desperation, rage, self-contradiction, strength and pathos, which he would reveal, as well, to other grown-ups." This could also be the description of a caring parent.

Caring means trusting that children will ultimately do well, succeed, and be good, even when at times the evidence may be to the contrary.

We often are reluctant to trust because we've been so constantly deluged with case studies of wayward and delinquent youngsters, case studies that quote the parents as exclaiming, "But I can't believe it!—Johnny was always a good boy—*he'd* never do a thing like that!"

Just because such an attitude may appear in a problem situation (or be alleged by a feature-writer in a newspaper) does not mean that this attitude is therefore unwise or the *cause* of the problem. Just as it's common for people to identify with the symptoms of medical case studies and instantly conjure up images of similar illnesses of their own, so it's a temptation to identify with the reporting of child and family pathology all around us. Strange biological and psychological creatures that we are, both abnormal and healthy functioning can present similar appearances. Symptom-hunting—medical or behavioral—quite possibly induces as much malfunction as it prevents.

In any case, a caring attitude can help sort out our concern for the *real* child — or teenager, or young adult — in our family from the question of how well he or she reflects on us. It's this type of caring, I think, that has been done by those parents who have survived the many changes of the past few years with their children. They have had to keep focussing on *this* child, holding onto him and believing in him by hook or by crook, even if, in the eyes of others or, compared to their own early expectations, they may seem to have failed as parents.

The questions become: "Am I treating this child according to how he is as I know him or according to what outsiders think?" "Am I responding to the way things are with us and our family — or to the way people will see me as a successful parent?" The answers to these questions may vary from time to time. When life is going smoothly, it's possible to make more accommodation to public opinion, particularly to the observations of grandparents or immediate neighbors. But when a serious situation develops, when a child is really troubled or faced with a major decision, the area of concern generally narrows.

Focussing on the child doesn't necessarily mean that it's what the child *demands* that we must consider, but rather what we now know and have known of this child through the years.

We need to keep these questions about our motivation in mind in all our decision making with our children, including our religion teaching. Especially in our ideas on morality, are we really subscribing to moral values or only to an elaborate, church-supported, paternalistic version of "What will the neighbors — or experts — think?"

This in no way suggests that there are not likely to be problems. Nor is it meant to imply that there should not be information and communication. But it is certainly *not* our duty to be full-time worriers and watchdogs. Whatever we do or say ought to be based first on belief in the child and in awareness of what he or she is *really* like. To proceed according to prevailing images of children in magazines and academic research, or to follow too trustingly the schedules and presentations of workbook-makers and audiovisual producers can cause us to judge the child in terms of categories and groups that are quite superficial. There are many cultural and tempermental differences in behavior to be taken into account in considering what educational and psychological experts would like to identify as norms. At least let's look at our own situation, not just follow the echoing voices of experts defining our duty with data drawn from random samples.

An observer from a much earlier period wrote:

> Hold childhood in reverence and do not be in any hurry to judge for good or ill. Leave exceptional cases to show themselves, let their special qualities be tested and confirmed, before special methods are adopted.

Give nature time to work before you take over her business, lest you interfere with her dealings. You assert that you know the value of time and are afraid to waste it. You fail to perceive that it is a greater waste of time to use it ill than to do nothing, and that a child ill taught is further from virtue than a child who has learned nothing at all.

Rousseau

To Be Specific. .

I'd like to consider how some apparently commendable procedures in recent educational experience (including religious education) may in reality have been damaging to the children and possibly to the culture itself.

A great many of the problems stem from projection on the part of adults. In some instances the problems arise from our projected guilt feelings, and in others from our personal fears and anxieties. Both guilt and anxiety take on additional significance when we hitch them to our sense of responsibility as parents.

In the great confusion of instant consciousness-raising during the sixties many people suddenly experienced enormous guilt over the multitude of social problems they apparently hadn't been paying attention to. There were plenty of guilt-inducers around to assure that the level of breast-beating was kept up. Ministers in pulpits, TV newscasters, and filmmakers pointed out at every turn how we had been self-centered and apathetic, akin to prewar Germans in our blindness, misreading or betraying the Gospel, failing our idealistic young (who were quickly pictured as perceptive as we were blind, and as vigorous as we were sluggish and complacent). We were told over and over that we were a sick society, and informed of our collective guilt in the horrors of the day—assassinations, poverty, war, and injustice. If we weren't part of the solution, we were part of the problem, the posters and graffiti incessantly reminded us.

What was there to do but become active and involved?—And where was it more logical and convenient to begin than in the schools? So into the schools went the collective guilt of responsible adults. We felt keenly the accusing eyes of our offspring, who had overheard and had begun to repeat the charges against us. Perhaps one of our major motives was trying to prove to them that we were as righteous and upstanding as they. Unfortunately, the result has been that we've dumped our guilts on them, and eased our own burdens of conscience only by adding to theirs.

As speedily as we moved to rename airports, highways, and grammar schools to memorialize Kennedys and Kings, just as speedily as we enacted legislation to require courses in ecology, in drug education, in peace and violence, and in racism. Sex education enlarged its scope to consider venereal disease and contraception, with a new concern for overpopulation added to the old questions of proper conduct. A new emphasis on "relationships" tied in well with the longing for smooth teamwork around the world as well as at home.

Here are some of the things that apparently went wrong:

1. Overawareness: too much too soon

We claimed to understand the insecurities of the young who had grown up under the threat of The Bomb. (We chose to ignore the impact of the same bomb on ourselves, the over-forties who were teen agers when the attack on Hiroshima occurred. I, for one, was fourteer at the time.) We didn't hesitate, however, to add to their insecurity b constant programmed discussion of cosmic disaster from pollution, overpopulation, and technological takeover. Rather than serving t celebrate the noble insight of the young, it's likely that the turnoff w all worried about might now come earlier and earlier as children car take no more talk of doom. Sending youngsters out to pick up trash i probably reasonable on ordinary principles of decency, but to preacl that trash collection is their duty as preventers of the planet's deatl simply unloads adult concerns onto the child.

In an essay several years ago, Kevin Walsh gave this view:

> Perhaps there is not even a need to daydream any more; we now live in an age of enlightenment where even the smallest child must know the evils of venereal disease, the pollution of our skies and waterways, and the crisis of the population bomb. Superman and Roy Rogers have faded into the sunset and have been replaced by shows tailored for the kindergarten intellectual set. There is no more mystery in life for the child, no more sandy beaches glistening with sparkling blue water (for we all know that the seas are clogged with oil and sewage) nor are there any green forests perfect for day-long adventures (for Americans have killed plant growth and wildlife with insecticides and poisons).[4]

Children can hardly escape contact with real life. But it would far better if their contact with real life came from real living. Jai Addams learned of the social evils that led to her vocation—soci work at Hull House in Chicago—from being taken along with her mi ister father as he went about his work and from later travels on h own. Her learning was organic and integrated; her father thought important for her to know the things he dealt with in his work.

4. Kevin Walsh, "When I Was Younger," *The New York Times*, December 19, 1972.

Instead, we now keep children separated from their parents' work; we relentlessly and graphically overexpose them to *every* kind of problem in life in the six-o'clock-news style, like newscasters milking the horror of the stories for various media-industry purposes. A look at the graphics of religion textbooks published during the sixties shows that schools and classrooms have served up generous portions of this stuff, helped along by the doctrine that the young can only be communicated with by high-powered media.

Many children in this country already live with trouble, whether poverty, hunger, or internal family discord. As Jonathan Kozol says in *Free Schools:*

> Most public schools, and a large number of the Free Schools, too, nourish an atmosphere which is devoid of almost all true, credible experience and in which only arduous simulations of real processes take place. The ultimate paradox to which such gruesome institutions finally arrive is the introduction of that paradigm vehicle of school-delineated alienation, the "simulation game." We close up the windows, pull down the blinds, etherize the heart, and neutralize the soul; and then we bring in "simulation games" to try to imitate the world we have, with such care and at such consummate expense, excluded.[5]

For some kids, their own lives are pain enough; for any kids, classroom handling of social issues can overwhelm and defeat. It's not just that this overaggressive programming is too much to bear for individuals whose major task is just to grow. This programming also promotes the idea of the world as a bad and fearful place, full of inhuman, careless, unreliable people, with a questionable future. It dumps on students the responsibility for correcting the world's wrongs, one following upon another in a relentless ten-month cycle.

Do we really want a nation of children who, when taken for a Sunday afternoon walk, can now see only garbage?

We not only increase their exposure, we urge action upon them before action is possible. We suppose that we are training their consciousness against the time they *are* able to take action — yet right now they aren't allowed to leave home, to vote, or to go to work. They cannot possibly comprehend — nor can many of us without extensive, critical study — the worldly subtleties and complexities of power, politics, and social ferment. Can they see beyond their guilty haste to throw soda cans in litter baskets to the company that overproduces the cans, or to the advertising that has made them believe that soda is essential? Stirring children up with naive philosophical notions about changing the world builds up a backlog of explosive energy with no satisfactory way of discharging that energy. Where does it go except

Jonathan Kozol, *Free Schools* (Boston: Houghton Mifflin Company, 1972).

to wear itself out in their own nervous systems—in worry, irritability, and in guilt? Perhaps by presenting children with these outsize problems for which they have no solutions, we unwittingly provide them with the experience of powerlessness and teach them how to fail when they encounter problems in their grown-up lives.

Further, while lamenting our supposed lack of influence on the young, we permit and approve such masochistic approaches as the television spot commericials in which adults are pictured as the enemy, while ingenuous children beg us to leave some of the world's resources for their future. By presenting ourselves as scapegoats, we let our children off the hook. Our overresponsibility sets the stage for lack of it in them.

Too much too soon is also a factor in the expanding insistence on career education, which reflects economic anxieties and fulfills one of the school's functions in producing an adaptable work force. College requirements have increased the pressure on youngsters at lower and lower grades to choose their activities with care, as credential-grubbing widens its scope beyond College Board scores and grade-point averages. "How will it look on my record?" they ask as they prepare to sign up for this or that extracurricular activity. Students, college and noncollege alike, are asked to think about their life's work at earlier and earlier ages, assisted by a myriad of audiovisual aids at every stage.

I certainly don't believe in the myth of childhood as "the golden period." Especially because I don't believe it, I think adults have little business making these years a dumping ground for either our guilts or our need to manipulate.

2. Invasion of Experience

We all want to give others the benefit of our insight. One evening when I was about eight, I delayed my parents' departure for a *Thin Man* movie—which I'd seen that afternoon—while I explained the entire plot in great detail. They surely missed the opening scenes, but I insisted that without my clarification they'd doubtless not understand what was going on. In 1952 when I had my first baby, my aunt told me of her plan to write down all the helpful things she'd learned in raising her children so I could be spared a lot of wasted time and effort. I was twenty-one at the time and as independent as most people are at that age. I thought irritably, "Thanks, but I'm going to have my own damn baby and figure it out myself."

Several years ago I previewed an extensive collection of sex education filmstrips that covered early grades through the beginning of college. The later ones included something about natural childbirth and showed the delivery room, green hospital gowns, and the like. The thought occurred to me again, "Why can't we just let them have their own damn babies and stop muscling in on their experience?"

Today controversies over childbirth practises (for instance, the popularity of Dr. LeBoyer's quiet delivery-room approach or the interest in midwives) make such materials seem a little one-sided. But in any case, the entire business smacks of an adult voyeurism that can hardly be justified.

The need for privacy is an important part of the "differentiation" I mentioned earlier. If we insist on sharing and inspecting all of our children's experience, might they not be forced to invent ever-newer experiences that we can't possibly comprehend or share? A great deal of what's involved in the need for privacy is distance and protection of one's own self. In their travels to adulthood, children *must* go underground at times—rather like astronauts who, for a brief period, inevitably are out of voice contact with the earth.

There is in particular the function of fantasy, which swings far and wide in an in-the-head exploration of a range of possibilities. Joyce Maynard, who frequently writes about teenage from her vantage point of having recently been there, says:

> They [her parents] even gave Stones records for my birthday. I think I felt some unease about that, as a girl would whose mother gives her a prescription for the pill, or a boy whose father drives him to pick up an ounce of hash. They were simply anxious to share in my enthusiasm, of course, but I didn't much want to make this a public concern, to take the Rolling Stones out of the dark caves I inhabited with them and into cheery yellow-curtained sunlight. It is a problem for most 12-year-old girls and it certainly was for me—that their bodies rarely match their minds. So while the young girl lies in the dark and dreams of being the one who will, at least, give Mick Jagger his Satisfaction, the next morning she must go to school and give an oral report on Bolivia.

And she further writes,

> The Rolling Stones were pretty clearly Bad Boys, and I was a Good Girl. What I liked about them, I think, was the sense of danger and anarchy they conveyed. As one who still cared desperately about pleasing her parents and getting into a good college, I admired the Stones for their appearance of not caring an awful lot about anything.... The Rolling Stones were not boys our mothers would like—which made them more appealing, of course.

In spite of all the *Music Man* kind of admonition to "Watch for the telltale signs of corruption" (e.g., printed checklists of suspicious indicators of drug use, handed out after mass), during teen years what *seems* and what *is* are not always that clear.

In spite of conflicting appearances, most young people, like Joyce Maynard, *do* care about pleasing their parents. Guidebooks and advice columns seem to want parents to make a career out of jumping to conclusions, but they forget the age-old caution about looking before you leap. Plunging in with overblown assumptions can fracture a much-needed sense of trust.

Another obsession of our time, "open communication" often verges on the voyeuristic, too, like filmstrips and courses. Sometimes it certainly is necessary to be candid and outspoken. But it seems quite unnecessary—and even hazardous—to start out too openly on every occasion and about every subject.

Paul Tillich writes:

> As long as the pupil lives in a dreaming innocence of critical questions, he should not be awakened. But our time is not favorable for a long preservation of such innocence. And if the first critical questions are asked by the child, the first cautious answers must be given. Later on, the questions will become more critical and the answers must become bolder and more fundamental.

Indeed, our time is *not* favorable for preserving innocence, but that doesn't mean that we must be the ones to lead the way to its destruction. Hearing so much that we must be honest with our children, many people are likely to be confused about the extent of this candor. Honesty does not suggest that we are obliged to give our grown-up position on a given subject when it clearly would be inappropriate for the child's present age. Nowadays there are many grown-ups whose views on sexual matters are rather more liberal than they once were, but their more relaxed attitude contains in it many modifiers and qualifiers. Even a carefully stated opinion that reflects a more tolerant attitude will probably not be helpful to a nine-year-old. Adults cannot always be "honest" in a sense that implies total frankness and total clarity in areas where there is enormous complexity or which require maturity to appreciate.

In dealing with children, it is probably prudent to handle the adult's matured or maturing thinking in questions of sex with a certain decent obscurity. The same could be said for the current concern for feelings—"affective education." However much adults may notice their own emotional responses, and however much they may identify the frustrations and inhibitions they believe have resulted from submerged childhood conflicts, what children choose to reveal about their feelings is really their own business. Instructing children about ventilating bad feelings of jealousy, fear, anger, and the like is to presume that these feelings are present and to expect that they will be present. Yet, not all children—and certainly not all at the same ages in life—experience these feelings. And some children just might prefer not to acknowledge their presence, and certainly not to display them for grown-ups.

Even though to some adults a certain self-consciousness can come as a relief, to others it can be a contemporary version of the nervous introspection of past religious practice. For adults to plot out children's emotional lives on a plan drawn from their own remembered wounds is, to say the least, presumptuous.

3. Overexposure

One area in which chronic worrying, leading to responsible "doing-something-about-it," hits near hysteria is in the matter of drugs and drug education. From the very beginning, drug instruction has resembled a modern-day variety of the old story "Don't Stick Beans Up Your Noses." The more we preach "Don't", the more we seem to dare our children to do; we constantly remind them of what we wish they wouldn't think about. From innumerable films, filmstrips, and textbook photographs it's possible to become familiar with models of all kinds of behavior, all kinds of environments, and all kinds of equipment for ingesting and injecting forbidden substances.

The message is, of course, that drugs are dangerous and to be avoided. A message these days supposedly is delivered effectively only by some highly-colored medium—film and filmstrips, or vivid, stylish kodachromes and solarizations in textbooks. But these fashionable tools are chiefly decorations, a means to advance the sales appeal of the product. Yet it's precisely these illustrations that deliver the strongest message, a message that opposes the verbal one droning along in the background. The pictures scream, "This is how it's done" while the words argue, "Don't." As we've been told for years, it's the pictures that win 1,000 to 1. Interestingly enough, it's been charged that films and television shows themselves, with their overstimulation and their hypnotic, brain-dulling, mass-audience approach, contribute to an attitude and climate congenial to drug use.

The conservative parent worries that we'll give our children wrong ideas. The radical or liberal parent says they already have wrong ideas. Unfortunately, with drug education as with sex education, the packaging and programming often contribute to problems whether the youngsters have any ideas or not. For the packaging and programming imply that adults expect all young people to be actively interested and likely to be engaged in these subjects. They suggest that adults accept the concept of young people as universally preoccupied with these subjects. And they heighten, dramatize, and reinforce these images on larger-than-life stages, with all the authority of glamorous audiovisual techniques.

There's a great difference between pretending not to know about problems and forbidding them to be talked about, and forcing information and discussion on students whether or not they want it or are ready for it. (The same distinction should be made in many discussions of censorship: forbidding access to books is not good, but requiring them to be read isn't necessarily good either.)

Is it conceivable that if we didn't constantly tell youngsters we don't approve of something and describe in graphic detail what it is we don't approve of, they'd really not know that we don't approve? Would they really think we do approve? Would they never hear that it's dangerous?

The grapevine spreads news quite rapidly without our help. Young people are likely to be way ahead of information processed through a text publisher's production and marketing schedule. Newspapers and news magazines report regularly on new cautions and hazards, many of them more distressing and more effective deterrents than our lectures and moralisms (e.g., threats of feminizing effects on boys, reports of loss of sexual potency, hazards to offspring, etc).

As Rousseau pointed out, the child badly taught is further from virtue than the one not taught at all. In drug education we are influenced by the same myth as in sex education, the notion that street teaching is vastly inferior to controlled, adult, schooled teaching. But if only because of rapidly changing data, the information presented in many teaching materials is itself of doubtful accuracy. It's naive too to suppose that teachers are always going to have the most reliable and up-to-date film or filmstrip. Pressures of scheduling often mean that teachers will descend on the local public library and thankfully book *any* available film to fulfill the requirements of a compulsory classroom unit. I've watched them do this time after time.

As for effectiveness, it's likely that drug-education-by-curriculum is at best ineffective, at worst counterproductive and dangerous. The problem of drug abuse may have little to do with ignorance of facts and, instead, involve many oblique factors of individual and social functioning. One writer says:

Can schools do anything to prevent drug abuse? The answer is murky—for there is little hard evidence. Indeed, what prevention *is not* is much

clearer than what it *is*. But a way to begin is to turn the question
around and ask what characteristics of schools, as they are usually found,
hinder drug prevention (and possibly stimulate drug abuse) . . . . Scruti-
nize the drug-education problem long enough and it becomes the school
problem. Drug abuse is a peculiar microscope magnifying many of the
flaws in education . . . that reformers have carped about from Rousseau
to Silberman.[6]

With both sex education and drug education, conservative parents argue that they have the primary responsibility for teaching as a moral
right and duty in areas involving behavior. More liberal parents take a
more practical position. They feel that teachers who today are often
incapable of teaching math or grammar adequately are hardly reliable
guides of behavior. Both kinds of parents are troubled about teacher
biases—whether overrigid or overpermissive—which may color the presentation of emotionally-charged questions.

I suggested at the beginning of this section that these difficulties in
education stem from projection on the part of adults. Two other topics—death and homosexuality—fall almost completely into the category of projection.

It may be profitable for grown-ups—especially those growing old or
facing serious illness, and their counselors—to work through their fears
of death. But it has to be either neurotic or plain silly to suggest, as I
read in a catechetical magazine, that the "happy-ending" view of life
shown in children's stories is unrealistic, calling for corrective courses
in death education in elementary grades. And while a philosophizing
adult might arrive at a liberating perspective through his reflection on
death (called in some places "The final stage of growth" or by similar
titles), current statistics on teenage suicide suggest that the question of
death ought not to be introduced as a curriculum item without extreme caution.

Not that the fact of death should—or can—be hidden from the
young. But the subject of death can be handled by reasonably healthy
adults in the normal cycle of events or by good literature. Trying to
make healthy adults and good literature available to young people is
hard enough work to keep us busy these days.

Vigorous direct assault on a subject may work well in math or biol-
ogy. But "Let's talk of graves, of worms and epitaphs" is more safely
said by Richard II than by a grade school teacher in search of "relevance" and "realistic adjustment."

Similarly, it's certainly a good thing to talk about accepting the ho-

6. Richard H. DeLone, "The Ups and Downs of Drug Education," *Saturday Review of
Education,* November 11, 1972.

mosexual members of society. Yet in the face of the confusions and
ambivalence of teenagers in their struggles for sexual differentiation—
especially in the light of feminist consciousness-raising—an uncritical
and virtuous emphasis on acceptance ought not to suggest that the
choice really doesn't matter. Church people have a generous and genuine purpose in addressing the question of homosexuality. But teenage radio stations, from other motives, seem to have a stake in creating
the impression that whether one will be homosexual or heterosexual is
simply another career-decision. The effect upon the youngsters of either church or disc-jockey arguments is likely to be essentially the
same.

Which aspects of masculinity or femininity are genetic and which
are cultural is of great interest in contemporary discussions. These are
confusing and often disturbing questions even to mature adults. They
can be most unsettling when young people's understanding of themselves is already in turmoil. The question "Who am I?" does not need
to be turned into "Which am I?"—*whether* to be masculine or femi-
nine. Yet judging from some youthful conversations, this is the way
the question is being presented.

Do We Just Ignore These Questions?

Every serious subject and every current concern need not be automatically pumped through youngsters like a therapeutic dose of salts simply because it's important. Some important questions are too potent
and too close to the bone to bear close scrutiny by a developing personality, however central to that development the question itself may be
Simply deciding that an issue is crucial and that it impinges in some
significant way on both adults and young people doesn't necessarily
justify head-on classroom analysis and discussion.

In questions of sexuality in particular—though to us the kids appear
cool, uninhibited, and light-years beyond where we were in sophis-
tication at their age—it's quite likely that some kids more than others
and most kids at one time or another, will be embarrassed by mixed
company presentations. In addition, with any questions that involve
personal emotions, the function of the adult—whether parent or
teacher—can be quite complex. There are questions of authority, psychological barriers (ranging from a need for privacy to an incest tabu
that makes it difficult for parents to be the communicators of sex information), the influence of the youngsters' associates, and unresolve
conflicts on the part of the adults.

We tend to think of humaneness in terms of lots of personal involvement, but in some instances it may be more humane to leave information-dispensing to a nonhuman agent such as books. Though there can be difficulties in agreeing on suitable materials, ordinary reference books—without a lot of sensational graphics—nevertheless maintain a neutrality and distance that can help to circumvent some of the trying and unpredictable elements inherent in charged questions.

Adults can be available informally and privately to supplement the reading if individual students or groups seem to want to talk things over. Again, however, care should be taken that such discussion not become an authorized version of busybody meddling and snooping, disguised and sanctioned by guidance-department rhetoric. In not a few school systems, youngsters have as much to guard against from their advisors as they do from what they are advised about and against.

Furthermore, it isn't just the drug question that suggests larger issues. How all of us—in the family and in the world—live and treat each other, how well we're able to love ourselves as well as our neighbors, how our science, politics, and industries function legitimately and humanely—all these elements underlie questions of drug use, sexual behavior, war, ecology, and civil rights. Some general moral principles always apply whatever the specific issue (I have never understood such designations as "sexual morality"), yet school courses separate and isolate these issues. Taking each subject as a separate focal point develops it out of proportion to its place in life at large and often aggrandizes and overglamorizes it. Too much time goes into defining, describing, and looking for examples, so that students end up knowing quite a bit about what the problem is and how it manifests itself but very little else. As each new concern takes the spotlight, time, money, and expensive materials are piled onto the bandwagon, but the fundamental ethical considerations—both personal and social—remain largely disconnected.

If we must address specific issues, a reverse approach is probably better. A study of ethical and moral principles is the base, with reference to specific issues where appropriate. Giving the major attention to ethics and morality may be old-fashioned and not as stimulating as developing high-powered, latest-thing curriculum programs. But this approach can restore a sense of the continuity in human life. And it can permit a shift in emphasis from an expectation of pathology to a consideration of the possibility that, despite a sometimes poor record, the human race throughout history has at least claimed for itself, and aimed for, decency.

Another Basic Attitude

So many of the things we do in educating children are based on fearsome "What ifs." All around us are sermons and case studies convincing us that pathology and dysfunction are everywhere. One of the bits of wisdom my own children have passed along to me is the occasional substitution of *"So what?"* for the chronic *"What if?"*

What indeed is the *real* likelihood that something catastrophic is going to happen? And suppose it does? How does this possibility balance out against the emotional cost, to us *and* to the children, of fretting and viewing with alarm? Chronic nervousness, my children point out, is likely to be far more malignant than any potential disaster. Do the corrective programs legislated as a result of collective anxieties do much good—or do they sometimes just make matters worse?

Better, perhaps, is teaching our children—and learning ourselves—that few of life's trials are irreversible, that people *can* survive problems and even tragedies. Instead of boxing ourselves in with boundaries made of known or nameless fears, we can trust our own good sense to keep us out of many difficulties and to cope with whatever difficulties do arise.

One might call this attitude wishful thinking or false optimism. Then why isn't our excessive moralistic anxiety called wishful worrying or false pessimism? Why is hope the only thing that we don't allow ourselves? Why don't we forbid ourselves to worry, despair, and literally scare ourselves to death?

After all, saying, "Few of life's trials are irreversible" is only another way of saying it's permissible to hope. And hope is supposedly the whole point of our theology.

> Hope is not contrary to soberness and realism. It can go along with a clear and hardheaded view of our own inadequacies, and those of the world. The form it takes will depend on our character and disposition. In some people it will be a deep and joyful thankfulness for everything that happens. In others it will be a struggle against innate pessimism. In others again it will be the ability not to become embittered and full of rancour. It is not merely a matter of being confident that our own eternal destiny is in good hands. It means that we are sure that the life of the world is in good hands. God has good things in store for all men.[7]

Throughout this chapter I have expressed misgivings about dependency on experts. The experts I distrust I have defined as manipulative, coercive, serving to confuse and to undermine parents' confidence. I

7. Herder and Herder, *A New Catechism* (New York: Seabury Press, Inc., 1967).

do, however, believe in drawing on any wisdom—from people in high places or from ordinary individuals—that will bolster belief in ourselves and in our children. Some of these people may indeed be experts, but it's the authority of their words that counts—how the words make sense in relation to the things that I know and believe. For example, in a profile of Erik Erikson, Robert Coles cites Erikson's approach to parents and problems:

> What really keeps the generations in lively touch with one another is each parent's "ability to face his children with the feeling that he was able to save some vital enthusiasm from the conflicts of his childhood." In other words, problems generate a good deal that is valuable. They are not things to be avoided (who can avoid them, anyway?) or worried over—or even analyzed, except under very special circumstances.[8]

Another writer who makes sense is artist/sculptor Frederick Franck:

> In the history of everyone in whom the artist-within has survived conditioning, schooling, training, there are persons, influences that have kept him alive, awake, who have encouraged him without even trying—just by being. They have been one's real teachers.... (A) teacher who comes to mind did not draw at all. He was a rather forbidding lawyer, my father's attorney. One day we went to see him unexpectedly. When the maid showed us into the stiff drawing room he was sitting at his piano, so absorbed in a sonata that it took polite coughs to make our presence known. I was deeply moved, felt a sudden leap of love for this man. He gave me hope about growing up.[9]

This is the kind of security and encouragement that children need most—direct evidence that it's safe to go on to become one of the older folks. This is much better than the evidence that the older folks are just as scared and overwhelmed as the kids themselves, either about themselves, about the world, or about the kids. I believe that there are not many clearer messages in much of our teaching and childraising than that the world is alarming and that the kids themselves are among the most alarming of the world's problems.

It is essential that youngsters have the presence of people around them who like and are reasonably confident about what they're doing, who eat three square meals a day, who can laugh, and who don't have their heads down their own throats investigating their own interior mechanisms or doing the same to anyone else.

8. Robert Coles, "Profiles (Erik Erikson, Part I)," *The New Yorker,* November 7, 1970.
9. Frederick Franck, *The Zen of Seeing* (New York: Vintage Books, Random House, 1973).

With all the talk about the breakdown of the family—and with all the finger-pointing about who's at fault—I wonder how much of this problem is actually a result of the undermining of parents' belief in themselves. And how much of it is a result of the emotional overload of parents who have been pushed to an impossible level of responsibility?

In this chapter I've also spoken disparagingly of the guilt-inducing truisms and cliches so often urged upon parents. These truisms are the kind that stiffly point to our responsibility and let us know where we frequently fail. But there's another kind of truism that belongs to a freeing, whimsical, ground-level wisdom. It's a good idea for parents to store up all this healing wisdom they can get, and to ignore the other kind with gusto. It sometimes can be a relief, in a sea of family tensions, to throw up our hands and say, as my father often did: "God gave you your relatives—thank God you can choose your own friends!"

10

THE TOOLS OF THE TRADE: WHICH TOOLS? HOW MUCH TRADE?*

[Too many materials] aspire to High Moral Purpose when they really want to Cash In on Hot Issues.

Susan Rice

Housecleaning

Housecleaning may seem a peculiar subject to start with in talking about resources for religious education. But the process of housecleaning is essential to keeping up to date on these resources. It's also quite instructive. It's a good means of accomplishing that most longed-for thing in education, evaluation.

In housecleaning I try to analyze the things I throw out to try to find out why and how I acquired, kept, or filed them in the first place. Choosing what to preview from all the promotional material on teaching aids is only the beginning. You sit down with the catalogs and brochures and say you'd like this, this and this . . . and pretty soon the dining-room table is covered with boxes and film cans and you have to start looking at all the stuff. When it comes to buying or renting, it's difficult to balance the many variables of usefulness, taste, theological nuance, and cost. Then there's the matter of age-level, topic orientation, and seasonal interest.

I keep hoping that the selection process will be helped and refined by discovering the misguesses of the past. But over several housecleaning seasons it has become clear that even a good guessing instinct isn't much help. In dealing with educational materials, there are some hidden notions that influence judgment.

In this chapter let us consider some of these hidden notions. In the preceding chapter I suggested that we might profit by doing less rather than more. This is true for teachers, too, especially when it comes to resources. And, like parents, teachers need to take an honest look at

* This chapter was written by Janet M. Bennett of Boonton, N.J.

their motives.   To what extent are teachers responding to outside influences such as fads in sociology and education?   How much teaching
involves real enthusiasm for the subject or interest in the student, and
how much is an effort to live up to an image of "successful teacher"?
Is "successful teacher" as much a siren song as "successful parent"?
These questions are important for the whole teaching enterprise, but
they also have a lot to do with how many, and which kinds of, resources teachers will require.

This chapter will consider only the most commonly-used resources—films, filmstrips, and books.   Though I may concentrate on
one medium more than another at various times, in general they all
come under the same classification as resources.   More exotic materials and equipment are around, of course; guidebooks such as *Practical
Guide to Classroom Media,* by Dolores and David Linton (Dayton,
Ohio: Pflaum/Standard, 1971; $3.50), give considerable detail on recent
products and ways to use them.

"A Diller, a Dollar, a Ten o'Clock Scholar."   In this old jingle, the association of dollar and scholar was made only for rhyming purposes.
But the relationship has become closer and closer, not only in schools
and in resource-selecting but in families as well.   Since education is
one of our highest priorities, a thing to which we give almost unconditional approval (regardless of how we individually think it ought to
be carried out), any expenditure can be justified by calling it "educational."   Somehow it's possible to bypass criticisms like "materialistic," "spendthrift," or "overindulgent" when whatever you're buying claims to further somebody's education.   As long as there's an
educational objective, books and creative playthings of all kinds can be
loaded onto youngsters.

The producers of these items quickly caught onto the idea, and now
any manipulable object, gooey substance, picture, or word-thing can be
said to "develop" one quality or another in the child—his or her motor
or mental ability, or emotional stability—*for a price.*   The children
with "the gimmes" recognize the game and they surround their dime-
store pleading with, "I need it for school!"

Educators and schools themselves now seem very much like children
with the gimmes, turned loose in the toy department with the tax-
payers' money and the same persuader: "I need it for school!"   Just as
toys for children have to be educational, education itself has to have
toys.

All along teachers have wanted to liven up the teaching process by
occasional diversions like spelling bees and guessing games, and maybe
some handmade flash cards.   But now that education is one of our big-
gest industries, educational psychology has gone to market with a mul-

titude of new toys and games in the form of films, filmstrips, tapes, records, and the king of authorized toys, the simulation game.

In New Jersey between 1964 and 1974, the cost of audiovisual materials rose from 4 million to 14 million dollars. In the same ten years, expenditure for teaching supplies—paper, paste, scissors, and such—increased from 11 million to 35 million dollars. A school superintendent in a large New Jersey school district complains:

> It's the influence of the manufacturers that bothers me. Every year after the conventions, we are urged to buy this or that latest overhead projector, or this or that set of teaching materials. This year, for us, the big items have been tape recorders and calculators. We are trying to hold the line but the pressures are enormous.[1]

At the same time, this superintendent says that although the use of a variety of materials is justified by the efforts to provide individualized instruction, it hasn't done much to improve the students' basic skill levels.

Teachers and administrators are constantly pressured—by salesmen or by a blizzard of promotional brochures—to buy not only hardware but also films, filmstrips, and the latest revision of the text series, complete with matching workbooks, teacher guides, slides, and records. Brides' magazines lure young ladies to believe in the necessity of a complete trousseau and travel-package honeymoon; later these same young ladies are urged to buy the complete approved layette for their first baby. In just the same way teachers are persuaded that they must have a whole catalog-full of educational necessities.

The process of housecleaning illustrates the amount of time we spend on materials handling—"getting and spending, laying waste our powers." There's the ordering and bill-paying and filing, and the cataloging and storing and evaluation, the scheduling and setting up.

For Ivan Illich, getting and spending is the name of the game. It's not just that education has increasingly become a big business, it's that business is the whole point of education. Students and teachers are trained to be consumers dependent on producers of materials and ideas.

Whether you pursue the argument as far as Illich does or not, you *can* cut down on some of the costly, time-consuming, space-requiring work of providing resources for religious teaching. As Bess Myerson says repeatedly (in a filmstrip that, at $48.50, isn't exactly a giveaway), "You don't have to buy it!"[2]

1. *The Sunday Star-Ledger*, February 22, 1976.
2. *The Exploited Generation* filmstrip (New York: Guidance Associates/Motion Media; $48.50).

Though the New Jersey school superintendent says that audiovisual and other materials are justified in the effort to individualize, you can individualize all by yourself, maybe with a blackboard and chalk, with pencil and paper, or only with your voice, and often much more successfully than with a mass-merchandised individualizer. Harold Mantell, whose *Films for the Humanities* productions are meant as a means of introducing students to literature and encouraging them to return to the printed word, once urged an audience: "Don't get hung up on hardware. Remember that the most worthwhile communication is the same one it's always been, one human voice speaking to another."

If you do want extra materials, you can buy just a few, resisting the temptation to grab everything in sight, just as you would in a department store full of pans or dolls or jeans. You can buy cheaper things—prices vary, and so does quality—and not just succumb to in-group name brands or the brochure's appeal to professionalism. You can rent or you can borrow. (Unless they're in a public library collection, however, materials described as "free-loan" can be a trap. The occasional really useful item is seldom worth all the time spent in wading through the stockpile of industry documentaries and promotional films, or in sweating out the long waiting time needed in booking.)

But more important, you can break out of the usual ways of thinking about and using resource materials, ways of thinking that generally require you to do more and harder work. How you approach and use teaching materials is as much influenced by marketing as is your wanting to use them in the first place.

"The Matched Set." This idea promotes the whole line of interconnecting materials included in a publisher's "program." The concept is similar to the department store/decorator dream of color-coordinated bedroom and bath. With impressive charts and other promotional papers, any items a publisher wants you to buy will be carefully tied into whatever materials you may already be using, in intricately interlocking patterns. In textbooks, neatly appropriate suggestions for audiovisual supports will be plugged in for every topic, chapter, age group, and season a harried teacher could possibly encounter. The brochures and title pages will carry impressive lists of the educational and psychological experts who developed the program and worked up these charts, in order to create and enhance an atmosphere of solid research.

Religious publishers make their suggestions with ex cathedra self-assurance. Secular publishers are suitably deferential, and their brochures are laced with key phrases so you'll know they understand and respect your spiritual and educational needs and ideologies.

This approach, of course, is great for sales. And in theory it may sound attractive enough, given the fact that religion teaching is so often turned over to anxious and inexperienced voluntɛers. But this "matched-set, color-coordinated" attitude can only cause greater insecurity and confusion.

Suggesting that audiovisual materials ought to match the text and the schedule gives the illusion that for every idea, theological point, historical fact, or sacramental nuance there will be a perfect audiovisual partner. Such correspondence of topic and material is not even possible, not only because of the vastness of the content but because of the variety of classroom situations in which the content is presented.

Among the users of my own four-year telephone-reference service, the hardest callers to help were the seminarians working in religious education. They'd ask for an in-depth, specific film or filmstrip precisely tailored as to theological nuance, contemporary and historical attitude and atmosphere, for use with a class of a special age group and social background, free or for an under-ten-dollar rental, for tomorrow afternoon. One seminarian called me at just the moment of the emergence of the state of Bangladesh, requesting a film to illustrate that event to a class of fourth-graders. With little likelihood that such a topic would be on the market, I desperately suggested the opening portion of "The World Is Born" section of Disney's *Fantasia*, on hand at the county library. Fortunately, seminarians are also invariably polite and grateful, and this one was, he said, happy with my choice.

Generally, the narrower the subject and treatment requirements the less likely you are to find a film about it. Marketing is one of the reasons for this, since a broad, multiapplication (even ambiguous) film will have a wider audience and potential sales value than a specific one.

Furthermore, there are differences in the kinds of things each medium can do, and limits to what any one medium can do. Filmstrips provide pictures to watch while you listen to a talk; they can therefore be more directly instructional than most films—and you can always tape your own material to go with the pictures. (Sometimes it's the pictures you ought to replace; in many filmstrips the pictures are so nonspecific, so hard to relate to the script even with the audible tone to guide you when to change pictures, that they could easily be done away with altogether. But then, everybody *knows* how hard it is to get a class to sit still for a tape.)

A film can be instructional if it's an interview or documentary, neither of which is popular with teachers who are bent on teaching by entertaining, since they've been taught that this is all students will tolerate. The story kind of film is not geared for specific, direct teaching of academic points:

> Movie directors sense the intellectual resistances of their medium and
> confine thinking in movies to references to ideas rather than attempts to
> develop and define them. Even the most advanced moviemakers rarely
> go beyond namedropping and ideadropping. . . .[3]

Another practical problem underlying the "matched-set" approach is
the fact that audiovisual recommendations in many texts are made by
individuals who, though they may be veteran educators or psychologists, actually have had only limited exposure to resources. Though
the audiovisual references seem thoughtfully selected, they are often of
poor quality, outdated, and impossible to procure. Often a textwriter
will simply lift somebody else's list, adopting the previous selector's
determination about the topic and its use, without personally looking
at or handling the item in question. More than once I've been asked
by phone, by letter, or by being buttonholed in a corridor, if I could
think of a film, a record, or even a whole list of materials for someone
who was writing a book. In each case my top-of-the-head suggestion
or mailed compilation was scooped up and included in the author's
manuscript without a second look. Yet I'm sure the readers of these
books dutifully followed the recommendations as though they were really worth something.

An awful lot of teacher time, effort, and money is expended because
of this compulsion to find a corresponding teaching aid for every point
to be presented. You can be a world traveller without owning a
matched set of luggage, or you can be a terrific cook without a collection of avocado-colored gourmet pots. You can also teach without
ever touching a piece of celluloid or plugging in an appliance, no matter how much your associates may sneer. If you do like to use audiovisual materials, you don't have to agonize over matching everything
you're teaching step-by-step and line-by-line.

The Age-Level Hangup. Like the matched-set mentality, this obsession with age-levels is another route to overspending of time and
money. Teachers have been led to look for something for every topic
under the sun, presented in modifications for each age-level. All the
abstractions (community, awareness, forgiveness), all the issues (poverty, war, abortion, drugs, ecology), all the gospel stories (each parable,
miracle, or event), all the time periods (Early Christian, Reformation,
1963 Council), all the personages (St. Paul, Mother Teresa, Tom Doo-
ley, John Kennedy), and all the sacraments—*all* must be presented by a
separate audiovisual *thing* projectable to each group from grade school
through junior high, through teens and golden-agers. I have received

3. Harold Rosenberg, "Notes on Seeing *Barry Lyndon*," *New York Times*, February 29,
   1976.

requests for materials narrowed down almost to month of birth of audience members. It's like looking for greeting cards for "My teacher's aunt's neighbor's dog's christening."

As with subject-matching, this kind of close age-matching often just can't be done. However, though I said earlier that audiovisual producers would rather reach a wide audience and market with a single item, as dependency on audiovisual materials increases and as expectation and demand create a bigger and bigger market, producers will increasingly oblige by providing more diversified subject and age products. This, in turn, will add to the inflationary spiral of problems, for as each new age-specific or subject-specific item appears, there's that much more stuff to look at, order, and store. And, as more and more materials are produced, a teacher who can't find a particular specialized item will worry that he or she just hasn't worked hard enough or been clever enough to locate it; it can't *possibly* be that the material just doesn't exist.

Related to this age-subject tangle is the whole problem of cataloging. Catalogs, librarians, description writers, and audiences can differ widely in what they say a filmstrip or film is about or who it's for. Catalog listings, ironically, can limit what's available to users as easily as expanding the offerings. The same film may be listed in different places as biography because of the person it's about, as adventure because of what this person does, as art because of the film technique employed (or if the subject is an artist), travel because of where the subject lives—or as documentary, history, or under a million other classifications. Or a film could even be listed under the name of the filmmaker if he or she is especially famous.

In my own public library film catalog, teachers hunting for material on the "Generation Gap" would have missed *Replay*, which is listed under Communications, a category that to me suggests Marconi or the TV industry. They never would have found a film useful for "Celebration of Life" or "Right to Life," *Leo Beuerman*, which is listed under the two categories of Biography and Handicapped. Other libraries include this film under Human Relations and Psychology categories. There are a lot of titles suggested under "Birth Control," but the films listed there are really about the population explosion, a topic that doesn't have a separate listing of its own.

The problem is not just that opinions vary. A newspaper friend of mine recently had to write the horoscope column for several days when the regular syndicated copy was delayed in the mail. The newspaper's readers had no way of knowing that the predictions they'd be basing their plans on had been dreamed up by the sports editor rather than by any consultant astrologer. I suspect that in the process of

making up catalogs a lot of subject headings are arrived at just as unre-
liably through weariness or rushing to meet a printer's deadline. A decision may be the result of a bored shout across the room, "Hey, do
you remember what that film was about?"

I have found in my own experience of running innumerable film pre-
views that age-level too is in the eye of the beholder. Preview audiences were given report forms on which they were to state the ages
they thought the films might suit. Except for a few titles specifically
about very young children, or described in catalogs as being meant for
very young children, the ages the audience members suggested for any
given film covered the entire life span. An occasional viewer might
point out that grown-ups would also like the children's films, but generally adults saw themselves as selectors of, but not legitimate enjoy-
ers of the category Children's Films. Yet it seemed obvious that these
grown-ups *had* really liked these selections; in fact it's quite likely
that such films, like so many children's books, are really aimed at the
grown-up's wishful remembrance of his own past rather than at the
present-day child.

Finally, the topic-age obsession often means that the teachers will be
satisfied to find a film that covers just the right subject, for just the
right age group, without worrying about how good a film it is. In fact,
quality ends up being low on the priority list in this resource rat race.
Sometimes it even seems that correctness of subject and audience is a
major standard of perceived value. Films and filmstrips don't have to
be masterpieces and award-winners—few of them are. In the combinations of story or theme and method of presentation, one facet or the
other may be flawed to some degree. But it doesn't pay to grasp too
eagerly at a product just because it's *about* the needed topic and *for* the
needed age, without concern for the adequacy of the idea and its rendition.

New Attitudes and Purposes

Shifting from the more obvious merchandising influences, other complicating factors in resource work arise from prevailing social and academic attitudes and methods. Though I don't want to belabor the image of publishers and producers as men like Robinson's *Aaron Stark*
"with eyes like little dollars in the dark," current attitudes are also
subject to the considerations of commerce. Too many materials, according to film critic Susan Rice, ". . . aspire to High Moral Purpose
when they really want to Cash In on Hot Issues." (*Media and Methods*, February 1971) Everything I've described in the previous chapter

applies here as well, but I want to be more specific in relating these attitudes to audiovisual use.

The emphasis on the social gospel, the role of the church in the modern world, meant that religious education felt compelled to involve itself with the "hot issues" Susan Rice speaks of. Some of these issues were there all along, some people were involved with them all along; for instance, Dorothy Day and the poor. But suddenly everybody was talking about the "inner city," and films, texts, and posters made use of newsclips showing all kinds of poverty situations. Some issues, of course, were in current focus because they were new happenings — the Vietnam war, peace and civil rights marches, assassinations, and middle-class drug abuse. In any case, anything you had read about in the newspapers could be found shortly afterwards in a religion class.

In defining what is meant by "involvement" the church pointed out that we should be concerned with, and related to, the affairs of all men; that is, we should be "relevant." Once having opened their eyes and looked around them, inevitably everyone suddenly noticed the distance between the church's customary reserved, self-involved, and structured identity, and the realities and complexities of the world it claimed to serve.

"Involvement" meant what we should do; "relevant" meant how we should be and sound. Even though, as mentioned before, there had been individuals in and out of the church who had recognized and dealt with the world as it was, suddenly multitudes of enthusiastic and well-meaning (and conscience-struck) people began to jump into the fray. Imperceptibly both "involvement" and "relevance" took on a life of their own. People became involved because involvement was *the thing to do*; preaching, teaching, and publishing became relevant for the sake of relevance. Interest in issues became not only matters of conscience but also matters of style.

Like the newspapers, religious education found that nothing is staler than yesterday's issue. New buzzwords and new issues tumbled along, accompanying the shifting headline issues, one following another in rapid succession. With so many new things to think about *now*, everyone, not just the youngsters, became a whole big Now Generation. An organization of historians recently lamented a widespread malady called "presentism," which means the practise of looking at current events taken out of historical perspective. A novelist, similarly, complains of the "Disease of contemporaneity."

Granted, there was some harking back to the early Christians — adoption of earthenware utensils for mass, burlap vestments, small-group liturgies. But this was all done *in terms of* now, in the haste to divest ourselves of our guilty wealth and specialness. *Everything* was done in terms of now. Again imperceptibly—and paradoxically—our new-found concern for others resulted in an enormous amount of *self*-preoccupation, self-involvement, and self-analysis. If there was an appropriate word for religious education in the sixties, it was "self-conscious."

This was probably an inevitable result of the permission to think which we had been granted by the Council. Middle-aged adolescents, as we called ourselves, we plunged into the long-delayed and fascinating business of finding out who we were. We thought we were teaching our children, but we were talking to ourselves at the same time. As we showed filmstrip after filmstrip and film after film, we were watching too. In most cases our interest was far greater than our students'. Teaching the youngsters became, like the audiovisuals, another medium for learning about ourselves and working out our new ways of thinking.

The audiovisuals, symbols of now, were a logical means of presenting new ideas. But at the same time they multiplied our reflection of ourselves and our children, our country, community, and world—our *now*. Together with our students, we watched our performance, inspected our behavior, matched our attitudes and functioning with those shown on celluloid. And for all of us, grown-ups and children alike, our living ran the risk of becoming artificial, ersatz, as we tried to locate each episode of community, to identify each evidence of loving, each burst of—of all things—spontaneity, in these captured images. Some of us began to look to the films and filmstrips for models, for clues to the right way to look and act. The Filmstrip Christian was not too far removed from the Cosmopolitan Girl and the Marlboro Man.

In living up to the current idea of religion we watched ourselves and our associates as if on closed-circuit television, performing a sort of catechetical choreography. There we all were, like glimpses in a store window, a parade of people of all colors and ages, faces beautiful and plain, mailmen and hippies, priests and babies, soldiers and housewives, a candid-camera commercial for the newest and brightest idea packages—community, alienation, communication, reconciliation, love.

Among the idea package was one called Awareness. The focus broadened from people and events to rays of sunlight, leaves, flower petals, and dewdrops—another fragmented view of *right now*. Again imperceptibly, the media idea backfired. Some people were so over-exposed to kodachrome that they came to hate it. Others suffered a more subtle—and unfortunate—psychological reaction: reverse conditioning.   The repeated view of kodachrome reality—a reality heightened by filming selectivity, technique, and style—came to be more compelling than real trees, real skin, the dull and uninspiring *real* world.   On film, poverty can be dramatic and challenging; in reality, it's only wearyingly miserable and monotonous.

There are even more concrete contradictions.   For one thing, there's something strange about a religion teacher using a 500-dollar projector to show a film about world poverty.   The film itself sells for 250 dollars and rents for 25 dollars a day.   Another film on ecology scolds about waste, destruction of forestry, and the use of energy, while the projector whirrs on and the duplicator pumps out the piles of dittoes the students will use to answer questions, along with the take-home announcements about the Earth Day celebration.

The media, if not the whole message, certainly have been part of the message, a part that badly needs sorting out.   Besides the loss of time sense and historical perspective, and the contradictions between what we thought we were doing and what the audiovisuals made us do, there was another difficulty.   The over concentration on present, combined with the use of quick-change media, meant that we were offering our students a superficial consideration of a series of brightly-spotlighted concerns—a smattering of ignorance in technicolor with sitar accompaniment.

In 1970 Harvard sociologist David Riesman wrote:

> Young people are often tempted today to suppose that the war against war and against injustice requires only will and courage, and not also trained intelligence.[4]

We are not now as naive as we once were about social change, but there doesn't seem to have been any appreciable progress in the effort to train intelligence.   Consciousness-raising still occupies much of our teaching time, but a raised consciousness can have only passing effect without the backup of a trained brain.

These problems related to audiovisual use in religious education were probably unavoidable during the shifting sixties.   Things happened so fast it was hard to figure out what was going on and why. We heard that rapid change was sure to continue ("Change" was a favorite lecture topic for awhile), so we didn't dare stop to reflect lest we be trampled by the next idea.

4. David Riesman, *Radcliffe Quarterly*, December 1970.

"Old Faithful" Attitudes and Purposes

Another hazard connected with attitudes in audiovisual use is an old familiar one. This is the matter of propaganda—tractarianism—whether conscious or unconscious.

Even if you manage to teach an old dog new tricks, he's likely to be basically the same old dog. Though some people painfully or enthusiastically shifted position during the sixties, many more learned some new tricks and bought some new toys but couldn't do much about the underlying habits of thinking. When a moralistic teacher said, "I'll show them a film" it was likely that the motive, just as in the old days, was "*I'll* show them."

A teacher came to my office one day looking for supporting materials for her seventh-graders. She was using one of the most psychedelic of the current text series, full of graffiti, cartoons, and such. I had done a lengthy review of this series and was bothered by the grimness of many of the stories. I asked this teacher if she felt that any of the stories seemed too strong for the children in her class and she exclaimed, "Oh, good heavens, they need this strong stuff. You can't let them have it too easy, you know!"

The film portrait *Phoebe* and its companion piece *The Game* continue to be favorite choices for delivering the age-old warning, "You're gonna get in trouble if you don't watch out." Even though a teacher may use a new and sophisticated medium, the point is to bring home the same old moral message.

When Shel Silverstein's *The Giving Tree* emerged on film in 1973, it was scooped up joyfully by religious education people because of its image of a perennial favorite, the unstinting self-sacrificer. This dumb tree allows itself to be chopped up a little at a time to serve the requirements of a snivelling ingrate. I suppose this unpleasant tale, with its cute drawings, is great for preaching dogmas like "turn the other cheek" and "lay down your life." But neither the inconsiderate, world-weary, self-pitying boy nor the neurotic tree is much of a model, and this film's use simply perpetuates a misreading of the meaning of service, sacrifice, and giving. Anyone attracted to this film might consider the following excerpt from a small book that—despite its inhibiting title—nevertheless contains several useful essays, among them one entitled "The Grace to be Well," by Gregory Baum:

> There is in man a seeking of sacrifice and self-abasement that is as destructive as selfishness ... Because the ascetical tradition did not acknowledge this hidden self-hatred in man, it advised people to flee from selfishness without warning them that by doing so they could fall into the terrible trap, equally displeasing to God, of their hidden self-hatred

... An uncritical insistence on fighting self-centeredness often encouraged men to follow their hidden desire to be unhappy.[5]

Guilt-inducing, another familiar activity, was a factor in the use of war-related films. I invited two nonteaching friends to a film preview one evening. On the program were the much-requested *The Hand, Occurrence at Owl Creek Bridge,* and *Peace and Voices in the Wilderness.* Afterward one of my friends exploded, "How these church people love their guilt! Now I know why my mother wouldn't let me go to Sunday school. She used to take me for walks in the woods instead."

Time and again teachers have called me to locate a source for *Night and Fog* in order to blast the youngsters out of their apathy; *St. Matthew's Passion* likewise was used as a bludgeon but with the added bonus of liturgical, seasonal pertinence.

Worst of all is Alpha's filmstrip *The Way of the Cross for Children,* top on my list of horrible examples. Young children can do little to alleviate the sufferings of the crippled or war-wounded children shown in this grade-school filmstrip. All they can do is feel uneasy because most of them themselves have never had any shattering affliction.

As usual with this kind of preaching, it's assumed that the audience has no problem of its own and should be grateful for such undeserved comfort. Consciousness-raising also assumes that consciousnesses *need* raising, without any acknowledgement that some children – and grown-ups too – are painfully oversensitive and aware, "thin-skinned" as they say, not only about themselves but about everything. It seems strange indeed that religious teaching can so passionately espouse sensitivity and compassion toward significant causes, with plenty of high-powered materials, but in its moral fervor and adulation of media ride roughshod over the sensibilities of its students.

Treating children as an undifferentiated group, as receptacles for the program's thoughts, is as much an injustice as any other. Children are entitled to keep their anxieties to themselves; in their growing-up years they may also be unable to define these anxieties to themselves, let alone to adults. But it's a mistake to assume they have no worries, or that they are insensitive unless we press on a nerve. And it's a mistake to think that children, in a children's context, perceive the problems we show them in the same way that we do.

When my daughter Martha was in eighth grade, feminist talk was just beginning. The girls in her class, taking arguments they had heard to their logical conclusion, understood that they, as soon as they

---

[5] Alfred R. Joyce and E. Mark Stern, *Holiness and Mental Health* (Paramus, N.J.: Paulist Newman Press, 1972).

were old enough, would be drafted. And they had begun making plans to go on starvation diets so they'd be too skinny to qualify, because, as Martha said, "They'd be so scared."

Another topic of interest at the time was speculation that an unseasonal heat wave was a result of the earth's rapid move in the direction of the sun. I overheard a conversation among Martha's friends in which they concluded soberly, "Well, it might be so—after all, the world has been getting pretty bad. Remember Noah!"

As for myself, I can remember hearing a great deal of conversation about the veterans' bonus in 1936. As a result of the importance attached to this issue by innumerable conversations (after all, this sum of about 600 dollars was, in that economy's terms, considerable wealth, enough to approach a downpayment on a house), I used to sit on my front steps watching for the President's arrival in a coach with liveried messengers to deliver our share.

Although this particular concern was somewhat exaggerated, it was not really worrisome, but other matters were. The tear-jerking *White Cliffs of Dover*, the *Reader's Digest* version of *The Diary of Anne Frank*, the newsreels of bombings and refugees, the Saturday matinees about the boy who worked in the drugstore, lived in the white house with the picket fence on the tree-lined street, and got killed in the war—not to mention all my boy cousins who were in Germany or Guam—this was all the awareness I needed in the 1940s.

Nobody—not *anybody*—had any idea how much the war was worrying me. Mercifully I had no guidance counselor to recommend talking the matter over singly or in a "pool-your-problem" group. The best antidote for me at the time—at age eleven, twelve, and thirteen—was knowing that my parents, who read the papers, listened to H. V. Kaltenborn and Walter Winchell, and who as far as I knew weren't stupid, were still able to listen to the ball game, play cribbage, and sing about "Pat McCarty, Hale and Hearty . . ." on the way home from our gas-rationed car rides. I remember feeling a little silly but getting myself calmed down enough to sleep when I imagined getting bombed while in the rapid transit or somewhere else, by imagining that if I put my head in my mother's lap (always with a flowered Fruit-of-the-Loom® apron) somehow she'd figure out a solution. I knew this was stretching things a little, but this was the game I played with myself and it worked. Now twelve and thirteen are supposed to be pretty old—junior high age—and nobody would have thought of me as anything but a quite grown-up, unconcerned kid at the time. I'm sure glad the only films I ever got to see in school were *The Scarlet Pimpernel* and a dumb thing about good posture!

On the other hand, once in a while children are protected from this unspeakable kind of "teaching" by their own innate good sense and logic.   As first-graders we were chronically exposed to that era's version of brutality, a horrid little magazine called *Manna*.   This publication was notable for heartrending stories of little boys in white first-communion suits who were incredibly holy and invariably in the process of succumbing to some indefinable and incurable malady.   Because of various spiritual machinations such a child would ultimately be permitted a rare privilege: to "carry the book" at mass, at the tender and unorthodox age of five, in order to fulfill a consuming desire, before being beautifully laid to rest in a white satin box.

We quickly got the point that it didn't pay to be too conspicuously good or holy, or you'd never make it to second grade.

Since there's no guarantee that this kind of logic is inherent in children, and since children, teaching materials, and circumstances vary so enormously, teachers should avoid trying to make youngsters holy or responsible by making them feel guilty.

Message-Plundering

Because of their broader scope, films more than filmstrips are pressed into service for a variety of purposes, acknowledged or unconscious, which may be quite different from the purpose the filmmaker had in mind.   *Phoebe* is a good case in point.   As stated previously, this film is a popular vehicle for preaching against premarital sex.   Its central characters are familiar in their dress, talk, and behavior—marvelously easy for a teenage audience to identify with in pressing home the point that it *can* happen to you.

Poor Phoebe is heartbreaking to contemplate in her predicament—so young, so lovely, and so unfortunate.   The film provides a great combination—a clear-cut moral backed up by vicarious emotional experience.   Yet filmmaker George Kaczender meant this film as a study of the psychological currents at work in connection with the dilemma of untimely and unwanted pregnancy, as a profile of human conflict, not a filmed sermon.   In the context of young people's lives, the tensions arise from the attitudes of parents and society, and from the sudden responsibility that will be demanded.   But an equally anguished portrait might just as well have been constructed around the unplanned pregnancy of a woman with only a short time to live, or of a woman who seems destined to give birth only to handicapped children.   For teachers, though, the psychological drama in *Phoebe* is just what makes it so terrific for shoving home the moral point.   Though *The Game* similarly concerns itself with adolescent culture and mores, Kaczender himself was more interested in the question of conscience and remorse than in the preachifying possibilities of the seduction.

Other films have been similarly raided for currently serviceable messages for religious education. The prevailing mindset can push perception in a direction that may be difficult to support. For instance, one of my film preview audiences saw in *Good Night Socrates* a vision of the young as highly adaptable, future-oriented, and undisturbed by change. Yet the narrator, looking back to his impressions of himself as a little boy watching the destruction of the way of life in Chicago's Greek Town, speaks of the lost harmony, the melody that was never recovered. Though he says at the end, speaking to Socrates Street, the scene of much of the urban renewal, "I will remember you always, with love and pain. Now I am free," this statement is, at least, ambiguous. The message of youth as having a trusting grip on the future was one that was widely promoted at the time of my preview (1971), and it was suitably programmed into the audience responses.

Discussion guides often begin by asking, "What was the filmmaker trying to say?" This is not the same question as, "What did you get from this film?" Nor is it at all the same as, "What are you using this film for in teaching?" Yet more often than not, religious educators think their purposes and the filmmakers' are the same. But just because you *can* use a particular film for a religion class and *can* extract all kinds of marvelously appropriate lessons from it, does not in any way mean that this is what the film is actually for or about. Quite possibly such message-plundering does the film an injustice. Film critic Pauline Kael once said that if you don't believe it's possible to destroy movies you underestimate the power of education.

On the other hand, some films, rather than being destroyed by religious education, have been elevated to a significance they haven't deserved. According to one friend of mine, anything inscrutable will sell. Films that are simply exercises in technique have been eagerly snatched up by wide-eyed symbol-hunters. *A Scrap of Paper and a Piece of String* is as profound, apparently, as "a loaf of bread, a jug of wine, and thou. . . ." You begin by playing with *A Dot and a Line* and maybe a little *Orange and Blue,* seeing all kinds of anthropomorphic goings-on, and soon you're awash in bits of colored glass and even a *Boiled Egg.* "I know why he made that film," a viewer once told me disgustedly, "To enter it in a film festival." This kind of nursery-level Rorschach-testing has slowed some as budgets have tightened—good thing, too.

Harder to give up are the allegory films, the "modern parables" that so it's said, would be what Jesus would be using if he were on earth today. (I once wrote in a magazine article that maybe that's why he *isn't* here today, but the editor deleted it before sending it to press. *Parable* is the most obvious example of the "allegory" genre, and a dreadful example it is. The only possible good I can see in it is tha this film introduces to a wide audience (it was originally shown at the 1965 New York World's Fair) the idea that there can be parallel as well as literal interpretations of scripture. But the parallel is imprecise and the context strained to suit the purpose of the message. The clown's assistance is gratuitous and suggests ego-tripping rather than genuine bearing of burdens. The circus is harsh and unhappy, with a sadistic acrobatic performance directed by a hysterical black-uniformed mario-netteer. This peculiar Christ-clown might have been of some *real* service if he had led the evacuation of the child-audience from this un-healthy place. Instead, he proceeds to demonstrate his poor judgment by facilitating his own demise at the hands of lunatics. (The "modern crucifixion" is one of the reasons for this film's continued use for Lenten programs. A far better version of the crucifixion concept, with logical underpinnings, is to be found in Chaim Potok's *My Name Is Asher Lev.*)

I think this film is nasty. But again, maybe some youngsters have their own built-in immunity. One of my young friends saw *Parable* recently at a parish program and found it "just dumb and unintelli-gible."

Mental Malnutrition

"Just dumb" isn't much consolation. What critic Jean Stafford says about books is true also of audiovisuals:

> Most children can smell a rat a mile off, but at the same time they can be intimidated by parents and teachers who, being bigger, can force-feed them fare ... that not only is unnourishing but may lead to functional disorders of the brain later on, the most crippling of which—and the most damaging to the republic—is stupidity.[6]

I'm always disturbed to see so many youngsters on their way to school armed with their "breakfast," a can of purple soda and a packaged pie. But what will be offered them by way of education when they arrive is quite likely to be just as unnutritious, as full of empty calories, as what goes into their stomachs. Too much of present-day teaching is unnutritious, empty-calorie education, especially when it comes to au-diovisual use. Films that are only snacks and seasonings are offered as the whole meal. Even worse, some materials are like food additives, which not only offer no food value but are possibly damaging, and in any case are included only to make the product more eye-catching and saleable.

6. Jean Stafford, "Books," *The New Yorker*, December 5, 1970.

It's not only the young bodies that are undernourished and over-stressed. Nutrition and public health are just as poorly considered in taking care of youngsters' minds and emotions. There's a special problem with film, whether it's well done or badly done. The problem is this: film experts say that film is an "experience." It can be a very potent experience, drawing the viewer vicariously into high-intensity situations and feelings. Youngsters have plenty to do these days in coping with the ordinary stresses of growth and the ordinary life experiences directly concerning them. If only from the standpoint of emotional exhaustion, which seems to be a real possibility with films like *Night and Fog* and *Phoebe* (both films of high quality), the matter of proper use of films deserves much more consideration than it gets.

We all know that teen-agers are subject to mononucleosis, whether directly or indirectly, resulting from overexertion and undernutrition. I also worry about mental and emotional mononucleosis. Many movies, or a regular fare of them, can demand so much of the young viewer that emotional reserves needed elsewhere may be depleted. In addition, the total religious education climate, which implies parent and church concurrence with the obvious or subliminal messages, can contribute to the youngster's difficulties in sorting out adequate responses.

The hazard of vicarious film experience is most evident in those films that consider the youngsters' own world. As Jean Stafford observes:

> Adolescence is so complex a season of life and frequently so miserable, that it would be merciful not to treat it realistically. Let the young go directly from E.B. White to Jane Austen. . . .[7]

The Passion for Parables

We have talked a good bit about films and film attitudes during the sixties. As time passed, areas of concern continued to succeed one another according to headline importance. Some of the earlier concerns just faded away, but others have settled into place as curriculum regulars. Certain films continue to be used because they have become automatically associated with a certain topic, because the textbook-writers go on including references to them in their new revisions, because word-of-mouth keeps the recommendations current among an ever-changing population of teachers who have no hope of keeping in touch with newer releases. *Parable* fits all of these categories. But in addition *Parable*

7. Ibid.

serves as an example of a favored concept, the translation of Bible material into modern terms.

Teachers and publishers really like this "parable" idea. I suppose it's understandable. After all, we are supposed to relate scripture to our own circumstances, to illuminate and find meaning and support for our lives. I enjoyed algebra's substituting because of the neat way that letters and numbers could stand for each other and the way a whole new package could be made by plugging in a new set of variables. I suppose that's why magic decoder rings were so much fun too. But what made algebra and codes so satisfying was the precision of the parts and their relationships. Precision is often pitifully lacking in audiovisual parables and allegories. The pieces just don't match.

Furthermore, in many of these allegories, pedestrian, dull parts are put together in stories that have no style, depth, or point, just for the sake of working out a parallel to the Gospel story. The Twenty-third Publications' *The Rescue* is a case in point. It's a modern version of the Good Shepherd parable, designed to be "A delightful way to convey to the first- to third-graders how much God loves them."

This is a cartoon story of Mr. Dobson, caretaker at the city pound, and of a fire in the kennels and cages. Mr. Dobson gets the animals out and the firemen are on their way. But as he checks his list of animals he finds that one little puppy has stayed behind in the burning building. So—what does Mr. Dobson do? Naturally he goes back to rescue the puppy. And, says the narrator, "This story is like a story that Jesus told once about a shepherd who rescued a lost sheep ... Was Mr. Dobson like the shepherd? Did he love the animals in the same way? Who would go out and find you, if you were lost?"

But, mothers, fathers, and teachers, do you, as I do, flinch at the implication that an imitation of Christ involves going back into a burning building to rescue a puppy?

Even with the teleKETICS film *The Stray*, which is, I think, a more satisfactory production, I had to object to the busdriver's leaving the children all by themselves in the bus while he races off to find the child left behind in the zoo. True, the shepherd left his flock to go find the lost sheep, but I'm not sure that you can predict the behavior of a busload of grade-school children in quite the same terms as that of a bunch of 30-A.D. Israeli sheep.

Referring again to *The Rescue*, when Christ was telling the story of the lost sheep, he was, after all, telling it to grown-ups who would have a different sense of prudence about going back into a burning building than would a class of first- to third-graders.

Besides, what's so hard or in-need-of-relevance in the story of the sheep and the shepherd?

This brings us to the matter of playing things straight; that is, using films and filmstrips that give straightforward presentations of the conventional academic material of religion. As mentioned earlier, theology is hard to depict on film. Many theology-related filmstrips are like overlong and illustrated master's theses disguised with pop music and a designer package. (*This Sunday Party*, for instance, is a very heavy meal.) As for the Bible, nobody dares to tell any of its stories straight or the youngsters would be bored. All the publicity about the film-generation children, and about the need to adopt the media world's entertainment techniques, persuades teachers that the original stories have to be given a new treatment.

It's possible that young people's boredom, if it does exist, does so because the whole subject of religion is a grown-up subject. That doesn't mean we shouldn't tell them about religion, but it does mean we shouldn't be too surprised if they aren't wildly enthusiastic about it. In addition, the lack of success of some materials may be due to the same old failings of school materials that have existed since the world began: they're pedantic, pedestrian, patronizing, and too darned long. Advertising may describe materials as "contemporary" as though this were a synonym for "good," "intelligent," or "interesting," when all it really means is "Now."

Quality

Religious education has an inflated view of its own importance. It tends to think that because it has important connections, that is, to God, everything it does is necessarily good. Yet religion teaching does its share to contribute to sloppiness of thinking and tastelessness in literary and artistic expression. Films and filmstrips aren't just teaching tools ordered up to do the bidding of the teacher. They're subject to the same observation Thomas Merton made about books:

> The fact that your subject may be very important in itself does not necessarily mean that what you have written about it is important. A bad book about the love of God remains a bad book, even though it is about the love of God. There are many who think that because they have written about God they have written great books. Then men pick up these books and say: If the ones who say they believe in God cannot find anything better than this to say about it, their religion cannot be worth much.[8]

8. Thomas Merton, *The Sign of Jonas* (New York: Doubleday & Co., Inc.).

In a chapter on teaching aids in *The Process of Education* Jerome Bruner identifies different purposes to which various materials can be put, but he points out, "Problems of quality in a curriculum cannot be dodged by the purchase of sixteen-millimeter projection equipment." And in one short phrase he characterizes my own judgment of much religious education material: "The pictographically vivid portrayal of the trivial."

A good artist or photographer cannot by himself compensate for a production with an ill-conceived idea. Nor can a skilled radio-announcer/narrator invest a script with depth and meaning that the writer has not given it. Wonderful thoughts miss their mark when delivered by a condescending narrator or when matched to witless graphics. Too many filmstrip and slide programs feature greeting-card nature photographs that produce dreamy "oohs" and "aahs" among certain adults, but they work with youngsters about as effectively as yelling at them to look at the scenery when they're out for a drive.

The concern for simplification is a major snare and delusion in audiovisuals. Teachers believe that students have little patience, limited imagination, and a passion for graphics that matches their distrust of the printed word. In both pictures and language, many filmstrips are nothing more than celluloid comic strips produced for the religion market. We claim our subject is the most important of all; must we sacrifice elegance and subtlety in offering it to our children? In removing the detail, the life, and the nuance of the Bible, in stripping it down to cereal-box language and clothespin-doll characters, can we really be doing the subject or the children any favors?

Pflaum's 1974 scripture filmstrip series (*Joseph, Jonah, Amos, Abraham*) is a fine idea—brief segments about people and incidents—but it misses the mark for the reasons mentioned above. The characters are like Dick and Jane, without faces or culture, invented to dramatize a moral. When Jonah hears that God wants him to go to Nineveh he exclaims, like Charlie Brown, "Good grief, Lord!" When Bill Cosby does this kind of colloquializing in *Noah* (for adults, and not to teach anything), it works far better—the language suits the character and situation he's developed and isn't just inserted to sound familiar.

Though Jonah's speech to God after being thrown overboard is called a "psalmlike prayer," a statement like "The belly of a fish is no paradise" sounds like Lou Costello. Jonah tells God, "Those Ninevites are our *worst* enemics! *I* should help them?", and the illustration wears a Charlie Brown expression of chagrin. Or maybe the models are Archie and Jughead. The stylized backgrounds, especially pictures of the fish, are attractive enough, but the characters could use more character.

The events—on the ship, in the whale, on the way home, outside

Nineveh (where Jonah "sat pouting")—are strung together like a crib-note outline, with minimal context or connective tissue. The story is decoded and denuded but it hasn't been especially clarified in the process. For the writer or teacher who knows the flavor and atmosphere of the original, this may be simplifying; for the student who hears it without such a background, perhaps for the first time, it's only meager and muddled.

Of all the filmstrips in this series, only *Abraham* escapes the kind of vernacular that not only diminishes the subject but is likely to date it as well. *Joseph* opens with, "Look at the dude . . ."; the brothers agree that "Dad always did like Joseph best." *Amos* begins decently enough, but soon the priest is calling Amos a hillbilly; the pictures suggest Hagar the Horrible.

Do we mean that our children should think *this* is what the big deal we're making is all about? Do we keep the poetry for ourselves and give our youngsters biblical bumper stickers?

Before they began eliminating such devices altogether, high schools often offered Shakespeare plays in modernized and abridged forms for the low-competence, unmotivated reader, on the theory that even these students should be exposed to great literature but on their own level. However, it isn't just the basic plots or ideas in Shakespeare that are of value. It's also the poetry and wit of the language, the depth of the insight and characterization, and the experience of life sweepingly portrayed. It's worth something to know the extent of such works, to know that a man lived who wrote like that, to hear what he wrote as he wrote it even if it does seem vast and mysterious. It's an error also to assume that poetry, drama, music, and art are tightly tied to intellectual ability; whether they address another part of the brain or another part of the soul, they speak to more than just an intellectual elite. Neither Shakespeare nor scripture should be subjected to the corruption of dilution and kiddyfying.

Children can handle big words if they're good ones; *Peter Rabbit* would be nothing without Beatrix Potter's schoolmarmish phrasings. As for the Bible stories themselves, they're plain enough for the ideas they convey. Many of the ideas of the Bible and of theology, however, are *not* simple stuff meant for children, nor can they be made so by modern drawings or lyrics.

A Weston Woods filmstrip, *The Holy Night*, treats scriptures more successfully by combining in two sections a careful retelling of the Christmas story with the biblical rendition of Luke 2, verses 1–18. The illustrations by Italian artist Celestino Piatti suit the narrative.

There doesn't seem to be enough critical judgment employed in religious education, for a number of reasons. Several of these reasons also afflict all of public education, for instance the capitulation to the publicity about what kids want and enjoy. Then there's the supreme criterion of applicability in education — what you use it for (and "using it for" requires elaborate "utilization guides") becomes much more important than how good it is.

But for religious education there's one other complicating factor: a combination of misguided Christian charity that demands constant sweet approval of publishers' materials, and an all-in-the-family, you-scratch-my-back-and-I'll-scratch-yours view of promotion. A great fraternal round-robin seems to go on perpetually, with tributes and testimonials seeding each other from friend to colleague and back again. If you work it right, anything under the sun can end up being "Highly recommended for . . ." somebody by someone. It's hard to explain to religion teachers that some of these "highly recommended" films, books, and other materials aren't available in public libraries and bookstores not because they're so specialized but because they're junk.

I am continually fascinated at the way religious education, which claims to be interested in the loftiest values, cooperates so readily in the destruction of literacy and the mediocritization of art, language, and culture. It's not only important that the materials used to amplify teaching be of decent artistic quality; it's also necessary to recognize that whatever has artistic merit is worth notice on its own, without the baptism or membership card provided by a utilization guide.

Finally, I'd like to comment briefly on several important matters connected with the ways and means of audiovisual use:

1. **Film teaching vs. teaching with film.** In the sixties a lot of teachers became involved with film instruction and went on to learn more about the process for themselves. That was fine. But for other teachers, the suggestion that they had to learn the inner workings of filmmaking only added to their woes — more work, more confusion. It *was* revealing to learn that the camera angle had as much to do with what the film was saying as what the film itself said. But religious education is really concerned mainly with the end result. While the knowledge of the intricacies of filmmaking can add to your appreciation of the film, it isn't imperative. Films are made for audiences, not just for secret societies who understand the esoteric code.

2. **Discussion.** This is another pressure point. In education, discussion has become the great certifier. A lot of talk means that you've learned something; the more talk, the more learning. ("Why, you couldn't shut them up! They kept going for two *hours!*") Discussion may be profitable or it may just be an exercise in joining the eyes, ears, and mouth without ever touching the brain. Many people would rather ponder the meaning of a film over days or weeks, or talk about it on the phone instead of in an auditorium. The Good Dis-

cussion is sometimes just another educational game, with skilled play-
ers mixed with awkward ones. Or it can be a case of conditioned response, with students trained to drool impressions as soon as the lights
go on. Try discussion if you want, but you don't have to throw yourself on your sword if it doesn't work.

3. **Preview.** This is just about the only professional rule that I acknowledge. You just don't know what's in a film or how it's presented unless you see it yourself. One line or even one word in the
narrative can wreck the whole presentation (maybe it's profane, or
maybe just pompous). You just can't take a film's reputation and run
with it.

I once stood at a library film counter beside a teacher who was picking up *The Dove* to show her freshman English class. She had not
seen it but had heard it was "hilarious." *The Dove* is a satire on Ing-
mar Bergman films. It opens with a long, meditative drive through
the countryside—but with a brief, graphic stop at an outhouse.
There's also a little nudity, a little incest, a little what-have-you as the
film parodies various Bergman themes. All this is not any enormous
problem, but the whole film is quite pointless unless the students have
had some background in Bergman. (I asked; they hadn't.) And unless
this teacher knew beyond a doubt that her students were in their un-
communicative-at-home phase, she could count on some parental pro-
test over her choice.

4. **Teacher guides.** If they help to organize the subject matter, provide
additional research, outline important questions, give biographical
background or helpful bibliography, that's one thing. But if they organize the child—or you—with behavioral objectives and cute classroom
activities, stand back. Some guides like to play "Let's all find the
scripture passage" with every reference. In the long run "Monopoly"
is more character-building.

5. **Kinds of stuff.** According to Charles Davis:

> The irreligion of today is closely associated with an impoverishment of
> symbolism. . . . Children need a rich and emotional and imaginative life
> for a meaningful encounter with Christian story and symbol. . . . At a
> later stage, immersion in the hopes and failures, the tragedy and joy of
> human existence through literature and drama is needed before the in-
> culcation of religious doctrines. The basic task of religious education is
> to widen and deepen human consciousness, so that religious questions
> make sense.[9]

9. Charles Davis, "Puzzling over Religious Education," *National Catholic Reporter,* Jun
    4, 1971.

If you agree with this statement, don't apologize for it and feel you have to justify it. It's destructive to try to make literature and art respectable by fine-tooth-combing them for the curriculum's needs. And allowing new stories to be made up by nonwriters in order to peddle a needed message is like burying the cod liver oil in the applesauce. I've had experience with both; both made me sick.

If you *don't* agree with Davis, go ahead with the conventional subjects, but be sure that in an attempt to offer variety you don't give the students variations on a theme but no theme. You may be offering alternatives—but do the youngsters know to *what?* In any case, remember that students deserve materials of quality, and that the standard of quality is not solely determined by how much these materials suit religion teaching's purpose.

One standard of quality is provided by a great religious educator:

> The riches of a soul are stored up in its memory. This is the test of character—not whether a man follows the daily fashion, but whether the past is alive in his present. When we want to understand ourselves, to find out what is most precious in our lives, we search our memory.... The things which sweep through our daily life should be valued according to whether or not they enrich the inner cistern. That only is valuable in our experience which is worth remembering. Remembrance is the touchstone of all actions.[10]

10. Abraham J. Heschel, *Man Is Not Alone: A Philosophy of Religion* (New York: Octagon Books, 1972).

BIBLIOGRAPHY

1. Community of Believers

Clarke, Stephen, B. *Building Christian Communities.* Notre Dame, Ind.: Ave Maria Press, 1972.

Community of Faith Manual, A Self-Development Process Booklet. Dubuque, Iowa: Diocesan Office of Education, P.O. Box 1180, 52001.

Dulles, Avery. *Models of the Church.* New York: Doubleday, 1974.

Farrell, Edward. *Disciples and Other Strangers.* Denville, N.J.: Dimension, 1974.

——. *Prayer Is a Hunger.* Denville, N.J.: Dimension, 1972.

Giving Form to the Vision, Process for Faith Community in Schools and Religious Education Centers. Washington, D.C.: NCEA Publications, Suite 350, One Dupont Circle, 20036.

McBrien, Richard. *Church: Continuing Quest.* Paramus, N.J.: Paulist Press, 1970.

Nouwen, Henri. *With Open Hands.* Notre Dame, Ind.: Ave Maria Press, 1972.

——. *The Wounded Healer.* Notre Dame, Ind.: Ave Maria Press, 1972.

Schmidt, Herman, ed. *Prayer and Community,* Concilium Series, "Theology in an Age of Renewal." New York: Herder and Herder, 1970.

2. Basic Teachings

God

An American Catechism. Mundelein, Ill.: Chicago Studies, Box 665, Fall 1973.

Greeley, Andrew. *What a Modern Catholic Believes About God.* Chicago: Thomas More Press, 1971.

Humitz, Robert. *Man Meets God.* New York: Benziger, 1972.

A New Catechism ("Dutch Catechism"). New York: Herder and Herder, 1967.

Revelation

Hellwig, Monika. *What Are the Theologians Saying?* Dayton: Pflaum, 1970.

Marthaler, Berard. *Catechetics in Context.* Huntington, Ind.: Our Sunday Visitor, 1973.

Sullivan, Thomas, and Meyers, John. *Focus on American Catechetics.* Washington, D.C.: NCEA, 1972.

Faith

Baum, Gregory. *Faith and Doctrine.* Paramus, N.J.: Paulist Press, 1969.

Forliti, John. *Faith Without Anger* (Infinity Series). Minneapolis: Winston, 1972.

Mitchell, Joan. *Me Believing?* (Infinity Series). Minneapolis: Winston, 1972.

Scripture

Farrell, Melvin. *Theology for Parents and Teachers.* Milwaukee: Hi Time, 1971.

Grispino, Joseph. *Bible Now.* Notre Dame, Ind.: Fides, 1971.

Hunt, Ignatius. *Understanding the Bible.* New York: Sheed and Ward, 1962.

McBride, Alfred. *A Short Course on the Bible.* New York: Macmillan, 1968.

Christ, Our Way to the Father
Creation and Fall

Kozlarek, Sr. Clare. *The Catechesis of Original Sin.* Collegeville Minn.: St. John University Press, 1969.

De Rosa, Peter. *Christ and Original Sin.* Milwaukee: Bruce, 1967.

Schoonenberg, Piet. *Man and Sin.* Notre Dame, Ind.: Notre Dame Press, 1965.

Person of Christ

Brown, Raymond. *Jesus, God and Man.* Milwaukee: Bruce, 1967.

Greeley, Andrew. *The Jesus Myth.* New York: Doubleday, 1971.

Padavano, Anthony. *Who Is Christ?* Paramus, N.J.: Paulist Press, 1971.

Vawter, Bruce. *This Man Jesus.* New York: Doubleday, 1973.

Trinity

Di Giacomo, James. *Would You Believe?* New York: Holt, Rinehart & Winston, 1971.

Kiesling, Christopher. *Any News of God?* Dayton: Pflaum, 1971.

Phillips, J. B. *Your God Is Too Small.* New York: Macmillan, 1969.

Smith, Robert T. *Spirit Seekers.* Minneapolis: Winston, 1972.

Mariology

American Bishops Pastoral. *Behold Your Mother.* Washington, D.C.: United States Catholic Conference, 1974.

Pope Paul VI. *Exhortation on Devotion to Mary (Marialis Cultus).* Washington, D.C.: United States Catholic Conference, 1974.

Eschatology

Montgomery, Mary. *Death: End of the Beginning?* Minneapolis: Winston, 1972.

Phelan, Richard, and De Cuir, George. *What's Now About Forever?* Minneapolis: Winston, 1974.

General Readings

Jerome Biblical Commentary, ed. by Raymond Brown et al. Englewood Cliffs, N.J.: Prentice-Hall, Inc., 1970.

U. S. Catholic Bishops. *Basic Teachings for Catholic Religious Education.* Washington, D.C.: United States Catholic Conference, 1973.

3. Moral Education

General Readings

Beck, C. M.; Crittenden, B. S.; and Sullivan, E. V., eds. *Moral Education.* Paramus, N.J.: Newman Press, 1971.

Baier, Curt, and Rescher, Nicholas, eds. *Values and the Future* (Free Press Paperback). New York: Macmillan, 1971.

Curran, Charles, *Christian Morality Today.* Notre Dame, Ind.: Fides, 1966.

——, *A New Look at Christian Morality.* Notre Dame, Ind.: Fides, 1968.

Dedek, John, *Contemporary Sexual Morality.* New York: Sheed and Ward, 1971.

——, *Human Life, Some Moral Issues.* New York: Sheed and Ward, 1972.

——, *Titius and Bertha Ride Again: Contemporary Moral Cases.* New York: Sheed and Ward, 1974.

Menninger, Karl, *Whatever Became of Sin?* New York: Hawthorn, 1973.

Mondon, Louis, *Sin, Liberty and Law.* New York: Sheed and Ward, 1965.

Moral Education: Five Lectures by James Gustafson, Richard Peters, Lawrence Kohlberg, Bruno Bettelheim, and Kenneth Kenniston. Cambridge, Mass.: Harvard University Press, 1970.

Shea, John, *What a Modern Catholic Believes About Sin.* Chicago: Thomas More Press, 1971.

Simon, Sidney; Howe, Leland; and Kirschenbaum, Howard, *Values Clarification: Handbook of Practical Strategies for Teachers and Students.* New York: Hart, 1972.

Kohlberg Bibliography
Articles written by Lawrence Kohlberg

"The Development of Modes of Moral Thinking and Choice in the Years Ten to Sixteen." Unpublished doctoral dissertation, University of Chicago, 1958.

"Moral Development and Identification." In H. A. Stevenson, ed., *Child Psychology 62nd Yearbook National Society for the Study of Education. Part I.* Chicago: University of Chicago Press, 1963 (a).

"The Development of Children's Orientation towards a Moral Order. I. Sequence in the Development of Moral Thought." *Vita Humana*, 1963, 6, 11–13 (b).

"Stages in Conceptions of the Physical and Social World." Unpublished monograph, 1963 (c).

"The Development of Moral Character and Ideology." In M. L. Hoffman, ed., *Review of Child Development Research*, Vol. 1. New York: Russell Sage Foundation, 1964.

"Psychosexual Development, a Cognitive-Developmental Approach." Unpublished mimeographed manuscript, University of Chicago, 1965.

"Cognitive Stages and Preschool Education." *Human development*, 1966, 9, 15–17 (a).

"A Cognitive and Developmental Analysis of Children's Sex-Role

Concepts and Attitudes." In E. Maccoby, ed., *The Development of Sex Differences.* Stanford, Calif.: Stanford University Press, 1966 (b).

"Moral Education in the Schools." *School Review,* 1966, 74 (1), 1–30 (c).

"Moral and Religious Education and the Public Schools: A Developmental View." In T. Sizer, ed., *Religion and Public Education.* Boston: Houghton Mifflin, 1967.

"Preschool Education: A Cognitive-Developmental Approach." *Child Development,* 1968, 9, 5–17 (a).

"The CHILD as a Moral Philosopher." *Psychology Today,* 1968, 7, 25–30 (b).

"Moral Development." *International Encyclopedia of the Social Sciences.* New York: Crowell, Collier and Macmillan, 1968, 483–494 (c).

"Stage and Sequence: The Cognitive-Developmental Approach to Socialization." In D. Goslin, ed., *Handbook of Socialization: Theory and Research.* Chicago: Rand McNally & Co., 1969, 347–480 (a).

"Stages in the Development of Moral Thought and Action." New York: Holt, Rinehart & Winston, 1969 (b).

4. Spiritual Education

Valuing Processes

Hall, Brian P., and Smith, Maury. *Value Clarification as Learning Process, A Handbook for Christian Educators.* Paramus, N.J.: Paulist Press, 1973.

Harmin, Merrill; Kirschenbaum, Howard; and Simon, Sidney. *Clarifying Values Through Subject Matter.* Minneapolis: Winston, 1973.

Metcalf, Lawrence E., ed. *Values Education, Rationale, Strategies and Procedures.* Washington, D.C.: National Council for Social Studies, 1971.

Paulson, Wayne. *Deciding for Myself: A Value Clarification Series Leader Guide and Sets.* Minneapolis: Winston, 1974.

Raths, Louis; Harmin, Merrill; and Simon, Sidney. *Values and Teaching.* Columbus, Ohio: Charles E. Merrill, 1966.

Shields, Sr. Kathleen Marie, ed. *Developing the Competencies of the Religion Teacher.* Washington, D.C.: NCEA, 1974.

Simon, Sidney, and Kirschenbaum, Howard, eds. *Readings in Value Clarification.* Minneapolis: Winston, 1973.

Youth Research Center. *Youth Research Mini-Survey: My Views, My Values, My Beliefs.* Minneapolis: Youth Research Center, 1975. (This project is cosponsored by the NCEA Forum.)

Spiritual Education

Fowler, James W. "Religious Institutions: Toward a Developmental Perspective on Faith." *Religious Education,* vol. LXIX, March-April 1974.

Higher Catechetical Institute at Nijmegen. *A New Catechism, Catholic Faith for Adults.* New York: Herder and Herder, 1969.

McBride, Alfred, O.Praem. *Heschel: Religious Educator.* Denville, N.J.: Dimension, 1973.

———. "Religious Experience: Public Utterance and Dogma Development." *American Ecclesiastical Review,* March 1974.

National Conference of Catholic Bishops. *On Moral Values in Society.* Washington, D.C.: United States Catholic Conference, 1975.

Faith

Haring, Bernard, C.Ss.R. *The Law of Christ.* Westminster, Md.: Newman, 1966.

Jurgens, W. A. *The Faith of the Early Fathers.* Collegeville, Minn.: Liturgical Press, 1970.

Kierkegaard, Soren. *Fear and Trembling.* Princeton, N.J.: Princeton University Press, 1954.

Lonergan, Bernard. *Method in Theology.* New York: Herder and Herder, 1972.

McBride, Alfred, O.Praem. "Spiritual Education: Fowler's Stages of Faith." *Momentum,* vol. VI, May 1975.

National Conference of Catholic Bishops. *Basic Teachings for Catholic Religious Education.* Washington, D.C.: United States Catholic Conference, 1973.

Rahner, Karl. *Theological Investigations, vol. V.* Baltimore: Helicon, 1966.

Rahner, Karl, and Vorgrimler, Herbert. *Theological Dictionary.* New York: Seabury Press, 1965.

5. Liturgy

Hall, Fred. *The Rite Maker.* Minneapolis: Winston, 1973.

Hellwig, Monika. *The Meaning of the Sacraments.* Columbus: Pflaum/Standard, 1972.

Hovda, Robert. *Dry Bones: Guides to Good Liturgy.* Washington, D.C.: Liturgical Conference, 1974.

Hurley, Karen. *Why Sunday Mass?* Cincinnati: St. Anthony Messenger Press, 1973.

Rabelais, Sr. Maria, and Hall, Howard. *Children Celebrate!* Paramus, N.J.: Paulist Press, 1974.

Shaughnessey, James. *The Roots of Ritual.* Grand Rapids: Eerdmans, 1973.

Sloyan, Virginia. *Signs, Songs, Stories.* Washington, D.C.: Liturgical Conference, 1974.

Sacraments of Initiation and Reconciliation

Buckley, Francis. *I Confess.* Notre Dame, Ind.: Ave Maria Press, 1972.

Champlin, Joseph. *The Mass in a World of Change.* Notre Dame, Ind.: Ave Maria Press, 1973.

Guzie, Tad W. *Jesus and the Eucharist.* Paramus, N.J.: Paulist Press, 1974.

Keating, Msgr. Charles. *Anointing for Healing.* Mystic, Conn.: Twenty-Third Publications, 1973.

Kelly, Francis. *Confirmation: Parent and Child.* New York: Wm. H. Sadlier, Inc., 1973.

McBride, Alfred, O.Praem. *The Gospel of the Holy Spirit.* New York: Arena Lettres, 1975.

MacNutt, Francis. *Healing.* Notre Dame, Ind.: Ave Maria Press, 1974.

Prieur, Michael, STD. *The Sacrament of Reconciliation Today.* Bethlehem, Pa.: Catechetical Communications, 1973.

Quinn, James. *The Theology of the Eucharist.* Notre Dame, Ind.: Fides, 1973.

Sacraments of Vocation

Champlin, Joseph. *Together for Life.* Notre Dame, Ind.: Ave Maria Press, 1970.

Hovda, Robert. *There Are Different Ministries.* Washington, D.C.: Liturgical Conference, 1975.

National Conference of Catholic Bishops. *Ministries in the Church.* Washington, D.C.: U.S. Catholic Conference Publications, 1974.

Powell, John. *The Secret of Staying in Love.* Chicago: Argus, 1974.

6. Adult Education (Courtesy of NCEA's Department of Continuing Education)

Articles

Bergevin, Paul. "Adult Education—The Chief Form of Catechesis." *Living Light*, IX, iii, Fall 1972.

Callahan, Sidney. "Family Religious Education." *Living Light*, II, ii, Summer 1974.

Coughlin, Kevin, "Adult Learning Research and Adult Religious Education, Some Implications." *Living Light*, II, ii, Summer 1973.

——. "A Pilot Program in Adult Christian Education." *Living Light*, VI, iii, Fall 1969, 51–61.

Hughes, Jane Wolford. Column, *Today's Parish*.

——. "Growing Together in Detroit." *Religion Teachers Journal*, IV, September 1970, 7–10.

Jacobs, William. "Adult Education and the Sin of Evasion." *Living Light*, V, i, Spring 1968, 23–29.

Knowles, Malcolm. "Sequential Research Needs in Evolving Disciplines of Social Practice." *Adult Education*, XXIII, iv, Summer 1973.

"Lights Are for Burning." *America*, CXIII, October 16, 1965, 425–426.

Lloyd, Arthur S. "Freire, Conscientization and Adult Education." *Adult Education*, XXIII, i, Fall 1972.

Losoncy, Lawrence. "The Year of Religious Education." *Religion Teachers Journal*, IV, September 1970, 4–6.

McCann, J. "Adult Education in Religion." *Furrow Supplement*, viii, Summer 1969, 15.

McKenzie, Leon. "Adult Education—Program Evaluation." *Living Light*, iii, Fall 1973.

Maves, Paul B. "Religious Development in Adulthood." *Research on Religious Development*, New York, 1971, 777–797.

Moran, Gabriel. "The Adult in Religious Education." *Continuum*, VII, Fall 1969, 414–419.

——. "The Future of Catechetics." *Living Light*, V, Spring 1968, 6–22.

Novello, R. "Adult Education." *Living Light*, IV, Fall 1967, 88–93.

Reid, A. "An Experiment in Adult Education." *Furrow Supplement*, VIII, Summer 1969, 6–9.

Ryan, Bro. Leo. "The Vatican and UNESCO Link Efforts for World Literacy." *Adult Leadership*, IX, October 1970, 120–123.

Savory, L. "Religious Education for the Catholic Adult." *America*, CXIX, July 20, 1968, 34–35.

Schaefer, James. "GIFT—An Adult Program That Works." *Living Light*, VIII, Fall 1971, 23–28.

Thorp, Nathan. "Programming for Adult Religious Education." *Adult Leadership*, XVII, November 1968.

Zahn, Jane C. "Differences Between Adults and Youth Affecting Learning." *Adult Education*, Winter 1967, 67–77.

Books

Apps, Jerold W. *How to Improve Adult Education in Your Church.* Minneapolis: Augsburg Publishing House, 1972. Offers some concrete recommendations for an alive, dynamic education program. Apps suggests a workable system based on relationship of the Christian faith to the life of the individual and society.

Bergevin, Paul. *Adult Education Procedures: A Handbook of Tested Patterns.* New York: Seabury Press, 1958.

——. *A Philosophy for Adult Education.* New York: Seabury Press, 1967.

Bergevin, Paul, and McKinley, John. *Adult Education for the Church: The Indiana Plan.* St. Louis: Bethany Press, 1970. A condensation of early work—a stimulating approach to training volunteers.

——. *Design for Adult Education in the Church.* New York: Seabury Press. A good balance of theory and practice. Describes the "Indiana Plan" as a model.

——. *Participation Training for Adult Education.* St. Louis: Bethany Press, 1965. Describes a purpose of learning that develops a favorable climate for learning through coming to understand one's relationship and responsibility to other persons in the learning process.

Carp, Frances. *Retirement.* New York: Behavioral Publications, 1971.

Clemmons, Robert S. *Dynamics of Christian Adult Education.* New York: Abingdon Press, 1958.

——. *Education for Churchmanship.* New York: Abingdon Press, 1966.

Ernsberger, David. *Education for Renewal.* Philadelphia: The Westminster Press, 1965. Let the world set the agenda for programs.

——. *A Philosophy of Adult Christian Education.* Philadelphia: The Westminster Press, 1959. A book in practical theology with special emphasis on work with small groups.

Fish, John. *The Edge of the Ghetto.* New York: Seabury Press, 1966. Ecumenical involvement in a racially changing area of Chicago. A research document on method and meaning.

Fry, John. *A Hard Look at Adult Christian Education.* Philadelphia: The Westminster Press. Stresses the importance of responding to varying needs in Church and society.

Gold, Samuel B. *Diversity by Design.* San Francisco: Jossey-Bass Publishers, 1974. The official final report of the Commission on nontraditional study funded by the Carnegie Foundation. It contains the findings and major recommendations on lifelong learning. It deals with degrees, institutions, faculty, new evaluation modes, educational technology, and college and community cooperation. It carries about sixty specific recommendations for action.

Goldman, Freda. *A Turning to Take Next: Alternative Goals in the Education of Women.* Syracuse, N.Y.: Syracuse University Press, 1967. Must reading for male chauvinists.

Havighurst, Robert J. *Developmental Tasks and Education,* 2nd ed. New York: David McKay, 1970. Basic, excellent.

Hesburgh, Theodore M.; Miller, Paul A.; and Wharton, Clifton R., Jr. *Patterns for Lifelong Learning.* San Francisco: Jossey-Bass Publishers, 1973. Presents three distinct explorations into how an institution of higher education can build systems of learning that institutionalize education as a lifelong process.

Johnstone, John, et al. *Volunteers for Learning.* Chicago: Aldine Publishing Co., 1965. Results of a NORC Study. The most comprehensive statement available on who participates in adult education.

Kaplan, Max. *Leisure in America: A Social Inquiry.* New York: Wiley Press, 1960.

Keeler, Sr. Jerome, ed. *Handbook of Catholic Adult Education.* Milwaukee: Bruce Publishing Co., 1959. Gives a good picture of where Catholic adult education was in 1959.

Kempler, Homer. *Adult Education Movement in the U.S.* New York: Holt, Rinehart & Winston, 1962.

Kidd, J. R. *How Adults Learn.* New York: Association Press, 1959. A good social science statement on how adults learn.

Knowles, Malcolm. *The Adult Education Movement in the U.S.,* New York: Holt, Rinehart & Winston, 1962. A good history of the adult education movement.

——. *The Adult Learner: A Neglected Species.* Houston: Gulf Publishing Co., 1973. Based on a good survey of the literature. Good bibliography of the area.

——. *A Handbook on Adult Education in the U.S.* Washington

D.C.: AEA, 1960. Articles by leaders in different areas of adult education. A good survey of what is going on.

———. *The Modern Practice of Adult Education*. New York: Association Press, 1970. Perhaps the most comprehensive volume available on adult education; andragogy vs. pedagogy.

Lanabee, Eric, and Meyershon, Rolf, eds. *Mass Leisure*. Glencoe, Ill.: The Free Press, 1959.

Leslie, Robert G. *Sharing Groups in the Church: An Invitation to Involvement*. Nashville: Abingdon Press, 1971. Combines insights of group dynamics and Christian faith.

Leypoldt, Martha. *Learning Is Change: Adult Education in the Church*. Valley Forge, Pa.: Judson Press, 1971. Reading this book is designed to be an adult education experience.

Little, Lawrence. *Wider Horizons in Christian Adult Education*. Pittsburgh: University of Pittsburgh Press, 1962. This book contains selected papers presented at a workshop in curriculum for the Christian education of adults.

Liveright, A. A. *A Study of Adult Education in the U.S.* Boston: Center for the Study of Liberal Education for Adults, 1968.

McKenzie, Leon. *Adult Religious Education*. Mystic, Conn.: Twenty-Third Publications, 1975.

Manes, Paul. *Understanding Ourselves as Adults*. New York: Abingdon Press, 1959.

Milka, Sebastian. *Principles and Problems of Catholic Adult Education*. Philadelphia: Westminster Press, 1962. Proceedings of workshop at C.U. on June 13–24, 1958. Covers definition, scope, and aims of Catholic adult education.

Miller, Cyr N. *Christians Are Not for Lions: Adult Religious Education Today*. New York: Bruce Publishing Co., 1971. A book for adult Christians of all denominations. It is "Christian" in keeping with human life, human values, and the Gospel message—the Good News that Jesus is life, love, and the ultimate meaning of human existence. Religious education deals with faith which shows that human existence is transparent with God.

Minor, Harold D., ed. *Techniques and Resources for Guiding Adult Groups*. Nashville: Abingdon Press, 1972. Provides a fruitful source for anyone seeking guidance in establishing effective adult groups. Uses newest concepts about the learning potentials of adults; presents fresh ideas for teachers and leaders for making group life a new source of satisfaction and challenge.

Moran, Gabriel. *Vision and Tactics, Toward an Adult Church.* New York: Herder and Herder, 1968. Largely theoretical; stresses need for parent education, need for mass media and small groups.

Pressey, Sidney, and Kuhlen, Raymond. *Psychological Development Through the Life Span.* New York: Harper & Row, 1957.

The Resource Guide, Mary Reed Newland, ed. Kansas City: NCR Press, 1975.

Rinehart, Bruce. *The Institutional Nature of Adult Christian Education.* Philadelphia: Westminster Press, 1962. This volume identifies some of the key reasons why adult education has not caught on better in the churches.

Robb, Thomas Bradley. *The Bonus Years: Foundations for Ministry with Older Persons.* Valley Forge, Pa.: Judson Press, 1968. Deals with the need to treat distinctive local needs with local response.

Schaefer, Rev. James R. *Program Planning for Adult Christian Education.* New York: Newman Press, 1972. Develops a methodology for planning adult Christian education programs and explains principles regarding the purpose, personnel, scope, process, context, and timing of same. It unlocks the planning process itself.

Seifert, Harvey, and Clinebell, Howard. *Personal Growth and Social Change; A Guide for Ministers and Laymen As Change.* Philadelphia: Westminster Press, 1969.

Smith, Robert M., et al., eds. *Handbook of Adult Education.* New York: Macmillan Co., 1970. A good cross section of what's happening in the various areas of adult education.

Thomson, Frances. *New York Times Guide to Continuing Education in America.* New York: Quadrangle Books, 1972. Good idea of the current diversity of program offerings.

Wyckoff, Campbell. *Theory and Design of Christian Education Curriculum.* Philadelphia: Westminster Press, 1961. The place of adult and parent education in the general education ministry of the Church.

Zeigler, Earl. *Christian Education of Adults.* Philadelphia: Westminster Press, 1958. A basic textbook of adult Christian education.

Zuck, Roy B., and Getz, Gene A. *Adult Education in the Church.* Chicago: Moody Bible Institute of Chicago, 1970. Affirms the proposition that adults are not a lost cause, and gives the A to Z of adult education. Twenty-eight Christian educators discuss the subject from almost every conceivable angle.

Pamphlets

Better Boards and Committees. Washington, D.C.: AEA.

Clyde, Robert, and Jayberg, Eugene. *The Use of Mass Media in Religiously Motivated Adult Education: Review of the Literature.* Syracuse, N.Y.: Syracuse University, 1970.

Conducting Workshops and Institutes. Washington, D.C.: AEA.

Conferences That Work. Washington, D.C.: AEA.

Effective Public Relations. Washington, D.C.: AEA.

Getting and Keeping Members. Washington, D.C.: AEA.

How to Lead Discussions. Washington, D.C.: AEA.

How to Use Role Playing. Washington, D.C.: AEA.

Leppert, Alice. *Guidelines for Adult Basic Education Volunteers.* New York: Church Women United, 1970.

Losoncy, Lawrence. *The ABC's of Adult Education.* Washington, D.C.: NC Publications, 1971.

MacLellan, Rev. Malcolm. *The Catholic Church and Adult Education.* Washington, D.C.: Catholic University, 1935.

Planning Better Programs. Washington, D.C.: AEA.

Reaching the Forgotten Adult: Proceedings of Bergamo Conference, May 9–14, 1971. Washington, D.C.: USCC, 1971.

Scott, Vaille. *Adult Education: A Proposal for Catholic Education.* Oak Park, Ill.: Argus Publications, 1968.

Streamlining Parliamentary Procedures. Washington, D.C.: AEA.

Supervision and Consultation. Washington, D.C.: AEA.

Taking Action in the Community. Washington, D.C.: AEA.

Training Group Leaders. Washington, D.C.: AEA.

Training in Human Relations. Washington, D.C.: AEA.

Understanding How Groups Work. Washington, D.C.: AEA.

Working with Volunteers. Washington, D.C.: AEA.

7. Delphi Technique and Futures Planning

Agel, Jerome, ed. *Is Today Tomorrow? A Synergistic Collage of Alternative Futures.* New York: Ballantine, 1972.

Baade, Fritz. *The Race to the Year 2000,* trans. by Ernst Pawel. Garden City, N.Y.: Doubleday, 1962.

Bell, Daniel. *The End of Ideology.* Glencoe, Ill.: The Free Press, 1960.

——, ed. *Toward the Year 2000.* Boston, Houghton Mifflin, 1968.

Brown, Harrison. *The Next Hundred Years.* New York: Viking, 1958.

Darwin, C. G. *The Next Million Years.* Garden City, N.Y.: Doubleday, 1952.

de Jouvenel, Bertrand. *The Art of Conjecture,* trans. by Nikita Lary. New York: Basic Books, 1967.

Flournoy, Don, ed. "Teaching a Course on Alternative World Futures." In *New Teachers.* San Francisco: Jossey-Bass, 1972.

Heilbroner, Robert L. *The Future As History.* New York: Harper & Row, 1960.

Kahn, Herman. *The Next 200 Years.* New York: William Morrow, 1976.

Polak, Fred L. *The Image of the Future.* Dobbs Ferry, N.Y.: Oceana, 1961.

Rojas, William. "Teaching the Future." *Change,* Vol 3, January-February 1971.

Teich, Albert H. *Technology and Man's Future.* New York: St. Martin's Press, 1972.

Theobald, Robert, ed. *Futures Conditional.* Indianapolis: Bobbs-Merrill, 1972.

Toffler, Alvin, ed. *The Futurists.* New York: Random House, 1972.

Vacca, Roberto. *The Coming Dark Age.* Garden City, N.Y.: Doubleday, 1973.

8. Teacher Talk (Courtesy of NCEA's Secondary Department)

Abbott, Walter M., ed. "The Declaration on Christian Education, *The Documents of Vatican II.* New York: Guild Press, 1966.

Abramson, P. "When Teachers Evaluate Each Other." *Scholastic Magazine,* September 1972, 26–28.

American Association of School Administrators, Educational Research Service. *Evaluating Teaching Performance.* Arlington, Va.: The Association, 1972.

Amidon, E.; Kies, K.; and Paliai, A. "Group Supervision." *The National Elementary Principal,* 45: 5, 54–58.

Annals of the Daughters of Charity. Emmitsburg, Md.: Archives of Saint Joseph's Provincial House.

Armstrong, H. *A Teacher's Guide to Teaching Performance Evaluation.* Worthington, Ohio: School Management Institute, 1972.

Bales, R. *Interaction Process Analysis.* Reading, Mass.: Addison-Wesley, 1951.

Bennis, Warren G. *Changing Organizations.* New York: McGraw-Hill Book Co., 1966.

Bennis, Warren G.; Benne, Kenneth D.; and Chin, Robert, eds. *The Planning of Change.* New York: Holt, Rinehart & Winston, 1969.

Bettman, Otto L. *The Good Old Days—They Were Terrible.* New York: Random House, 1974.

Biddle, B., and William, Ellena, Jr. *Contemporary Research on Teacher Effectiveness.* New York: Holt, Rinehart & Winston, 1964.

Blum, Virgil C. "School Teachers—The Architects of Society." Unpublished lecture. Philadelphia: Meeting of Consortium Perfectae Cartatis, 1973.

Blumberg, Arthur. *Supervisors and Teachers: A Private Cold War.* Berkeley, Calif.: McCutchan Publishing, 1974.

———. "A System for Analyzing Supervisor-Teacher Interaction." In *Mirrors for Behavior,* VIII. Philadelphia: Research for Better Schools, Inc., 1970.

Blumberg, A., and Amidon, E. "Teacher Perceptions of Supervisor-Teacher Interaction." *Administrator's Notebook,* 14:1.

Blumberg, A., and Cusick, P. "Supervisor-Teacher Interaction: An Analysis of Verbal Behavior." *Education,* November 1970, 126–134.

Blumberg, A., and Weber, W. "Teacher Morale as a Function of Perceived Supervisor Behavior Style." *Journal of Educational Research,* 62:3, 109–113.

Bredeweg, Frank H., ed. *National Conference on Catholic School Finance.* Washington, D.C.: National Catholic Educational Association, 1974.

Burns, James A. *The Principles, Origin and Establishment of the Catholic School System in the United States.* New York: Arno Press, 1969 (reprint of 1908 ed.).

Castetter, William B. *The Personnel Function in Education Administration.* New York: Macmillan Co., 1971.

Clark, David L., and Guba, Egan G. "An Examination of Potential Change Roles in Education," *Rational Planning in Curriculum and Instruction.* Washington, D.C.: NEA Center for the Study of Instruction, 1967.

Coleman, James S. *Youth: Transition to Adulthood.* Chicago: University of Chicago Press, 1974.

Commager, Henry Steele. "The School as Surrogate Conscience." *Saturday Review*, January 11, 1975.

Crumlish, John Mary. "The History of St. Joseph's Academy, Emmitsburg, Md., 1809–1902." Unpublished master's thesis, Catholic University of America, 1945.

Daniels, Steven. *How Two Gerbils, Twenty Goldfish, Two Hundred Games, Two Thousand Books and I Taught Them How to Read.* Philadelphia: Westminster Press, 1971.

Dirvin, Joseph I. *Mrs. Seton: Foundress of the American Sisters of Charity.* New York: 1962.

Dunn, Rita, and Dunn, Kenneth. *Educator's Self-Teaching Guide to Individualized Instructional Programs.* Nyack, N.Y.: Parker Publishing Co., 1975.

——. "Learning Style as a Criterion for Placement in Alternative Programs." *Phi Delta Kappan*, December 1974.

Elford, George. "Toward a Catholic School Philosophy." *Today's Catholic Teacher*, February 1975, 20–21 and 36–38.

Getzels, J., and Jackson. "The Teacher's Personality and Characteristics." In Gage, N. L. ed., *Handbook of Research on Teaching.* Chicago: Rand McNally and Co., 1963.

Gibb, J. "Defensive Communication." *Journal of Communication*, 11:3.

Goldhammer, Robert. *Clinical Supervision.* New York: Holt, Rinehart & Winston, 1969.

Goodlad, John I. "An Emphasis on Change." *American Education*, January-February 1975.

Harris, T. *I'm OK—You're OK: A Practical Guide to Transactional Analysis.* New York: Harper & Row, 1962.

Hebeisen, Ardyth. *Peer Program for Youth.* Minneapolis: Augsburg Press, 1973.

Hellwig, Monika. *Tradition.* Dayton, Ohio: Pflaum Publishing Co., 1974.

Kindall, Alva, and Gatza, James. "Positive Program for Performance Appraisal." *Harvard Business Review*, November 1963.

McNally, Harold J. "What Makes a Good Evaluation Program?" *National Elementary Principal*, Fall 1973.

Melville, Annabelle M. *Elizabeth Bayley Seton.* New York: Charles Scribner's Sons, 1976.

Meyer, H. H.; Kay, E.; and French, J. R. P. "Split Roles in Performance Appraisal." *Harvard Business Review*, March-April 1964.

Morehouse, Clifford P. *Trinity: Mother of Churches.* New York: Seabury, 1973.

Mosher, R., and Purpel, D. *Supervision: The Reluctant Profession.* Boston: Houghton Mifflin, 1972.

Murdick, Olin J., and Meyers, John F. *Boards of Education: A Primer.* Washington, D.C.: National Catholic Educational Association, 1972.

National Catholic Educational Association. *Giving Form to the Vision.* Washington, D.C.: The Association, 1974.

——. *Guidelines for Selected Personnel Practices in Catholic Schools.* Washington, D.C.: The Association, 1975.

National Education Association. *The Elementary School Principalship in 1968.* Washington, D.C.: The Association, 1968.

——. *Evaluation Systems for Education: Descriptive Abstracts.* Washington, D.C.: The Association, 1973.

O'Connor, Elizabeth. *The Eighth Day of Creation.* Waco, Texas: Word Books, 1970.

Ownes, Robert G. *Organizational Behavior in Schools.* Englewood Cliffs, N.J.: Prentice-Hall, Inc., 1970.

Postman, Neil, and Weingartner, Charles. *The School Book.* New York: Delacorte Press, 1973.

Redfern, George. *How to Appraise Teaching Performance.* Columbus, Ohio: School Management Institute, Inc., 1963.

——. *How to Evaluate Teaching.* Worthington, Ohio: School Management Institute, Inc., 1972.

Sacred Congregation for the Clergy. *General Catechetical Directory.* Washington, D.C.: United States Catholic Conference, 1971.

Sheehan, Lawrence Cardinal. "Mother Seton." *The Catholic Review,* June 13, 1975, A–16.

Simon, A., and Boyer, G., eds. *Mirrors for Behavior.* Philadelphia: Research for Better Schools, Inc., 1970.

Stufflebeam, Daniel L. "A Depth Study of the Evaluation Requirement." *Theory Into Practice* 5, June 1966.

"Supervisory Behavior and Interpersonal Relations." *Educational Administration Quarterly,* Spring 1968, 34–45.

Weller, R. *Verbal Communication in Instructional Supervision.* New York: Teachers College Press, 1971.

Williamson, Joseph. "A Pedagogy for Christians." In John H. Westerhoff, *A Colloquy on Christian Education.* Philadelphia: United Church Press, 1972.

9. Parents Are "The People" Too

In my most recent bout of housecleaning I took a good look at the bookcases as well as the file folders. There were just too many books—all good, instructive, or enjoyable and all worth keeping—but taking up too much space. I finally put them all in the attic—neatly and where I can still get at them if I want them—and kept only two downstairs in plain sight.

I could recommend all or portions of the books in the attic and would sound knowledgeable and erudite in listing them. There are titles by Charles Davis, Charles Curran, Eugene Kennedy, Karl Rahner, Alfred McBride, John Macquarrie—as well as Erich Fromm, Carl Rogers, Gordon Allport, John Holt, Ivan Illich, Paul Goodman, Abraham Maslow, and Abraham Heschel. There are also some historical items for counterpoint, like *Cana Is Forever* and a Baltimore Catechism. But I've followed a very meandering route in going from one book to another. The route is very much a part of their value for me, and a different process would be necessary for someone else. So would other titles and other authors. In some cases I've read the books bit by bit over a long time; in some cases I only like or would recommend certain sections or chapters. And even picking out a list of books or chapters wouldn't begin to cover all the things I'd like to suggest—the clippings from *The New York Times*, the quotes from magazines I've read in the dentist's office, even one or two items from the telephone bill flyer.

Instead I'll tell you about the two books I have kept downstairs, since they're worthwhile no matter how or when you get to them, no matter what your special tastes or interests. Just seeing them sitting there on the shelf and knowing what they represent is enough to improve my day.

The first one says on its flyleaf: "To Martha with love from Nina, Christmas 1965. This was my favorite story when I was growing up. . . ." Nina is my mother, Martha is my daughter, and the book is *The Secret Garden*.

The jacket reads:

> This is the secret garden, mysterious, walled and locked, that is the center of Frances Hodgson Burnett's beautiful and moving story of a lonely, willful little girl and how she finds friends, health and happiness when she comes to live in a great house on the Yorkshire moors. It is a story that has been loved by boys and girls since its first publication in 1912, never losing its charm, its magic, its deep satisfaction.

A review by Rumer Godden is also quoted:

It will rapt most children away, for after fifty years its spell is just as strong, a blend of power, beauty, vivid interest and honest goodness. Yes, if this is magic, it is good magic.

The Secret Garden will "rapt away" most adults too. There's something so refreshing, so consoling about a turnabout from sickness to health and about the nurturing of a garden in the same way that teachers ought to view teaching and parents ought to view parenting. Though my mother and Martha had read this book while growing up, for some reason I had never read it myself until this copy arrived. By then I was the mother of four children, and I've never forgotten this image:

> "Why, I thought tha' didn't know nothin' about gardenin'," he exclaimed.
> "I don't," she answered, "but they were so little, and the grass was so thick and strong, and they looked as if they had no room to breathe. So I made a place for them."
> "Tha' was right," he said. "A gardener couldn't have told thee better. They'll grow now like Jack's bean-stalk."

Only removing the obstacles to growth, and letting seeds sprout and children laugh seems so simple a process, yet growing today has been made to seem so treacherous, complicated, and unlikely. This book is a good antidote, for it reminds us of something we once knew:

> One of the new things people began to find out in the last century was that thoughts—just mere thoughts—are as powerful as electric batteries—as good for one as sunlight is, or as bad for one as poison. To let a sad thought or a bad one get into your mind is as dangerous as letting a scarlet fever germ get into your body. If you let it stay there after it has got in you you may never get over it as long as you live.

Thinking good and happy thoughts is not at all fashionable now, nor is the reading of good and happy books. But I recommend both of these things, for both children and parents. This one book alone has all the elements of Heidi and Clara in the fresh mountain air, nourished by bread, milk, and cheese; of Anne of Green Gables, whose sturdy common sense saved the baby with croup; and Dr. Alec in Louisa May Alcott's *Eight Cousins*, who kicked the pill bottles off the porch railing and sent Rose for a run around the house to brighten her cheeks. When Amanda, who is almost 24, comes home to touch base after too many deadlines, these are the books she asks for, to soothe, revive, and encourage herself. But *The Secret Garden* is the best of all.

Burnett, Frances Hodgson. *The Secret Garden.* Philadelphia: J. B. Lippincott Co., 1962.

The second book, once the focus of controversy — charges and countercharges — isn't talked about much any more. But it too has a capacity for healing and encouraging. Because of its origins, it's generally referred to as *The Dutch Catechism.* (Its actual title is *A New Catechism.*) This is a sound book, broad and tolerant in its outlook but respectful of convention and careful of feelings. It's good for both adults and young people.

So many of the recent books for teen-agers have been so anxious to counteract past rigidities that newer and seemingly more liberal interpretations have been offered with grand and sweeping assurance. Yet the authors of these books carry in their own minds all kinds of modifying attitudes that their maturity or past experience takes for granted. Students may or may not be able to discern these modifiers.

The Dutch Catechism weighs its words carefully. It provides a context; it provides nuanced explanations. It avoids the problem of seesawing reaction that can too often result from overenthusiastic generalizing. It allows those of more cautious and traditional temperament to maintain their position, yet it also defines a liberal viewpoint in a way that may ultimately make sense to some who might be confused and threatened by stronger statements.

Teachers seem surprised to realize that they are not the only ones who were taught "the old way." The Council, that frontier of observable change, occurred in 1962–1963. This means that any child who had even one year of religion teaching before that time — at minimum a child born in 1955 and in his or her early twenties now — will have encountered "the old way." Considering the fact that the Council's effects were slow to take hold, children born two, three, four, or more years later may still have been learning many things the same way. My older chldren — now twenty-five, twenty-two, and twenty — all began their religious education in the conventional mode and did not notice any change in approach or attitude until about 1968. This meant that they had, respectively, ten, seven, and five years of essentially the same kind of instruction that I did. Yet this is the age group that is thought of as being inherently liberal, even radical, because of being *from the beginning* free of the thought patterns of their elders.

This group of young people is likely to be at least as much in need of a coherent review, a reasoned and unified survey of their religion, as we who are their parents. We who are middle-aged at least had the benefit of a developed capacity for observing and processing new developments, however immature our religious psychology may have been. The younger ones were caught by the frontal edge of this great religious storm system while they were necessarily preoccupied with their own growing up—physically, emotionally, and intellectually. They could in no way have been equipped to work through and synthesize the shifting patterns with which they were confronted.

Perhaps it's no wonder that these are the children who are so quick to respond with cliches and to make such uncritical judgments. When everything is spinning and blurred, it is perhaps imperative to fix your attention on something loud, bright, and definite, regardless of its worth or staying power.

For such young people—or for anyone who likes to ponder in private, without a discussion leader or program director—*The Dutch Catechism* is ideal. It contains no photographs or cartoons, but it's kind and sensible, wise and hopeful. In this book even a worried or anxious person can find support, and even direct answers in an age that sometimes takes perverse pride in having none. And when it's not shoved down their throats, youngsters seem to like it.

Higher Catechetical Institute of Nijmegen, Holland. *A New Catechism.* New York: Seabury Press, Inc., 1967.

10. The Tools of the Trade: Which Tools? How Much Trade?

Listmaking is always a problem, whether in packing, grocery shopping, or resource selecting. You're always likely to forget something; if you do think of everything, you don't have the space, money, or energy to take care of it all. In resources, new things are produced—or withdrawn from distribution—faster than you can write them down, so your list is always running behind.

Librarians solve the problem with the word "selected." "Selected" implies thoughtful, serious choice—which may actually be true—while at the same time it compensates for memory lapses, time lags, and exhaustion. The selected list that follows is subject to such failings of mind and body. But the titles included do represent a selection process, one that incorporates all the observations made in the previous chapters. There are, of course, many other materials around that are equally good and cover similar subjects. But the materials cited here are the ones I've seen and read myself.

These materials are stimulating and informative but they're not just message-mongers. There are plenty of Significant Issues among them—war, poverty, prejudice, loneliness, the future, feminism, handicaps. But they're presented in ways that give viewers space and distance, without excessive control of their responses. So if your situation requires that you consider such issues, at least these materials won't browbeat your viewers or grind them down.   There are also Important Curriculum Topics—comparative religions, marriage, vocations, sacraments, morality, Christmas, Easter.

A good number of these titles deal with particular individuals—some famous and some not.   Both in what they have to say and how they say it, they are of immediate and long-range value.   Many of the biographical sketches are about older people, but they should not be tossed into the "Aging" file.   The chronology of these people is obviously important, whether it be because they've processed a large quantity of experience and thought, or because of their enthusiasm and optimism even when their personal time allotment on earth is running out.   But there is no reason for turning older people into another case-study group or another stereotype-able cause.

Many items resist categorizing.   For instance, Margaret Mead talks about religion, prejudice, race relations, and other subjects in her British television interview; this is not simply a profile of a personage.   In *If You're Not There, You're Missed*, Jean Vanier has some telling things to say about church and world, and though this film focuses on the particular community of retarded adults in Trosly-Breuil, France, the nature of community itself and the basic needs of all individuals also are considered.   In *Pilgrimage*, which covers an international gathering of retarded people at Lourdes at Easter 1971, the same themes appear, as well as some important observations about liturgy, celebration, and the mixture of religion and commerce.   *Anansi the Spider* not only presents a traditional Ashanti spider story, but it also suggests the way in which stories have been used in understanding the world.   This is done in the portion of the film explaining the moon, and in a useful introduction describing how stories help to ground the individual in his culture.

A few of these titles are simply light and bright, useful for introducing a subject, as counterpoint, or for making a point without making a production of it.   Still other things on the list are just stories, sufficient unto themselves.   It's best to let the storyteller do the talking and to resist the urge to interpret the story after it has been told.

All kinds of combinations are possible.   How Teilhard de Chardin (*The Heart of the Matter*) and Buckminster Fuller regard the world and the future might be considered together.   A profitable year's viewing could consist of a series of film profiles (Antonia, I. F. Stone, Mother Teresa, Eric Hoffer, . . .).   Or a series could be done about all the world religions.

A course could consider all the women (Antonia, Joyce, Helen Keller, . . .), though such categorizing amounts to resegregation rather than desegregation of women. I dislike the category "vocations," but it could be broadened into a consideration of what people do with their lives, with some mention of the fact that it's possible to have several life-periods, as Edward Steichen and Kurt Vonnegut suggest. In this grouping you might include *The Plutocrats, If You're Not There . . .* (Jean Vanier is the wealthy son of Canada's former Governor-General, had once commanded a ship, had also once thought of being a monk, but more or less by chance, found his career in developing homes for retarded people); *The Weapons of Gordon Parks, Art of Age,* and any of the other biographies, as well as *The Priest, The Cloistered Nun, The Shakers,* and the marriage films.

Then there's the possibility of combining with other school groups, for instance English or history classes, or the drama club, perhaps mixing study and performance. This plan would work especially well with the medieval material or the material having to do with historical personages, though, because the presentations are stimulating and well done, few of them need to be strictly confined. Such a cooperative venture can serve to overcome tight "religion-class" image and at the same time spread the costs around.

Or just a random selection of films or filmstrips, based mostly on what you can get with the time and money you have available, is likely to be quite satisfactory. Among the million cliches in the field of education is the one about poorly-prepared teachers using films as crutches. Some of these teachers are presumably goof-offs, while others may just have stayed up too late the night before. The audiovisual dogmatist makes it clear that anyone using a film had better do his or her homework, have a lot of neat discussion questions ready, and have thoroughly prepared the class ahead of time so that the film will fit suitably into the great scheme of things. Fiddledeedee! The majority of these films *can* be used without preparation, and in most cases it would be better to use them that way. The filmmaker is the prepared teacher; the filmmaker has done your work for you. He or she knows what should be said and can probably say it best without outside help. You *can* plug these materials into your curriculum like raisins on a gingerbread man, of course, but you can also just order them, then sit back and watch. Either way, you don't need to be obsessive about supplementary ditto-pumping and homily-hunting.

Films for little children are marked with one asterisk; those for fourth grade and up are marked with two asterisks. For the rest, it's up to you, keeping in mind all the questions we've been talking about—too much, too soon, invasion of experience and privacy, hidden agenda, etc.

Many of these films, and some of the Weston Woods filmstrips, will be available for free loan at public libraries. Others can be rented from universities that have film libraries, usually at lower fees than from commercial distributors. You may write or call the sources listed for purchase prices, previewing arrangements, or rental outlets near you.

To find out what's new in films, three reliable sources are:

The Educational Film Library Association, 17 West 60th St., New York, N.Y. 10023. Membership is fairly expensive (individual membership is thirty-five dollars per year), but it includes monthly mailings of film reviews, eight issues of *Sightlines* magazine with reviews and articles, plus descriptions of entries and winners of the American Film Festival held yearly in New York.

Film and Broadcasting Review, U.S. Catholic Conference, 100 First Ave., New York, N.Y. 10022. This newsletter, published twice monthly, concentrates on feature films but also regularly includes reviews of shorter films for religious education, other resources and bibiliographies, as well as occasional position statements and analyses of trends in movies, television, and theater. Subscription is ten dollars per year, including first class mailing.

Media and Methods, North American Building, 401 North Broad St., Philadelphia, Pa. 19108. This magazine is published nine times a year; it features film reviews and articles for teachers. Subscription is nine dollars per year.

Asking for catalogs from any of the film distributors listed on page 389 is helpful, but such requests tend to cross-fertilize to other companies, so you might want to proceed slowly in order not to become inundated with advertising materials.

Books

Listmaking here is too monumental to be worthwhile. Try looking in the public library first. Titles in the religion category (Dewey 200's) tend to be dull, especially in the children's collection, but they sometimes surprise you. The general collection works out quite well once you've figured out what you have in mind.

Of the books I've reviewed in seven years of newsletters, there are a few really exceptional ones, theoretically for middle-age children but equally good for adults. These are:

Charlip, Remy; Beth, Mary; and Ancona, George. *Handtalk.* New York: Parents Magazine Press, 1974. This book contains photographs both in color and in black and white, giving the alphabet, common words, and signs (like "peanut butter and jelly"). It was produced with the help of the National Theater of the Deaf; an alphabet poster is included.

The Hastings Institute of Society, Ethics and the Life Sciences. Offers in-depth study of particular ethical questions, in The Hastings Report (bimonthly), bibliographies, reprint packages, and assistance in designing courses. Individual membership costs eighteen dollars, fulltime student membership costs fourteen dollars, and institutional membership costs thirty dollars. (Write to the Institute, 360 Broadway, Hastings-on-Hudson, New York, N.Y. 10706.)

Langstaff, John. *St. George and the Dragon.* New York: Atheneum Publishers, 1973. This book, drawn from many versions of the play from around the world, includes the acting script, the music for the traditional songs to accompany it, instructions for performing the sword dance, and stage and costume directions. No set, scenery, or elaborate stage are necessary. The play, with its symbols of triumph of life over death, light over darkness, and spring over winter, was customarily performed as the Old Year turned and the New Year was about to begin, and concluded with audience participation in eating, singing, and dancing.

Macaulay, David. *Cathedral: The Story of Its Construction.* Boston: Houghton Mifflin Company, 1973. This is the story of the decision of the people of Chutreaux to build a cathedral that would be the longest, widest, highest, and most beautiful cathedral in all of France. Though the people of Chutreaux are imaginary, the story of their singlemindedness, spirit, and courage, and the details of the methods of construction are typical of the people and architecture of twelfth, thirteenth, and fourteenth-century Europe.

Rudstrom, Lennart. *A Home* (with paintings by Carl Larson). New York: G. P. Putnam's Sons, 1974. The original version of this book was published in Sweden in 1899. This edition combines a selection of watercolor paintings from the original book, with a text for children. This is a picture book to look at and a story book to read, about Sweden, a past time, and a particular family.

Shahn, Ben. *The Cherry Tree Legend.* This illustrated book tells of Mary and Joseph, and of her wish to have cherries to eat while waiting for Jesus to be born.

——. *A Partridge in a Pear Tree.* This illustrated book contains the music and an endnote explaining the connection of this song with penances exacted for failure to observe fine points of ritual in the ceremonies between Christmas and Epiphany. (These two small paperbacks can be ordered for ninety-five cents each from the Museum of Modern Art, 5200 Lenox Hill Station, New York, N.Y. 10021.)

Films
Biography, Film Profiles

Antonia: Portrait of the Woman (58m, color)	Phoenix Films
At 99 (24m, color)	Eccentric Circle
Carl Gustav Jung (38m, b/w)	Time/Life
Einstein (42m, b/w)	Time/Life
Eric Hoffer, The Passionate State of Mind (52m, b/w)	Carousel
Helen Keller (15m, color)	Contemporary
Helen Keller in Her Story (45m, b/w)	American Foundation for the Blind
I. F. Stone's Weekly (60m, b/w)	Open Circle Cinema
J. B. Priestley (30m, b/w)	Time/Life
Joyce at 34 (29m, color)	New Day
Kurt Vonnegut, Jr.: A Self-Portrait (29m, color)	Films for the Humanities
Leo Beuerman (11m, color)	Centron
Lorraine Hansberry: The Black Experience (35m, color)	Films for the Humanities
Margaret Mead (27m, b/w)	Time/Life
Mother Teresa of Calcutta (51M, color)	Time/Life
Nahanni (18m, color)	Contemporary
Norman Rockwell's World: An American Dream (25m, color)	Films, Inc.
Ruth Stout's Garden (23m, color)	Arthur Mokin Productions
A Third Testament (Kierkegaard, St. Augustine, Bonhoeffer, Pascal, Blake, Tolstoi; each 57m, color)	Time/Life
This Is Edward Steichen (27m, b/w)	Carousel
Weapons of Gordon Parks (28m, color)	Contemporary
The World of Buckminster Fuller (90m, color)	Grove Press
The Heart of the Matter (Teilhard de Chardin) (45m, b/w)	Time/Life

General (covers all kinds of topics, even though only the major emphasis is given)

**Anansi the Spider* (An Ashanti folktale; 10m, color)	Landmark Ed. Media
Anything You Want to Be (A girl tries to choose an occupation; 8m, b/w)	New Day
Art of Age (Four older people and how they see things; 27m, color)	ACI

At 99 (23m, color)	Eccentric Circle
Bach to Bach (Intimacy and intellectual conversation between strangers; 6m, color)	Contemporary
Beauty Knows No Pain(The training program of the Kilgore Rangerettes; 25m, color)	Benchmark
Birth Without Violence (Dr. Frederick LeBoyer's quiet delivery techniques in a mesmerizing study; 21m, b/w)	New Yorker Films
Blessing of Love (A bittersweet overview of courtship and marriage; 8m, color)	Macmillan
**A Chemical Feast*(Comedian Marshall Ephron describes "creative playfoods"; 11m, color)	Benchmark
Cornet at Night (A brief encounter, a musical memory; 15m, b/w)	Contemporary
The Critic (A 72-year-old Jewish viewer cuts the art film down to size; 5m, color)	Macmillan
**Dear Kurt* (Competition in the Soap Box Derby; 24m, color)	Weston Woods
Dr. Heidegger's Experiment (A Nathaniel Hawthorne story about good intentions and bad habits; 22m, color)	Encyclopedia Britannica
End of Summer (Teenagers reflect as time passes; 27m, b/w)	National Film Board
Essay on War (A thoughtful look at the subject; 23m, color or b/w)	Encyclopedia Britannica
Flowers (Very short but very nice—a bouquet and an elderly couple; 2m, color)	Tom Davenport
Friends and Aliens (Events on a downtown Denver bus at Christmastime; 21m, color)	Oxford Films
Glass (Beauty, machinery alternating; 16m, color)	Contemporary
Good Night, Socrates (The passing of an era, through a boy's memories; 34m, b/w)	Contemporary
Harold and Cynthia (Plain love, surrounded by advertising; 9m, color)	Eccentric Circle
He's Not the Walking Kind (A very able person, though quite handicapped; 29m, color)	Centron
If You're Not There, You're Missed (Retardation and a lot more; 42m, b/w)	Carousel
The Interview (Mostly questions; 7m, color)	Contemporary
Is It Always Right to be Right? (Two sides to everything; 8m, color)	Stephen Bosustow

Koestler on Creativity (Arthur Koestler
   examines the nature of the creative
   process; 40m, color)   Time/Life

**Lady of the Light* (Solving a
   communication problem in a lighthouse;
   19m, color)   Walt Disney

Living with Peter (Miriam and Peter, not
   married; see also *We Get Married Twice*;
   22m, color)   Miriam Weinstein

Mint Tea (A young man alone in a crowded
   cafe in Paris; 20m, b/w)   Contemporary

Munro (Bureaucracy and a four-year-old
   draftee; 8m, color)   Contemporary

Not Together Now (A marriage that didn't
   work out; 25m, color)   Polymorph

The Old Woman (Death hath no sting for a
   woman who's too busy to accommodate him;
   2m, color)   ACI

One-Eyed Men Are Kings (Sometimes a
   handicap is better than none; 15m, color)   Contemporary

Overture/Nyitany (A chicken hatches in
   triumph, with Beethoven accompaniment;
   9m, color)   Contemporary

Pilgrimage (Retardation, celebration;
   50m, color)   Sr. Patricia Hewitt

The Plutocrats (The super-rich in Texas;
   51m, color)   Time/Life

Pysanka: The Ukrainian Easter Egg (Crafts,
   poetry, fine filmmaking; 14m, color)   Filmart Productions, Inc.

The Red Kite (Thoughts about meaning;
   17m, color)   Contemporary

Replay ("Life is a replay—or is it?";
   10m, color)   Contemporary

Ruth Stout's Garden (Comments on life,
   gardening, and nutrition; 23m, color)   Arthur Mokin Productions

Sad Song of Yellow Skin (Vietnam—the war
   and the country, without hysteria;
   60m, color)   Films, Inc.

***The Soap Box Derby Scandal* (The pressure
   of the 1973 race; 24m, color)   Weston Woods

Somebody Waiting (A careful and encouraging
   look at changes made in supposedly
   hopeless children in an institution;
   24m, color)   University of California

Storm of Strangers (The changing wave of
immigration on New York's Lower East
Side; 27m, b/w)   ACI

The String Bean (A French woman and her
plant; 17m, color)   Contemporary

Sylvia, Fran and Joy (Three views of
marriage; 25m, b/w)   Churchill Films

That's Me (The social worker socialized
by a canny Puerto Rican "client";
15m, b/w)   Contemporary

This Is No Time for Romance (French
Canadian marriage and family, beginning
with a fuss; 28m, color)   Perennial Education

A Very Special Day (A little girl lost,
and the conflicting loyalties of the boy
who helps her; occurs at Coney Island;
19m, color)   Universal Education

The Violinist (What price genius?;
8m, color)   Macmillan

We Do! We Do! (Pros and cons of young
marriages; a bit hyper but covers a lot
of ground; 11m, color)   St. Francis

Weekend (Working through some middle-years
marriage strains; 15m, color)   St. Francis

We Get Married Twice (An informal and a
formal wedding, same people; see also
Living with Peter; 22m, color)   Miriam Weinstein

You Haven't Changed a Bit (Old patterns of
behavior emerge in a new marriage;
15m, color)   St. Francis.

Zlateh the Goat (An Isaac Bashevis Singer
story about a boy and a goat, filmed in
a snowstorm in Bavaria; 20m, color)   Weston Woods

Note: *The following films are generally funny, depending, of course, on personal bents:* Anything You Want to Be; Bach to Bach; A Chemical Feast; The Critic; The Interview; Is It Always Right to Be Right?; Munro; The Old Woman; One-Eyed Men Are Kings; Replay; That's Me; The Violinist.

Religion-related (directly and indirectly)

a. Art of Silence:

The Creation of the World (11m, color)   Encyclopedia Britannica

The Hands (good and evil) (7m, color)   Encyclopedia Britannica
(These are Marcel Marceau pantomimes)
Bread and Wine (5m, color)   St. Francis
Buddhism: Be Ye Lamps Unto Yourselves
   (25m, color)   Xerox
The Cloistered Nun (18m, color)   Films, Inc.
The Crusades: Saints and Sinners
   (26m, color)   Learning Corp.
Eucharist (10m, color)   St. Francis
The Hasidim (Lubavitch-Habad)
   (29m, b/w)   Vedo Films
The Heart of the Matter (Teilhard de Chardin)
   (45m, b/w)   Time/Life
Hinduism: The Many Paths to God
   (25m, color)   Xerox
The Jesuits: The Hated Society
   (51m, color)   Time/Life
Many Different Gifts (liturgy-planning;
   50m, color)   Mass Media
Mother Teresa of Calcutta (51m, color)   Time/Life
Morality: A Matter of Choice
   (29m, color)   Xerox
Plain People (30m, color)   Films, Inc.
The Priest (15m, color)   Archdiocesan Comm. Ctr.
Pysanka: The Ukrainian Easter Egg
   (Primitive and Christian symbols;
   14m, color)   Filmart
The Question (10m, color)   Contemporary
Road Signs on a Merry-go-Round
   (56m, color)   Mass Media
The Shakers (29m, color)   Tom Davenport
Something Besides Rice (28m, color)   United Methodist
Stained Glass (7m, color)   Films, Inc.
The Sufi Way (25m, color)   Hartley Prod.
A Third Testament (Kierkegaard,
   St. Augustine, Bonhoeffer; each
   57m, color)   Time/Life
The Vatican (52m, color)   Time/Life
Where Her Gifts Are Respected
   (28m, color)   Mass Media
Windows (11m, color)   ACI

b. **The Bible as Literature:**
Saga and Story in the Old Testament
(27m, color)   Encyclopedia Britannica

History, Poetry and Drama in the Old
Testament (27m, color)   Encyclopedia Britannica

The Bible: Literary Heritage
(27m, color)   Learning Corp.

Early English Drama: The Second
Shepherds' Play (This includes the
Quem Quaeritis Easter ceremony,
Abraham and Isaac, The Second
Shepherds' Play; 52m, color)   Films for the Humanities

Medieval Life: The Monastery
(15m, color)   ACI

Medieval Theater: The Play of Abraham
and Isaac (25m, color)   Encyclopedia Britannica

Filmstrips
Religion-related

Christmas in the Stable   Weston Woods
Covenant God and His Covenant People   Family Filmstrips
The Four Gospels   Family Filmstrips
The Life and Message of Jesus Christ   Family Filmstrips
Old Testament Life and Times   Family Filmstrips
Survey of the Bible (And others from
Family Filmstrips)   Family Filmstrips
Great Religions of the World (set of 12)   Time/Life
The Holy Night   Weston Woods
The Little Drummer Boy   Weston Woods
Martin Buber: The Life in Dialogue   Union of American Hebrew
                                              Congregations

Men Who Made History (David; Gautama
Buddha; Plato; Alexander; Caesar
Augustus; Augustine)   Encyclopedia Britannica
They Are My People (M. Teresa of Calcutta) St. Francis
This Is Judaism   Union of American Hebrew
                                              Congregations

Classics of Medieval Literature

("The Nun's Priest's Tale;" *Everyman; The*
Second Shepherds' Play; others in set:

"Gawain and the Green Knight"; *Beowulf*;
  Morte d'Arthur)   Encyclopedia Britannica

Great Classics of Literature

(Goethe's *Faust*; *Paradise Lost*; Prologue
  to the *Canterbury Tales*; "The Pardoner's
  Tale"; others in set: *Iliad*; *Odyssey*;
  Aeneid; *Oedipus the King*; *Don Quixote)*   Encyclopedia Britannica

Medieval Europe

(Especially "The Crusades and Their
  Significance"; others in set: "The
  Medieval Manor;" "The Knight and His
  Training"; "The Town and Its Guilds.")   Encyclopedia Britannica

Stories

*The Cat and the Collector	Weston Woods
*The Crystal Apple	Weston Woods
*Could Anything Be Worse?	Weston Woods
*Let's Be Enemies	Weston Woods
*Millions of Cats	Weston Woods
*The North Wind and the Sun	Weston Woods
*The Rich Man and the Shoemaker	Weston Woods
*Stone Soup	Weston Woods
*The Twelve Days of Christmas	Weston Woods

Other

*The Joy of Being You	Scholastic
*Nothing Is Something to Do	Scholastic

*Note: *Most of these filmstrips cost between eleven and fifteen dollars
each, with cassettes.*

Distributors

ACI Films, Inc., 35 W. 45th St., New York, N.Y. 10036

American Foundation for the Blind, Public Education Division, 15 W.
  16th St., New York, N.Y. 10011

Archdiocesan Communications Center, 50 Oak St., San Francisco,
  Calif. 94102

Arthur Mokin Productions, Inc., 17 W. 60th St., New York, N.Y. 10023

Benchmark Films, Inc., 145 Scarborough Rd., Briarcliff Manor, New York, N.Y. 10510

Carousel Films, Inc., 1501 Broadway, New York, N.Y. 10036

Centron Educational Films, 1621 W. Ninth St., Lawrence, Kansas 66044

Contemporary/McGraw-Hill, 1221 Ave. of the Americas, New York, N.Y. 10020

Eccentric Circle, P.O. Box 315, Franklin Lakes, N.J. 07417

Eccentric Circle Cinema Workshop, P.O. Box 1481, Evanston, Ill. 60204

Encyclopedia Britannica Educational Corp., 425 N. Michigan Ave., Chicago, Ill. 60204

Family Filmstrips, 5823 Santa Monica Blvd., Hollywood, Calif. 90028

Filmart Productions, 3926 Macalester Drive, Minneapolis, Minn. 55421

Films for the Humanities, P.O. Box 378, Princeton, N.J. 08540

Films Incorporated, 1144 Wilmette Ave., Wilmette, Ill. 60091

Grove Press, Film Division, 53 E. 11th St., New York, N.Y. 10003

Hartley Productions, Inc., Cat Rock Rd., Cos Cob, Conn. 06807

Sr. Patricia Hewitt, 6444 S. Dante Ave., Chicago, Ill. 60637

Landmark Educational Media, Inc., 1600 Broadway, New York, N.Y. 10019

Learning Corporation of America, 711 Fifth Ave., New York, N.Y. 10022.

Macmillan Films, 34 MacQuesten Parkway S., Mt. Vernon, N.Y. 10550

Mass Media, 2116 N. Charles St., Baltimore, Md. 21218

Miriam Weinstein, 36 Shepard St., Cambridge, Mass. 02138

National Film Board of Canada, 1251 Ave. of the Americas, New York, N.Y. 10020

New Day Films, P.O. Box 315, Franklin Lakes, N.J. 07417

New Yorker Films, 43 W. 61st St., New York, N.Y. 10023

Open Circle Cinema, Ltd., P.O. Box 315, Franklin Lakes, N.J. 07417

Oxford Films, 1136 N. Las Palmas Ave., Los Angeles, Calif. 90038

Perennial Education, Inc., 1825 Willow Rd., Northfield, Ill. 60093

Phoenix Films, 470 Park Ave. S., New York, N.Y. 10016

Polymorph Films, 331 Newbury St., Boston, Mass. 02115

Scholastic Books, 902 Sylvan Ave., Englewood Cliffs, N.J. 07632

Stephen Bosustow, 1649 Eleventh St., Santa Monica, Calif. 90404

St. Francis Productions, 1229 S. Santee St., Los Angeles, Calif. 90015

Time/Life Multimedia Distribution Center, 100 Eisenhower Parkway, Paramus, N.J. 07652

Tom Davenport Films, Pearlstone, Dept. DM, Delaplane, Va. 22025

Union of American Hebrew Congregations, 838 Fifth Ave., New York, N.Y. 10021

United Methodist Church—distributed by Cokesbury Regional Services Centers in Detroit; Cincinnati; Nashville; Dallas; Richmond, Va.; Teaneck, N.J. Chicago and Park Ridge, Ill.

Universal Education and Visual Arts, 221 Park Ave. S., New York, N.Y. 10003

University of California, Extension Media Center, Berkeley, Calif. 94720

Vedo Films, 85 Longview Rd., Port Washington, N.Y. 11050

Walt Disney Educational Materials, 800 Sonora Ave., Glendale, Calif. 91201

Weston Woods, Weston, Conn. 06880

Xerox Educational Publications/Xerox Films, 245 Long Hill Rd., Middletown, Conn. 06457

INDEX